# The Jewish Action Reader

# The Jewish

Published by

# Action Reader

A selection of stimulating articles
of vital interest to every
thoughtful contemporary Jew

Volume 1

**THE JEWISH ACTION READER VOL. I**
© *Copyright 1996*
by Union of Orthodox Jewish Congregations of America
333 Seventh Avenue / New York, N.Y. 10001 / (212) 563-4000

FIRST EDITION
*First Impression . . . January 1996*

*Distributed by*
**MESORAH PUBLICATIONS, Ltd.**
4401 Second Avenue
Brooklyn, New York 11232

*Distributed in Europe by*
**J. LEHMANN HEBREW BOOKSELLERS**
20 Cambridge Terrace
Gateshead, Tyne and Wear
England NE8 1RP

*Distributed in Israel by*
**SIFRIATI / A. GITLER — BOOKS**
4 Bilu Street
P.O.B. 14075
Tel Aviv 61140

*Distributed in Australia & New Zealand by*
**GOLDS BOOK & GIFT CO.**
36 William Street
Balaclava 3183, Vic., Australia

*Distributed in South Africa by*
**KOLLEL BOOKSHOP**
22 Muller Street
Yeoville 2198, Johannesburg, South Africa

**All rights reserved.**
*This text, prefatory and associated textual contents and introductions, including the typographic layout, cover artwork, charts and maps have been designed, edited and revised as to content, form and style.*

*No part of this book may be reproduced* **in any form** — *without* **written** *permission from the copyright holder, except by a reviewer who wishes to quote brief passages in connection with a review written for inclusion in magazines or newspapers.*

**AND THE RIGHTS OF THE COPYRIGHT HOLDER WILL BE STRICTLY ENFORCED.**

ISBN: 0-89906-594-5 (hard cover)
0-89906-595-3 (paperback)

Printed In The United States Of America by
Noble Book Press Corp., New York, NY

# Table of Contents

Preface — 13

## ✺ Biography and Autobiography

One Soul's Adventure: Spiritual Growth Through Halachah / *Anthony S. Fiorino* — 16

Personal Glimpses of the Rav, zt"l / *Dr. Allen Goldstein* — 32

The Prophet of Spiritual Renewal / *Matis Greenblatt* — 38

Sensitization to Holiness: The Life and Works of Rabbi Kalonymos Kalmish Shapiro / *Rabbi Nehemia Polen* — 43

Rav Aharon Lo Meit: The Legacy of Rav Aharon Kotler / *Marvin Schick* — 51

The Rav's Philosophical Legacy / *Dr. David Shatz* — 67

A Word of Thanks / *Herman Wouk* — 79

## ✺ Contemporary Issues

The Truth about Homosexuality / *Dr. Joseph Berger* — 84

Orthodox Soul-Searching After Goldstein / *Rabbi Hillel Goldberg* — 94

Of Patting (and Breaking) Backs / *Rabbi Yaakov D. Homnick* — 99

Why There Was No Gabbai at the Regency Theater / *Chava Willig Levy* — 101

## ✺ Education

Teaching Thinking Skills in the Judaic Studies Curriculum / *Rabbi Aharon Hersh Fried* — 104

Nobody's Business / *Charlotte Friedland* — 111

## ➤ Halachah and Talmudic Interpretation

The Brain Death Controversy in Jewish Law /
*Rabbi Yitzchak Breitowitz*    120
From What Point Should the Megillah Be Read? /
*Rabbi Nachman Cohen*    134

## ➤ Health

Helpful Tips to Insure an Easier Fast / *Ira Milner*    142

## ➤ History

The Frankfurt Secession Controversy / *Dr. Judith Bleich*    148
A Purim in Every Generation / *Rabbi Shlomo Jakobovits*    169
Resettlement of the Land as Viewed by the
Vilna Gaon's Circle / *Dr. Aryeh Morgenstern*    176
The Wrong Response to Modernity /
*Rabbi Bernard Rosensweig*    185
From the Caves of Qumran / *Lawrence H. Schiffman*    206

## ➤ Holocaust

Remembering the Living / *Rabbi Nachum Muschel*    214

## ➤ Humor

Is There a Cure for Shalach Manot Syndrome? /
*Charlotte Friedland*    222
A Pre-Schooler Confronts Divinity / *Elisheva Schlam*    227

## ➤ Jewish Thought

Illuminating Faith / *Dr. Yehuda Gellman*    230
Kabbalah as Experience: Moshe Idel's Critique
of Gershom Scholem / *Micha Odenheimer*    239
Fundamentalism Reconsidered / *Rabbi Dr. Jonathan Sacks*    247
To Radically Alter Our Lives / *Rabbi Mayer Schiller*    261

## ~§ Outreach

| | |
|---|---|
| From a Mother With Love / *Judy Berg* | 266 |
| At the Forefront of the Baal Teshuvah Movement: The Beginnings of NCSY / *Rabbi Pinchas Stolper* | 269 |

## ~§ Poetry

| | |
|---|---|
| Kolk / *Eleanor Freemer* | 278 |
| Reaching In / *Chevy Schwartz* | 280 |
| Conversations / *Devora K. Wohlgelernter* | 282 |

## ~§ Science and Judaism

| | |
|---|---|
| Holy Alliance: Reflections on Contemporary Science From the Tents of Torah / *Rabbi Yitzchok Adlerstein* | 284 |
| The Revolution in Evolutionary Thinking: Role of Divine Providence / *Professor Nathan Aviezer* | 291 |
| The Age of Our Universe / *Dr. Gerald L. Schroeder* | 298 |

## ~§ Sources of Faith

| | |
|---|---|
| Credo of Credence / *Rabbi Aharon Feldman* | 304 |
| Reflections on Emunah / *Dr. Judith Grunfeld* | 310 |
| The Source of Faith Is Faith Itself / *Rabbi Aharon Lichtenstein* | 314 |

# Contributors to this Volume

**Rabbi Yitzchok Adlerstein** teaches Jewish studies and directs outreach at Yeshiva of Los Angeles (YULA). He is a Contributing Editor to Jewish Action Magazine.

**Professor Nathan Aviezer,** of the Department of Physics at Bar Ilan University, is the author of *In the Beginning: Biblical Creation and Science* (Ktav, 1990) and has developed a lecture series based on his research on creation and evolution.

**Judy Berg** lives in Butler, PA with her husband, Larry. She is a homemaker, mother and grandmother.

**Dr. Joseph Berger** is a consulting psychiatrist in private practice in Toronto, Canada. He is a Board Examiner for the American Board of Psychiatry and Neurology, and has authored many papers in American, Canadian and British journals.

**Dr. Judith Bleich** is Associate Professor of Judaic Studies at Touro College. The subject of her doctoral dissertation was: *Jacob Ettlinger, His Life and Works: The Emergence of Modern Orthodoxy in Germany.*

**Rabbi Yitzchak Breitowitz** is the Rabbi of the Woodside Synagogue in Silver Spring, Maryland and Assistant Professor of Law at the University of Maryland Law School. He is the author of *Between Civil and Religious Law: The Plight of the Agunah In American Society* (Greenwood Press).

**Rabbi Dr. Nachman Cohen** is the spiritual leader of the Young Israel of North Riverdale/Yonkers, and the Director of Torah Lishmah Institute and Chairman of the Board of the AOJS — Association of Orthodox Jewish Scientists. He is currently completing a major work on the roots of midrashic disputes.

**Rabbi Aharon Feldman** was formerly Dean of Yeshivat Ohr Somayach, Jerusalem and is founder and Rosh HaYeshiva of Yeshivat Be'er HaTorah. His most recent book is the *Juggler and The King*, an elaboration of the Vilna Gaon's interpretation of difficult aggadata.

**Anthony S. Fiorino** is a student at the Albert Einstein College of Medicine.

**Eleanor Freemer** is a freelance writer from Atlanta, GA.

**Rabbi Aharon Hersh Fried** received his Ph.D. in Psychology from the New School for Social Research. He is best known for his pioneering work in Jewish Special Education with the Learning Disabled. He is the founder of the Jewish Centers for Special Education in New York and Jerusalem with affiliated programs in various cities in the U.S., Canada and Europe.

**Charlotte Friedland** is Editor of *Jewish Action*. Her articles have frequently appeared in Jewish magazines.

**Dr. Yehuda Gellman** is Senior Lecturer in Philosophy at Ben Gurion University, Beer Sheva, Israel and the author of *The Fear, The Trembling and The Fire: Kierkegaard and Hasidic Masters on the The Binding of Isaac* (University Press of America).

**Rabbi Hillel Goldberg** is the Executive Editor of *The Intermountain Jewish News* and a Contributing Editor of *Jewish Action,* and is the author of *Between Berlin and Slobodka* and *Israel Salanter, Text, Structure, Idea* among other works (Ktav).

**Dr. Allen Goldstein** is a prominent physician in Forest Hills, NY. He was a student of the Rav.

**Matis Greenblatt** is Literary Editor of *Jewish Action.*

**Dr. Judith Grunfeld** was an associate of Sara Schenierer in the founding of the first Beth Jacob Seminary (1925-1932). She was later Headmistress of the famed Jewish Secondary School of London. When the children were evacuated from London to the countryside during World War II, she stood at the helm of the reconstituted Jewish school in Shefford, and wrote *Shefford* describing that period.

**Rabbi Yaakov D. Homnick** is the author of *Prayer of Love* (1987), a collection of essays on Jewish subjects. He has also published several volumes of Talmudic commentary.

**Rabbi Shlomo Jakobovits** is the principal of the Eitz Chaim Schools of Toronto. He has lectured and written widely on Jewish history and education.

**Chava Willig Levy** is a freelance writer from Manhattan. She has lectured frequently in the U.S. and Canada on subjects including *"Gam zu l'Tovah," chesed* and disability awareness.

**Rabbi Aharon Lichtenstein** is a Rosh HaYeshiva of Yeshivat Har Etzion, Israel and Rosh HaYeshiva of the Gruss Institute in Israel of Yeshiva University. Rabbi Lichtenstein is a leading spokesman of Modern Orthodoxy.

**Ira Milner, R.D.,** is a nutritionist.

**Dr. Aryeh Morgenstern** is the Director of History Instruction for the Misrad HaChinuch and a Fellow of the Dinur Historical Institute. A well-known Israeli historian, Dr. Morgenstern is the author of *HaRabanut HaRashit B'Eretz Yisrael, Meshecheyus B'Yishuv Eretz Yisrael* and *Geulah B'Derech HaTevah B'Kisvei HaGrah V'Talmidav,* among other works.

**Rabbi Nachum Muschel** is Dean Emeritus of Yeshivat Hadar Avrohom Tzvi, Monsey, New York and Instructor in Jewish Education at the Azrieli Graduate Institute of Yeshiva University.

**Micha Odenheimer** is a teacher and writer living in Jerusalem.

**Rabbi Nehemia Polen** is Rabbi of Congregation Tifereth Israel in Everett, Massachusetts and is Associate Dean of students and Associate Professor of Jewish thought at Boston's Hebrew College. His book on Rabbi Shapiro, *The Holy Fire* was published by Aronson.

**Rabbi Bernard Rosensweig** is the Rabbi of Adath Yeshurun Synagogue, Kew Gardens, New York and an adjunct professor of Jewish history at Yeshiva University. He is a former president of the Rabbinical Council of America.

**Rabbi Dr. Jonathan Sacks** is Chief Rabbi of the British Empire. He is the author of numerous articles and books.

**Marvin Schick** is president of the Rabbi Jacob Joseph School, and the founder and first president of COLPA — The National Jewish Commission on Law and Public Affairs. Well-known for his contributions to Jewish communal life, he is an outspoken analyst and critic of the state of the Jewish community.

**Lawrence H. Schiffman** is Professor of Hebrew and Judaic Studies in the Skirball Department of Hebrew and Judaic Studies at New

York University. He is recognized as a leading scholar of the Dead Sea Scrolls on which he has written four books. His most recent book is *Reclaiming the Dead Sea Scrolls* (JPS). He was featured on the PBS Nova Documentary, "Secrets of the Dead Sea Scrolls."

**Rabbi Mayer Schiller** teaches Talmud and Jewish Philosophy at the Yeshiva University High School for Boys. He is a well-known writer and lecturer.

**Elisheva Schlam** is Director of Media Relations for the National Kidney Foundation and a freelance writer. She is the mother of two children.

**Dr. Gerald L. Schroeder** holds a Ph.D in Nuclear Geophysics and Oceanography from M.I.T., and is the author of *Genesis and the Big Bang: The Discovery of Harmony Between Modern Science and the Bible,* published by Bantam Books. He lectures widely on the topic of his book.

**Chevy Schwartz** teaches the learning disabled in Jerusalem.

**Dr. David Shatz** is Professor of Philosophy at Yeshiva University. He is a *musmakh* of Rabbi Isaac Elchanan Theological Seminary. He has co-edited several books, including *Contemporary Philosophy of Religion,* and has published numerous scholarly articles on both general and Jewish philosophy.

**Rabbi Pinchas Stolper** is Senior Executive of the Orthodox Union and author of *Love, Dating and Marriage: The Jewish View.*

**Devora K. Wohlgelernter** was a brilliant, multi-faceted figure. A few years before her own untimely passing, she wrote *Conversations,* after the tragic death of her 12 year old daughter.

**Herman Wouk,** the noted novelist, shared a close relationship with the late Rabbi Leo Jung. His thoughtful and poignant work, *This Is My God,* continues to inspire both Jews and non-Jews the world over.

# Preface

*Why were the arrangement of the banners (displayed by the Israelite tribes in the desert) delayed for a full year? The answer is that seemingly the banners were a source of divisiveness. Each banner reflected the individual striving and goal of each tribe, whose nature was unique and different from the others. Thus, the banners could have resulted in conflict. However, since all were encamped around a common center, the Tabernacle, their differences could not be a source of discord. They were like the human body in which each individual organ performs its function while working together with all the others.*
(Rabbi Yaakov Kaminetsky zt"l, *Iyunim BaMikro, Bamidbar*)

From its inception, JEWISH ACTION has sought to demonstrate the relevancy and vibrancy of Orthodoxy. By definition, a Torah life must be responsive to the needs of the time. However, no one segment within Orthodoxy has a monopoly on what that response should be; rather each segment makes its own positive contribution. But presenting one's view with passion and conviction should not preclude appreciation of the position of one's ideological opponent; not because of a liberal tolerance but rather out of a profound sense of the complementary role each plays in the overall spiritual state of Judaism and the Jewish people in our time.

It is appropriate that the magazine of the Orthodox Union serves as a forum for honest diversity within Orthodoxy. JEWISH ACTION's criteria for publication of a particular article have been its ability to enlighten and/or inspire us, even if we do not necessarily agree with its conclusions. It is to the credit of the Union that it has supported this goal.

JEWISH ACTION has striven to reach the growing population of intelligent, well-educated men and women who need to be addressed with reason and respect. THE JEWISH ACTION READER contains a sampling of articles on a wide range of perennial as well as contemporary issues. Hopefully, it will contribute to a deeper recognition that true unity can only come from diversity.

*Joel M. Schreiber*
Chairman
O.U. Publications Commission

*Charlotte Friedland*      *Matis Greenblatt*
Editor      Literary Editor
*Jewish Action Magazine*

# Biography and Autobiography

- ☐ *One Soul's Adventure:*
    *Spiritual Growth Through Halachah*
- ☐ *Personal Glimpses of the Rav, zt"l*
- ☐ *The Prophet of Spiritual Renewal*
- ☐ *Sensitization to Holiness:*
    *The Life and Works of*
    *Rabbi Kalonymos Kalmish Shapiro*
- ☐ *Rav Aharon Lo Meit:*
    *The Legacy of Rav Aharon Kotler*
- ☐ *The Rav's Philosophical Legacy*
- ☐ *A Word of Thanks*

*Anthony S. Fiorino*

# One Soul's Adventure: Spiritual Growth Through Halachah

*"How does halachah cause spiritual growth? The answer requires an examination of what led me to Judaism."*

IN THE FADING DAYS OF THE SUMMER OF 1989, I BEGAN A JOURNEY of self-discovery, a journey in which my long-neglected soul has grown from an atrophied state into an all-encompassing spirituality — to the point where the single most prominent characteristic of my identity is that of a religious Jew. On the most infertile of soil — the mind of an atheist — the seeds of *ahavat Hashem* (love of God) fell and, to my amazement, have grown and blossomed. As I reflect upon the process of my *gerut* (conversion), it has become clear to me that this transformation was brought about through the observance of *halachah*. My experience has been counter to what I had intuitively thought of as the path of religious awakening — my commitment to religion and observance preceded and caused my spiritual transformation. Now, I seek to understand this process, to glimpse an answer to the question "How does *halachah* cause spiritual growth?"

The answer requires an examination of what led me to Judaism. I grew up in a fairly religious Italian Catholic home, but I never had any real feeling for Catholicism. From an early age I found the imagery repelling, the rituals empty, and the theology cold; I never felt that I would or could be a practicing Catholic. As education assumed a primary role in my life, religion became merely an issue which caused arguments on Sunday mornings, when fights over church attendance would inevitably break out. Attending public school in a heavily Jewish, although not religious, community on Long Island gave me an elementary knowledge of Judaism and more importantly, a tremendous, and permanent, affinity for the Jewish people. But what really set the stage for the future transformation was the education I was receiving. The emphasis placed on the rational thought and the scientific process by American society had an enormous impact on my developing personality and vision. Technology is viewed as the answer to all wants; the media, schools, government, and the scientific establishment contribute to a secular yearning for a technological *mashiach* — a science which will cure diseases, feed the hungry, increase leisure time, bring world peace. A young and eager mind endowed with the gift of scientific aptitude is particularly sensitive to these societal influences. By the end of high school, I had learned to value scientific information above all other information, and what science had lured me into — an unexamined agnosticism.

The decision to pursue a career in the biological sciences led me to the Massachusetts Institute of Technology, where I received rigorous training in the methodology of science as well as an enormous quantity of information. This intense scientific training expanded my belief in the supreme value of reason and rationality; at the same time, excursions into existential philosophy led to my assessment of morals as both relativistic and arbitrarily defined. As my reasoning ability was challenged and forced to develop further, in the context of an existentialist world view, I was able to carry my view of science to the inescapable conclusion that only that which is observable is believable. The methods of scientific inquiry, I believed, yield "truth" in the absolute sense and furthermore, that which is not open to scientific evaluation and verification must be valueless. This reductionist approach provided answers to some otherwise difficult questions: for instance, the philosophical problem of body and mind was no problem at all — there is no aspect of "mind" separate from the brain. The trouble with the dualists, as I saw it, is that they mistakenly assign intentional and moral states to units of action which in reality are valueless — there are no morals in electrical impulses and chemical reactions. From such a position, one must inevitably conclude that human beings, and thus human behavior, cannot have any moral content. If a single bioelectrical impulse traveling along a neuron in a petri dish is not a moral action, then the same must be true of human thought and behavior — merely a complex system of such impulses. From this perspective, "right" and "wrong" are meaningless, and God is denied.

I believed in this . . . yet somehow, I was still an ethical person. It was not simply the fear of being caught breaking the law which shaped my behavior, because I found myself drawn to humanitarian issues, expending time and energy on behalf of others, sometimes at expense to myself. In fact, this deep feeling of a responsibility to others was a major factor in my decision to pursue medicine. I looked to the character Rieux in Albert Camus' *The Plague* as the model of a man, a physician, creating value in a world which he recognized to be devoid of meaning. He appealed to me so much more than Meursault of *The Stranger* precisely because he creates value and does good. I concluded that morals are the natural product of rationality and reasoning.

## ☙ The Process Is Set Quietly in Motion

Slowly, cracks began to appear in my carefully constructed world vision. Ironically, it began at M.I.T., where the environment of intense rationality had contributed greatly to my atheistic reductionism in the first place. Two specific events had a lasting impact on me and began the path to Judaism. First, I read Noam Chomsky's critique of B.F. Skinner's behavioral theory of linguistic development. Then I researched intelligence testing while writing a paper describing the use of the IQ test in supporting racist social policies. Both of these cases profoundly impressed upon me the effect that dogma can have on the ability to reason. I saw the scientific process twisted — scientists misrepresenting data, making unsubstantiated claims, sometimes lying, in order to generate results that were consistent with their preconceived notions. I wondered if dogma could influence the scientific process in the physical sciences, which deal directly with the material reality of the world, the final truth to which I thought all else must answer. Indeed, biology, chemistry, and physics lay at the core of my reductionist outlook. My initial reaction was "No," since the very nature of the physical sciences is objective — they study not ideas but matter, and matter is not subject to debate in the way that ideas are. I entered the M.D.-Ph.D. program at the Albert Einstein College of Medicine confident in my reductionism, not recognizing that the process which would shatter this vision had been set quietly in motion.

The issue that would topple my reductionism arose during my first few months at Einstein. All though high school and college, and then again in graduate classes, I had heard the classic biological explanation of the origin of life. And it had always seemed reasonable. But when considering the awesome complexity, structure, and order within even single cells, *in the context of how dogma can influence reason,* I cam to the realization that molecular biology too is gripped by dogma. It postulates the origin of life as a tremendous, complex series of events, each of which alone has an infinitesimally small chance of occurring. Forced by its basic tenets to deny even a hint of transcendence, biology must explain the beginning of life as a cumulation of events the possibility of which occurring is so slight that it is essentially zero. Nobel laureate Jacques Monod has written: "Life appeared on the earth: what, *before the event,* were the chances that this would occur? . . . its *a proiri* probability was virtually zero."[1] Constrained by reductionism, the scientist can draw only one conclusion; in the words of the Nobel laureate Salvador Luria, "each human being is the actualization of an extremely improbable chance — in fact, a series of improbable chances, extending all the way back to the unique event that more than three billion years ago started life on the earth on its chancy course."[2] Biology is forced by its basic premises to postulate that life began as a "unique event" — an event which has no possibility of occurring, yet which must have occurred — an idea which is not only absurd, but scientifically unsatisfying. Freed of this burdensome dogma, I could contemplate the origin of life without bias. Instead of attempting to convince myself of the unreasonable, I had to admit that for there to be a creation — the physical reality of existence — there could be, perhaps there must be, a Creator.

This insight radically altered my approach to the world around me. No longer could I view science, and the scientific method, as providing absolute truth, for if science yielded absolute truth, then dogma could not impact its results; but this was not the case. Consequently, as I reconsidered the value of scientific information, I realized that science

---

1. Monod, Jacques. *Chances and Necessity.* NY: Alfred A Knopf, 1971, p .144.
2. Luria, Salvador E. Life — *The Unfinished Experiment.* NY: Charles Scribner's Sons, 1973, p. 11.

is a belief system. Like all other belief systems, it has a set of basic assumptions and a methodology which generates information that is meaningful only in the context of those assumptions. Understanding that each belief system has its own language or symbolism which gives meaning within the belief system to the results of inquiry, and that there is incompatibility between the symbolism of different beliefs systems, was a critical step. Somehow I had given science a greater status, viewing the results generated by all other belief systems, if unintelligible under or contradicted by the basic tenets of science, as "untrue" in an absolute sense. No longer could I reject what history, philosophy, or religion might say about the nature of a human being simply because it disagreed with the rational view of science.

I subsequently began to examine what I had been forced to reject as untrue while I held science supreme. I had viewed morals, and moral behavior, as the natural outcome of reason alone. But this idea withered under scrutiny. There were too many instances in which reason clearly indicated a course of action, but I acted in another way, the "right" way. If morals were the outcome of reason, how could reason and morals demand a contradictory course of action? As a rationalist, I had been compelled to deny that anything could transcend or supersede human reason, but this belief had forced me to postulate something unreasonable and untrue — that because I clearly possessed morals, they must be the result of reasoning. Just as biologists, when considering the origin of life, must reject other views and postulate something unreasonable — that because life clearly exists, it must be the result of a unique biochemical event. Liberated from the confines of rationalism, I could for the first time consider the idea that morals have an existence independent of and sometimes contrary to human reason.

## ◆§ Unsettling Experiences — and Considerations of Conversion

Obviously, this was a time of marked transition. What are described as "liberating" experiences in retrospect were at the time much less defined and rather unsettling. To move from a position which denies all but empirical, observable reality to a position which recognizes transcendence is an enormous philosophical leap. But there is a still longer way to becoming an Orthodox Jew. As I started Einstein, my knowledge of Judaism contained nothing particularly compelling, but I happened to develop close friendships with several religious classmates very quickly. I found the idea of my peers being religious intriguing, and I wondered why they chose such a demanding lifestyle, sacrificing so much, in the absence of anyone forcing them to do so. Curiosity led to questioning; eventually, I searched through boxes of books in the basement of my parents' house to find the Bible I had received for my confirmation in the ninth grade (still unopened). As I read through the *Old Testament*, it became clear that Judaism is not a random collection of arbitrary rules, a view I inherited from my high school friends, but rather it is an organized and practical system. And not only did I find the ethics and values of that system compelling, but also the results — the numerous observant Jews whom I had come to know as classmates.

As I read and learned more, I began to consider the idea of conversion. The first bits of observance began spontaneously. Without a particular plan, or even a conscious decision, I stopped eating pork and shellfish, then I stopped eating meat and milk together. Shabbat observance began slowly, with no television on Friday night. Exactly how that process occurred remains somewhat unclear. Part of the motivation, perhaps, was a desire to reduce the differences between myself and my religious friends; I was certainly aware of the limitations that were inherent in any friendship between Orthodox Jews and a non-Jew. But more important was the tremendous amount of respect I developed for the religious people I knew. They were smart, thinking, and principled people who were not religious only because they were expected to be; rather, to be religious was a decision reaffirmed every day, and reaffirmed with joy. If they saw value and importance and truth in Judaism, I knew that Judaism might offer something for me. Having lost faith in science as the ultimate source of truth allowed me to be open to the issues before me without prejudice — I no longer considered religious experiences to be valueless.

As my knowledge grew, I found myself viewing Judaism not as an interested outsider, but as a potential insider — the thought of Judaism as a way of life for me was appealing. Yet I had to repeatedly justify to myself the idea of being religious; years of ranking all epistemological methods as inferior to science were hard to erase. I consequently developed a set of practical reasons for my continued interest. I saw the closeness of Jewish families and the Jewish community, and the emphasis that Judaism places on education and scholarship. I saw a means of transmitting a set of values and tradition to my children. My own somewhat

*One Soul's Adventure: Spiritual Growth Through Halachah* / 21

limited participation in the rituals of Judaism had been positive experiences. But these were aspects that could be found in many religions; there was much more to Judaism specifically which called to me. I found the theology pure and accessible, unlike the mystery-shrouded, complex morass that I had previously known. Because of an intense dislike of missionary activity, I found Judaism's view of the non-Jew to be enlightened. Also appealing to me, especially after struggling for years to eliminate all vestiges of the Catholic view of pleasure, was that Judaism allows, even requires, enjoyment of what is in this world. But the most appealing aspect was the freedom that Judaism offered — demanding a specific set of behaviors, yet allowing the mind to wander, to explore, to question, even to doubt — the idea that the way in which one acts is at least as important as what one thinks made intuitive sense to me.

This was no spiritual awakening. My attraction, my experience, was purely pragmatic, carefully reasoned and justified, and it continued to be. Pesach 1990, I attended two *Sedarim*, and after participating in the unique religious-political-historical event that a *Seder* is, I decided that I wanted to experience Judaism fully, to see if my intuitive feelings of affinity were strong enough to support both the lifestyle and the emotional stress of conversion. For the rest of my life, when I read from the *Haggadah* every year *kol dichfin yeitei v'yeichul, kol ditzrich yeizei v'yifsach*, I will remember my first Passover, and I will remember those Jews who welcomed me into their homes when I suffered not from physical hunger, but from a spiritual one. Essentially, I made a conscious decision to accept the faith issues of Judaism — *Matan Torah, Torah shebe'al peh* (divine giving of the Torah Oral Law) and the traditional principles of halachic decision-making — as by definition true. These were the basic tenets of a new belief system that I was building, an experimental framework which I could test, probe, experience. It was completely isolated from my other belief system — that of a scientist — and I did not feel any conflict between them because I viewed the information each provided as being value only within its original context; for instance, to compare how each views the origin of life was a meaningless exercise. My mental state could be that of either a scientist or a Jew at any given moment, and I could switch from one to the other simply by changing which set of basic assumptions I was accepting as true at any given moment. The systems were not ordered hierarchically — I did not consider one to provide answers closer to the "ultimate truth" than the other — but there was one important consequence of this mode of existence. Although my mind could be occupied by either belief system, I had to always act like a Jew. That was part of what experiencing Judaism involved, one of its attractions for me — my mind could wander, could be a scientist's mind, while my observance remained intact.

The change which proceeded from this was spectacular, if not in rate then in magnitude. Assumed faith has led to genuine faith, and being *shomer halachah* (observant of Jewish Law) has awakened a spirituality which has consumed the boundaries of my "scientific" and "Jewish" belief systems. It has grown, not as a blazing flame, but rather as a slow burning, blurring the distinction between my two selves before I was even aware of the process. What was an ultimately untenable duality has been replaced by a new, unitary identity — a cold rationality and a hot spirituality linked by, nurtured by, and restrained by *halachah*. As I considered this process, I first wondered if I had perhaps replaced the old supreme belief system, reason and rationality, with another. Indeed, the basic assumptions of Judaism had been elevated to a higher status, to the level of "absolute" truth which transcends the lines of all belief systems. But this elevation had occurred not by a conscious effort, but rather through the nourishment by Judaism of a part of my humanity which science had forced me to deny and neglect.

It is not immediately apparent how simply behaving as a Jew leads to spiritual growth, but the observation has been made throughout the ages. In the *Gemara,* the following is said to have been spoken by God: "Would that they had forsaken Me and kept My Torah, since by occupying themselves with Torah, the light which it contains would have led them back to Me" (*Yerushalmi Chagigah* 1,7). Yehuda Halevi observed it in *The Kuzari:* "Men cannot approach God except by means of deeds commanded by Him";[1] Moshe Chayim Luzzatto in *The Path of the Just*: "Outer movements awaken inner ones . . . for as a result of the willed quickening of movements there will arise in him an inner joy and a desire and a longing";[2] Abraham Joshua Heschel in *God in Search of Man:* "By living as Jews we may attain our faith as Jews. . .we may attain faith through sacred deeds."[3] But these are just observations; they add no insight into the process.

---

1. Halevi, Yehuda. *The Kuzari,* NY: Schocken Books, 1964, p. 111.
2. Luzzatto, Moshe Chayim. *The Path of the Just.* NY: Feldheim Publishers, 1966 (1990), p.91.
3. Heschel, Abraham Joshua. *God in Search of Man.* NY: Farrar, Strauss and Giroux, 1955 (1990), p. 282.

## ☙ How Does Halachah Cause Spiritual Growth?

In *Halakhic Man*, Rabbi Joseph Soloveitchik describes the halachic man, who can look into his psyche and see a synthesis of *homo religiosus*, the man of God who hopes to transcend the world, and cognitive man, the man who wishes to comprehend and categorize the world.

For the halachic man, these two personalities have been present and growing, together, intertwining under the guidance of *halachah*, from birth. My experience, and perhaps that of many who became observant later in life, differs. Developing under the influence of a secular society without the benefit of *mitzvot* allows cognitive man to grow and flourish at the expense of spirituality. Through *shemirat halachah*, the corresponding half of the synthesis — *homo religiosus* — is forced to develop. If that spiritual growth were not to occur, the synthesis would remain incomplete, leaving unintegrated, mutually exclusive identities of "scientist" and "religious Jew." But the spirituality does come, and I believe it comes inevitably out of observance and *mitzvot*; the relevant issue then is not "if" but "how" — how does *halachah* cause spiritual growth? Fitting my experience of spiritual growth through *halachah* into the Rav's construct of the halachic man has proven to be a fruitful approach to this question.

Cognitive man is very powerful. Science defines the world as purely material; it is thus anti-spiritual and in that way suppresses the growth and development of the soul. The Rav beautifully captures the essence of cognitive man:

> *When theoretical and scientific man peers into the cosmos, he is filled with one exceedingly powerful yearning, which is to search for clarity and understanding, for solutions and resolutions. Cognitive man aims to solve the problems of cognition vis-a-vis reality . . . [he] does not tolerate any obscurity, any oblique allusions and undeciphered secrets in existence. He desires to establish fixed principles, create laws and judgments, to negate the unforeseen and the incomprehensible, to understand the wondrous and sudden in existence.* [1]

The nature of his belief forces him to deny all but the physical; "he has no relationship with any mode of being that is beyond empirical

---

1. Soloveitchik, Joseph B. *Halakhic Man*. Philadelphia: The Jewish Publication Society, 1983, p. 5.

reality and scientific understanding."[1] When cognitive man perceives the world around him, his well-trained mind automatically and relentlessly disintegrates reality into progressively smaller units — human beings are collections of tissues, which are collections of cells which are collections of molecules, which are collections of atoms, which are collections of subatomic particles — and at each of these levels are sets of laws which precisely determine the behavior of the units. He is trapped by the principle that the whole must not be greater than the sum of its parts; therefore it is the parts and their interrelations which have ontic significance. The result is cognitive man's inability to grasp or appreciate the whole.

Because he defines any given state as an assembly of simpler states, cognitive man cannot look at the world with "radical amazement." This ability to stand in awe of the world is for Heschel an essential part of the religious experience: "What we encounter in our perception of the sublime, in our radical amazement, is a spiritual suggestiveness of reality, an allusiveness to transcendent meaning. The world in its grandeur is full of a spiritual radiance,"[2] a spiritual radiance which cognitive man cannot see because his eyes are turned not upward towards the whole, but ever downward, trying to identify and examine smaller, simpler units. The Rav echoes this understanding of the spiritually sensitive person who "encounters the universe in all its colorfulness, splendor, and grandeur, and studies it with all the naivete, awe, and admiration of the child who seeks the unusual and wonderful in every ordinary thing and event."[3] But cognitive man, focusing down on the tasks before him, has no part of this sensitivity; while he may feel excitement at the units or laws which he has identified, this excitement is missing an awareness that "the light of Your own presence, O Lord, our God, is imprinted on the laws that govern life."[4] My interest in molecular biology began not because the cell is an awesome manifestation of God's presence, but because it is a complex puzzle to be solved,

---

1. Soloveitchik, *Halakhic Man.* p. 13.

2. Heschel, Abraham Joshua. *Man is Not Alone.* NY: Farrar, Strauss and Giroux, 1951 (1990), p. 22.

3. Soloveitchik, Joseph, "The Lonely Man of Faith," *Tradition* 7:2, Summer 1965, pp. 5,6,7.

4. Kook, Abraham Isaac. *Abraham Isaac Kook.* NY: Paut Press (*Classics of Western Spirituality*), 1978, p. 222.

one molecule at a time. The prophet Isaiah exhorts, "Lift up your eyes round about and see" (*Isaiah* 60:4): don't look down, but *lift up your eyes*; don't merely observe, but *see*. Yet cognitive man is unable to heed the call — he is spiritually numb, blind to the testimony which all of creation gives, "Your judgments are far above out of his sight" (*Psalms* 10:5). *Moshe Rabbeinu* declared, "I call the heaven and earth to witness against you this day" (*Deuteronomy* 30:19), and they continue to bear witness every day: "The heavens declare the glory of God, and the firmament shows His handiwork" (*Psalms* 19:2). Still, cognitive man remains aloof and insensitive, unable to appreciate the splendor which is manifest in the world around him. Even an occasional glance up, a rare appreciation of God's presence, will not suffice: "Unless the awareness of the ineffable mystery of existence becomes a permanent state of mind, all that remains is commitment without faith."[1] "Commitment without faith" describes the state of dual identity, of individual belief systems of "scientist" and "Jew"; it is obliterated by the development of a permanent sense of God's presence. This ability to feel "radical amazement," to stand in awe before God's creation, is at the core of spiritual growth, and is an essential part of the developments of *homo religiosus* within cognitive man. It is the result of *shemirat mitzvot*. But this is description, not explanation; the question endures in an altered form. If shifting the gaze of cognitive man from the minute subdivisions to the whole causes his spiritual growth, how then does *halachah* shift his gaze?

The gaze of the cognitive man is lifted by the constant recognition of God's presence which is the inevitable outcome of being *shomer halachah*. *Mitzvot* constantly remind him of the limitations of rational science, of a metaphysical truth beyond his empirically defined reality, and a divine significance becomes attached to the objects and events of the world:

> *When halakhic man comes across a spring bubbling quietly, he already possesses a fixed, a prior relationship with this real phenomenon, the complex laws regarding the halakhic construct of a spring. The spring is fit for the immersion of a zav (a man with a discharge); it may serve as a mei chatat (waters of expiation); it purifies with flowing water; it does not require*

---

1. Heschel, *God in Search of Man*, p. 137.

> *a fixed quantity of forty se'ahs, etc. When halakhic man approaches a real spring, he gazes at it and carefully examines its nature. He possesses, a priori, ideal principles and precepts which establish the character of the spring as a halakhic construct, and he uses the statutes for the purpose of determining normative law: does the real spring correspond to the requirements of the ideal halakhah or not?...When halakhic man looks to the western horizon and sees the fading rays of the setting sun or to the eastern horizon and sees the first light of dawn and the glowing rays of the rising sun, he knows that this sunset or sunrise imposes upon him anew obligations and commandments.* [1]

Virtually every object, event, or experience has a halachic significance; therefore the world is appreciated not only in a physical sense, but also as having an inherent religious quality. A spring is not merely a physical entity; it has a religious significance and I must relate to it in the manner commanded by God. *Halachah* demands an appreciation of and interaction with the world on a divine plane; with increased knowledge, physical reality assumes an ever increasing halachic significance. Thus, the will of God is placed at the center of one's vision, balancing the crushing rationality of cognitive man and keeping his gaze lifted above and beyond his mundane reductionist activities.

Furthermore, *halachah* forces one to explicitly recognize God's presence regularly and repeatedly. The simple act of uttering a *brachah* has profound implications: It is first, a recognition of the existence of God; and, an admission that what is in this world comes from God; third, an act of submission to the will of God. Even a trip to the supermarket, as one searches for kosher items, reiterates this statement of recognition of, dependence on, and submission to God. In this manner as well, *halachah* places God as the central focus of one's activities.

There is a more mystical understanding of the relationship between *halachah* and spirituality: through performing *mitzvot*, we increase God's presence in the world, and we feel spiritual by sensing His presence, by sensing holiness in our world and in ourselves. "Halakhic man craves to bring down the divine presence and holiness into the midst of space and time, into the midst of the finite, earthy existence."[2]

---

1. Soloveitchik, *Halakhic Man*, p. 20.
2. Ibid., p. 41.

Indeed, it is not just a craving but an obligation: "You shall be holy, for I the Lord your God am holy" (*Leviticus* 19:2). This *mitzvah* of holiness is followed by a description of how it can be fulfilled: The next thirty-five verses describe a variety of commandments. Thus, the way to holiness as individuals and as a nation is through the adherence to God's will. This relationship between *mitzvot* and sanctification is reflected in the text of the *brachot* recited over *mitzvot*: "Blessed are You, Lord our King, King of the universe, Who has sanctified us with His commandments, etc." All halachic acts are endowed with the power to sanctify because they are the method by which we may fulfill God's desire and command for us to be holy; they are the means through which God sanctifies us. Halachic acts reverse the *tzimtzum*, the contraction of God's presence in the world: Each *mitzvah* sanctifies by reducing this contraction, by increasing God's presence. Our awareness of this *kedushah*, of God's presence, is spirituality. While it is easy to feel spiritual in holy places — standing before the *Kotel* — or at holy times — during *Ne'ilah* on Yom Kippur — we have the ability, by living halachic lives, to bring spirituality and holiness to every place we might be, to bring *kedushah* to our excursions into and involvements with that which is *chol*.

*Halachah* sanctifies by regulating human activity, limiting the promptings and attractions of the body. For the greater good, impulse can be conquered, and to do so for the will of God is holy. Heschel asks, "Does not a work of art represent the triumph of form over inchoate matter?"[1] Without the starting materials, without "inchoate matter," there can be no form, no works of art. And just as form depends upon matter, so too *kodesh* depends upon *chol*: Our impulses are the "inchoate matter," the *chol*, of humanity, and *halachah* is the holy form superimposed on that matter, sanctifying it; "And now, Lord, You are our Father; we are the clay and You our Molder" (*Isaiah* 64:7). Thus actions are not categorically forbidden by *halachah*, our impulses not banished; instead, they are modulated. It is in this modulation of impulse, the imposition of a holy form onto the "inchoate matter" of human nature, that *kedushah* rests. Because this holy form is dependent upon raw materials, *halachah* does not deny our physical bodies and its physical needs and is based firmly in the world as we experience it. This is a singular truth of Judaism: There is no *mitzvah*

---

1. Heschel, *God in Search of Man*, p. 306.

to transcend the physical world, and the sum total of the *mitzvot* does not result in an escape from this world — "...if God had wanted man to become an angel and do everything as such, He simply would have created more angels. But His wish was to create *man.*"[1] Attempting to transcend the world which God has given us is futile, for "the heavens are the heavens of the Lord, but the earth he has given to the sons of man" (*Psalms* 115:16). It is only by living as God has created us and by interacting with the world in the manner which God has prescribed that one is sanctified.

Our appreciation of the synthesis of *kodesh* and *chol,* our inability to divide the sacred and the profane into completely unconnected spheres, reflects the human unity of soul and body: "The Holy One brings the soul and joins it to the body and judges them as one" (*Sanhedrin* 91b). *Halachah* gives expression to the transcendent yearnings of a soul bound inextricably to a physical man, and only by relating to the world through *halachah* can soul and body be satisfied not as discrete entities, but as an integrated one. And in this is the recognition of and imitation of God's unity, a unity which we acknowledge every day: *Shema Yisrael Hashem Elokeynu Hashem Echad.* The *Gemara* relates that when Rabbi Akiva was martyred, he died proclaiming God's unity, saying *Shema,* the word *"echad"* still on his lips. And a *bat kol* rang out: "Happy are you, Rabbi Akiva, that your soul departed with the word *echad"* (*Brachot,* 61b). Happy is the person who testifies to God's unity.

In *Numbers* 15:39-40, the relationship betweeen spirituality and *halachah* is clearly, succinctly stated in the *mitzvah* of *tzitzit*:

> *And it shall be tzitzit for you, that you may see it and remember all the commandments of the Lord and perform them, and not follow after your heart and after your eyes after which you stray. So that you may remember and perform all My commandments, and be holy to your God.*

Israel is commanded to wear *tzitzit* as a visual cue: Seeing them will result in remembering and performing. But the two verses understand differently the relationship between the *mitzvot* and these two activities. In the first verse, remembrance and performance are two separate, independent processes; Israel will see *tzitzit,* thus they will remember

---

1. Steinsaltz, Adin. "Human Holiness" in *The Strife of the Spirit,* Northvale, NJ: Jason Aronson Inc., 1988, p. 38.

the commandments, and then they will perform them. There is, however, a subtle change in the phrasing of the second verse: "So that you may remember and perform all my commandments." Now, the remembrance is coincident with the performance; they are intrinsically linked, a single process. *Remember* and *perform* God's commandments. This is the performance of *mitzvot* with *kavanah,* performance coupled with the remembrance that God's will is being done.

This difference in phrasing has further significance because there is a causal relationship between the two verses. What is the purpose of wearing *tzitzit*? To remember the *mitzvot,* and then to do them — thus one who remembers the *mitzvot,* and does them, will not stray; he will have modulated his impulses. But this is not spiritual growth; it is merely good behavior. How then does spirituality come about? Because obeying the first verse will cause fulfillment of the second verse. Obey the first verse: "remember . . . perform . . . not explore after your heart and after your eyes." Why? So that you *remember to perform* all My commandments" — so that the performance of *mitzvot* will be with *kavanah.* The simple adherence to *halachah* will certainly keep one from acting the wrong way, but that is not the end — rather it is the means through which one comes to perform *mitzvot* with the remembrance of God. And the result of combining performance with remembrance is that one becomes holy: "so that you remember and perform all My commandments, and be holy to your God." This holiness, closeness to God, is sensed as spirituality. However, such holiness requires more than a passing interest or a partial commitment, more than adherence to some fraction of God's commandments; rather, it requires fulfilling "all the commandments of the Lord."

I did not recognize the initial manifestations of my nascent spirituality; the unique experience could not be placed into any of my previously existing categories of emotional states. Unsure of how to characterize the feelings, I did not reflect upon them. Even upon arising from the *mikvah,* literally a new person, the single most important and intensely spiritual moment of my life, I was unsure of how to interpret my feeings. There was joy, happiness, relief, and a bit of trepidation, but there was something else which I could not articulate. I began to seek understanding of this feeling when I noticed its effect — a heightened desire to perform *mitzvot,* a desire which could not be attributed to some personal gain I would receive from their performance. The need to justify or rationalize *mitzvot,* to look for reasons for *mitzvot* that had meaning aside from the will of God, was fading. It has been noted that "as long as man sees religion as a source of satisfaction for his own needs, it is not God whom he serves but his own self."[1] As my spiritual awareness grows, my actions are performed increasingly for God's sake, not for my own satisfaction. Not that the satisfaction which I receive from *mitzvot* has declined, but my reasons for pursuing *mitvzot* are no longer as dependent upon that personal satisfaction. A pleasant consequence is that my enthusiasm for certain areas of *halachah* had improved greatly. This increased *kavanah* and devotion to *mitzvot* further increases my spirituality, which in turn increases my devotion to *mitzvot*. "Faith and works — *emunah* and *maaseh* — are indissolubly intertwined: Right conduct, the life of Halakhah, is a functional manifestation of *emunah,* and reciprocally, inspires the trust which informs it."[2]

To feel God's presence . . . it certainly was not part of my original set of pragmatic reasons for conversion, but it has been the most significant outcome. My experience reiterates a lesson taught long ago by Hillel: Three potential *gerim* approached Shammai with what he considered unacceptable demands — the first considered only the Written Law valid, the second wanted to be taught all of the Torah while standing on one foot, and the third wanted to be made the *Kohen Gadol* upon his conversion. Shammai rejected all three, but Hillel converted them (*Shabbat* 31a). He saw that in each of these cases, the *gerim* were not rejecting specific *mitzvot,* in which case a conversion cannot be performed, but rather they were simply misinformed. Thus the three were accepted as converts on the basis of their commitment to Judaism, while their level of knowledge was of secondary importance. Hillel recognized that for the newly religious, more important than a well-formulated theological position is an unwavering commitment to Judaism and to *halachah,* for the *halachah* is the way to holiness. And for those who find *halachah* spiritually empty, perhaps there is need to embrace the *halachah* in *every* area of life, for spiritual fulfillment demands more than a half-hearted commitment.

---

1. Heschel, *God in Search of Man,* p. 350.
2. Lamm, Norman. *Faith and Doubt,* NY: Ktav Publishing House, 1971, p. 9.

Dr. Allen Goldstein, MD

# Personal Glimpses of the Rav: The Human Side of Rabbi Joseph B. Soloveitchik, zt"l

FOR THE RAV, *ZT"L*, WHETHER IN *HALACHAH, AGGADAH, DRUSH* or personal relationships, there always seemed to exist two aspects to everything: *din/rachamim, yotzer/borei, zochor/nekeyva, cheftza/gavra*. My relationship with the Rav was also a dual one.

My initial encounter with the Rav was upon arriving at Yeshiva University as a freshman. After seven years of learning in the Telshe Yeshivah in Cleveland, I had a rather inflated image of my capabilities as a scholar. Rav Mendel Zachs, *zt"l*, also seemed impressed and I was assigned to the Rav's *shiur*. Needless to say, after the first *shiur*, my self-esteem quickly vanished. My classmates and I rapidly developed acute cases of fear. We all sat in the *shiur* with great trepidation, lest he call on us to read or explain a passage in the *Gemara*. I quickly learned that in the pursuit of intellectual honesty and "truth in learning," nothing can be an impediment. Respect, honor, dignity or esteem became meaningless in the pursuit of the true interpretation.

However, with the passage of time, even as we cowered in our seats, we learned to admire the Rav's genius as a *rebbe*, teacher, and, as he used to say, a *"melamed"* par excellence. We listened in awe and reverence as he clarified the most enigmatic and obscure passages. My favorite and most descriptive episode of this talent dates back to a *shiur* of two hours' length that consisted of a single *Tosafos* of six small lines. It was truly an inspirational and enlightening intellectual trip. By the end of *shiur* every choice of word, every letter in those six lines "danced and saluted." On the way out, my *chavrusa* turned to me guilelessly and said, "I will bet you *Tosafos* didn't understand that *Tosafos* as well as the Rav does."

It is, however, the other side of my relationship with the Rav that I would like to share with you. After the passing of Rebbetzin Tanya Soloveitchik, *a"h,* I was privileged to help care for the Rav's medical needs. I would see him routinely on Tuesday afternoons and on being called.

During these encounters, I began seeing an aspect of this brilliant intellectual giant that he painstakingly hid from the world. The world recognized the Rav as a *gaon* in creativity in the intellectual challenges to man. They did not realize that he was also a *gaon* in the moral, ethical challenges.

The *Gemara* (*Yebamoth* 79a) states that the nation of Israel is distinguished by three characteristics: *Rachmanim* — merciful, *Baishanim* — bashful, and *Gomlei Chassadim* — benevolent. During his weekly two-and-a-half-day stay in New York, in addition to teaching three lengthy *shiurim* to the students, giving a lengthy *shiur* to *baalei batim* at Congregation Morya in the evening, and occasional lectures in universities and graduate schools, the Rav was continuously badgered and beleaguered by *Roshei Yeshivah,* students, politicians and organizations seeking an audience for answers to *she'elos,* clarifications of positions, and advice on all number of topics. Nevertheless, no matter how busy he was, he found time each week to visit a wheelchair-bound rabbi, who had been stricken by a neuromuscular disorder.

~§ Every Erev Yom Tov, the Rav placed long-distance calls to a number of widowed *rebbetzins* of *musmachim* who had learned with him. A postcard with the Rav's unique handwriting brought *Leshanah Tovah* greetings unfailingly every year. Good Yom Tov wishes by telephone enhanced the simchas Yom Tov in our house.

~§ The Rav spearheaded the creation of an anonymous fund for a widow of one of his students, who had been left in a difficult financial position. He also contributed generously from his own pocket. I was astounded when I happened to learn of the vast dollar amounts that the Rav himself distributed to various *yeshivos* and other charities.

◆§ A graduate of Yeshiva University, married with 3 children, who had never been the Rav's student, lay terminally ill in Mount Sinai Hospital. Upon discovering the gravity of the situation, the Rav asked to visit him.

◆§ The maid who cleaned the Rav's apartment was retired by Yeshiva University without fanfare. When he became aware of this, he sent one of the boys to buy a cake and a present and himself hosted a farewell party.

◆§ The class was once puzzled when suddenly the lengthy *shiurim* became obviously shortened. The Rav had become aware that a student who had developed a serious hematologic disorder would have had to leave before the end of *shiur* to receive his treatments, and discreetly shortened the length of the *shiur*.

◆§ The birth of a son on Shabbos to a *musmach* with a pulpit in the Midwest presented a problem which was referred to the Rav. No *mohel* was available for a Shabbos *bris*. The Rav personally arranged a weekend trip for a *mohel* from New York.

A discussion once developed among several of us as to what the Rav's custom was regarding the recitation of the *p'sukim* and the *Ribono Shel Olam* prayer during *Birkhas Kohanim*. The answer came from a respected rabbi. He related that a congregant of his had been orphaned as a very young child. The boy davened in the Maimonides Shul. During *Birkhas Kohanim*, the Rav would take the young orphan under his own talis.

I once had to hospitalize the Rav on an Erev Shavuous. My decision to stay with him in the hospital was overridden by him. He opened the Rambam to *Hilchos Yom Tov,* 7:17 and insisted that I join my family. A *minyan* was arranged, and the nurses were instructed to attend to the "special patient." After Yom Tov, the nurses reported that visitors had been continuously present all day. The nurses were so overwhelmed by this scene and by the Rav's pleasant conduct, that a gentile nurse exclaimed to me, "I understood that he was a special rabbi, but I didn't know he was the world's greatest rabbi."

One year, *Shabbos Parshas Vayikra,* our family visited Boston. We *davened* with the Rav. Following *Minchah,* as was the custom in Maimonides every Shabbos, we all sat around and hurled questions on the *sidrah* at the Rav. The Rav had invited me to sit near him. My son,

> During one of his trips to New York, the Rav passed out in the plane. I was called to meet him at the airport. When he was brought out by wheelchair, it became evident that he was merely dehydrated. To ascertain his mental status, I asked him the day of the week and the date. He correctly answered Tuesday but missed the month and date badly. Noticing the surprise on my face, he said: "You know you don't ask a Brisker dates. Ask me a Rambam."

aged 8, was on my lap. After several beautiful and brilliant explanations by the Rav, my son suddenly called out in a very loud stage whisper: "Daddy, is the Rav smarter than *Hashem*?" The Rav chuckled and flashed him a big smile. The encouragement inspired my son to try to stump the Rav. He asked him "Why is *Vayikra* written with a small *aleph*?" The Rav praised the question and rephrased it for the audience. He explained: If the purpose of the small *aleph* is to differentiate between Moshe and Bilaam, why did the Torah not do this in *Sh'mos* where *vayikra el Moshe* first appears? After again commending my son on the excellence of the query, the Rav proceeded with a beautiful explanation. A large set of Rambam, with a poetic handwritten *brachah* on the front leaf of the first volume, was a Bar Mitzvah gift from the Rav to my son which is, of course, a cherished treasure today.

On occasions when he was not feeling well, the Rav stayed in our home. During breakfast one morning, my 3-year-old daughter climbed on the Rav's lap, sampled his cottage cheese, and then proceeded to engage in a very serious give-and-take about her favorite doll.

Following the last time the Rav was *Mesader Kiddushin* in New York, I stayed with him near the *chupah* until the dancing crowd cleared the hall. As we were walking out, a little old lady approached the Rav and asked him for a business card. She explained that her granddaughter was about to be married. She was so impressed by the Rav's performance that she would like him to officiate. Politely and gently, he replied that he was soon returning to Boston and would have to decline.

According to the Rav, the prohibition of *lo tesaev mitzri ki ger hoyisa b'artzo* was commanded to Jews to inculcate in us the *midah* of *hakoras hatov*. The theme recurs numerous times in the Torah to establish it as a basic component in the Jewish ethic. Kindnesses to the Soloveitchik family were never forgotten and always repaid in excess. For many

*Personal Glimpses of the Rav* / 35

> In the later years, one of his students was given the privilege of serving the Rav in his apartment. One ambitious fellow used the opportunity frequently to ask the Rav difficult and perplexing questions. When I witnessed this, I asked the Rav about it. He smiled; "He thinks that I don't realize that I am writing his Ph.D. thesis for graduate school."

months he traveled to the Bronx every Wednesday to visit a *rebbetzin* receiving chemotherapy for a malignancy. Her only tie to the Rav was that her father had done a kindness to Reb Moshe, the Rav's father. When Professor Louis Ginzberg of the Jewish Theological Seminary died, the Rav went to visit the mourning family. They asked if the Rav knew the deceased. He replied that he had met him once. Later, he explained that the meeting occurred when Professor Ginzberg came to pay a *shiva* call after Reb Moshe's *petira*.

It is well known that Reb Chaim was *machmir* in *pikuach nefesh*. The Rav extended this position. The father of a student developed a severe post-operative infection that baffled the infectious disease team of a hospital on Long Island. A preeminent specialist from a university hospital, formerly a student of the Rav, refused all calls and invitations to consult on the matter. A personal call from the Rav, including a definition of *pikuach nefesh*, had him at the bedside within two hours.

The Rav amassed a phenomenal wealth of medical information in many areas. When the *Rebbetzin* was ill, the Rav was more familiar with medical literature on her condition than many of her attending physicians. At a medical ethics seminar, a noted oncologist was introduced to the Rav. After a lengthy conversation, the doctor commented to me that he thought that he had been speaking to a medical colleague.

When the early signs of Parkinson's appeared, the Rav described his symptoms precisely and clearly to the doctors. They suspected that he had consulted the medical books on the subject. In fact, it was only many years later that the Rav began suspecting that he was suffering from the disease.

The Rambam on the *pasuk* "*vayikra lo kel Elokei Yisrael*" (*Genesis* 33:20) quotes the *Gemara Megillah* to explain that God called Yaakov *kel*. The Rav explained: We are commanded (*Deuteronomy* 28:9) *Vehalachta b'derachav* — you should walk in His ways. The *Gemara*

(*Sotah* 14a) asks: "How can we walk after the *Shechinah*? Is it not a consuming fire?" Rather, it means that one should imitate His ways. This is the meaning of the *pasuk*: If you want to know what are the ways of God, then look at the Yaakovs, the *talmidei chachamim*, and the *Roshei Yeshivah* — they represent God on the earth. The Rav, though well concealed, was such a model.

Rev Velvel Brisker was once asked why the world recognized the Chofetz Chaim as a great *tzaddik* but not as a profound *talmid chacham*, despite his authorship of the monumental halachic work of the *Mishnah Brurah*. He replied that the Chofetz Chaim prayed daily that God keep his scholarly abilities hidden, and so they were. Why then did he not pray for a similar camouflage of his ethical behavior? The reply was that the Chofetz Chaim was aware of his talmudic abilities — but he was not aware of his *tzidkus*. Similarly, the Rav's ethical behavior was so ingrained that he did not feel it to be extraordinary. Thus, the entire world unanimously acknowledged him as a giant in *talmud Torah* and intellectual creativity. Those of us who had the privilege to get close to him knew him also as a giant in *midos*.

יה"י זכרו ברוך

*Matis Greenblatt*

# The Prophet of Spiritual Renewal

*Thoughts in honor
of the 50th Yahrzeit of
Rav Avraham Yitzchak Kook zt"l*

"There are souls which serve as receptacles for the 'light.' But there are more sublime souls which are themselves the 'light.'"
(Sfas Emes)

A S THE YEARS SLIP BY SINCE RAV KOOK'S PASSING, HIS figure grows larger and more impressive. The problems he grappled with and the solutions he proposed can be even better appreciated today than they were in his own day; the intensity and reality of his faith inspire us and strengthen our own faith; and his vision, breadth and courage can help to guide us through the seemingly overwhelming problems of our own tumultuous and difficult era.

## ৵ Faith and Divine Mission

From the vantage point of our basically cynical, secular world, perhaps the most striking factor about Rav Kook was the certainty and reality of his faith. For Rav Kook, the Divine Presence was a daily, tangible experience, and Providence, he felt, had selected him to bridge the great and growing gap between the religious establishment and the irreligious builders of the new *Yishuv*.

Shabbetai Don-Yahia, the late editor of *Hatzofe* and a former disciple of the Rav, once said: "Rav Kook was different than normal human beings. He . . . at times could detach himself completely from his terrestrial surroundings and communicate with higher spheres. If you should ask me, what is *Ruach Hakodesh,* I would not be able to answer you. But in the presence of Rav Kook I felt what *Ruach Hakodesh* must be like."

Isaac Halevy, the brilliant historian and founder of Agudas Yisroel, wrote to Rav Kook, "I well know and make known publicly that God has sent you to Eretz Yisroel to be a sustainer of life."

The profound inner harmony of the Rav's soul was reflected in his face. Dr. Pinchas Cohn, political secretary to Chaim Weizmann during the London period, relates: "In the midst of the dark, anxiety-ridden days of World War I, I was undergoing a personal crisis and decided to visit the Rav and relate to him what troubled me and surely he would be able to provide me with words of encouragement and strength. To visit the Rav one needed no entrance pass, not even prior notification. His home was open to all and the Rav helped each needy person as best he could. Between visitors, he went back to his study and writing.

"When I entered the hall where the Rav sat, no one else was present and the Rav sat at the head of the table completely immersed in learning a *sefer*. I looked at his face and it was exceptionally serene. A quiet sublimity surrounded him, a peacefulness out of place in the stormy world about. I remained as if glued to my spot and so I stood and continued to peer at him. Gradually, my anxiety dissolved, my heart was quieted and my soul was restored. I had no need to speak. I quietly backed away and left. From the peacefulness of the Rav, I had derived all that I needed."

Rav Kook's two leading disciples, the Gaon and Zaddik Rabbi Y.M. Charlop and Rabbi David Hakohen, were both first drawn to the Rav by hearing him pray. That experience changed the course of their lives.

## ↦ Emphasis on the Thought, Spirit and Ethics of Judaism

Rav Kook never ceased to stress that religious Jewry's inability to influence contemporary Jewry was in large measure due to our failure to emphasize and communicate the inner spiritual force of Judaism as expressed in the whole range of our ethical, philosophic, *Kabbalistic* and *Aggadic* literature.

*Maran,* the late *Rosh Yeshiva,* Rabbi Yitzchak Hutner zt"l, was greatly influenced by Rav Kook's emphasis and even utilized the Rav's precise terminology,[1] "Hilchos Dayos V'chovos Halevovos" in describing his own profound *mamorim* (lectures).

## ◆§ Creating a Devout, Learned, but Self-Confident Generation

The Rav's faith enabled him to confront the whole range of modern-day problems with confidence and courage. He strove to help create a thoroughly learned and devout generation, who at the same time could contribute to and influence the shape and character of the exploding renaissance going on around them. He sought to replace the image of the *Golut* Jew as a bent, fearful, somewhat pathetic figure, with a deeply spiritual but joyous, self-confident new generation.

## ◆§ One Nation

Rav Kook sharply decried and was deeply pained by all forms of irreligiosity, but never gave up on all Jews who continued to identify themselves as part of *Klal Yisroel*. He was strongly opposed to dividing religious and irreligious Jews into separate camps as if the irreligious were no longer part of *Klal Yisroel*. In this regard he pointed to the symbolism of the *arava* on Succos and the foul-smelling *chelbana* used in the *ketores* (incense). He wrote with great feeling:

> "The pure Zaddikim do not complain about evil, but increase justice; do not complain about lack of faith, but increase faith; do not complain about ignorance, but increase wisdom."

Once a group of workers who were unable to finish constructing a building before *Rosh Hashanah* continued their work on the Holy Day itself. The neighbors immediately notified the Rav, and shortly thereafter, the Rav's messenger arrived at the building site, *Shofar* in hand.

---

1. In his essay *Tchiyat Hakodesh.*

## Rav Kook on Education

On the individual level, Rav Kook emphasized the necessity of providing each child with the opportunity to develop in the specific fields for which he had a unique gift or inclination, rather than forcing him into a prescribed learning mold. He warned that such compulsion could and did lead to defections from the ranks of Judaism which could easily have been avoided. (Orot HaTorah pps. 43-44)

On a broader level, he recognized the importance of knowing secular subjects as well as gaining familiarity with the spirit of the times as a prerequisite to making an impact on the contemporary world (*Ikvay Hatson* p. 129). He also recognized the need for and supported vocational education.

On the other hand, he warned against under-estimating the continuing value of the old style *cheder*. In a letter to Rabbi Fishman (Maimon), who had spoken disparagingly of an old style yeshiva, Rav Kook sharply rebuked him for his remarks and pointed out that the pure, unadulterated method of Torah education was still the main source for sanctity and outstanding scholarship. (Letters v. 2, pps. 206-7)

And in his frequently referred to (but seldom read) address at the dedication of Hebrew University, Rav Kook underscored the profound apprehensions which must accompany education partaking of outside knowledge.

His perspective did not reflect an empty tolerance of diverse approaches, but rather a profound grasp of the legitimacy of different approaches, each in its own way, contributing to *Kavod Shamayim*.

In the end, the primary goal of education, was seen by Rav Kook as a means to develop the best in man by attaching himself to the divine through the medium of Torah. All other considerations are secondary. (Letters v. 1, pps. 218-9; Orot HaTorah p. 14)

---

He approached the startled workers, blessed them with a good year, and informed them that the Rav had asked him to blow *Shofar* on their behalf, so that they could fulfill their obligation. He therefore asked if they would interrupt their labor to listen, whereupon he said the *bracha* and began to blow.

The Rav's words and the *Shofar's* blast fulfilled their purpose. With each blast the Jewish core was touched and aroused. The workers left their tools and work, gathered round the blower and some began to cry. They recalled the images of their parents, the *shtetl* and the synagogue and asked themselves, "What happened to us?" After the blasts were completed, they said little but all agreed to discontinue their work. They changed their clothing and joined the prayers at the synagogue of the Rav.

## ~§ Material and Spiritual Renewal

Rav Kook's perspective was panoramic and all encompassing. Though renowned for his love of every Jew, he was also an extremely penetrating, perceptive and sophisticated critic.[1] While discerning sparks of Yiddishkeit in the intense devotion of the irreligious settlers to the physical rebuilding of the land, he was sickened[2] by their disregard of Torah observance. However, he saw their generation as transitional, to be ultimately supplanted by descendants loyal to Torah.

With prophetic insight he predicted 80 years ago that the irreligious pioneers' ideological zeal would wane and wither, and that believing Jews would launch the true, spiritual renewal.

## ~§ Unity

Besides his interpretation of the return to and renewal of *Eretz Yisroel*, Rav Kook provided a world view unmatched by any other modern Jewish thinker in its scope, originality and loyalty to the mainstream of Jewish thought. He enabled intelligent, observant Jews to view the world as a place which must be improved rather than neglected. He sought for the spiritual unity of life and demonstrated that Torah was not removed and distant from the flow and flux of everyday life.

But perhaps his greatest contribution was to provide meaning, by his inspired thought and extraordinary deeds, to the profound historical changes that *Klal Yisroel* was and is experiencing in the modern era. He clarified the special role that our generation has to play in the dramatic unfolding of Jewish history.

Herman Wouk has written that to present Judaism to our age requires two qualities: prophecy and monumental scholarship. In the person of Rav Kook, both qualities were present in abundance. Yet unfortunately, the true nature of his life and works have been clouded by misunderstanding. The time is right to clarify and communicate his message for our confused generation.

---

1. Space does not permit discussions of his thoughtful criticism of Zionism, Mizrachi, Agudah, Mussar etc.
2. It should be emphasized that he was never reconciled to irreligiosity. There is much misrepresentation on this point.

*Rabbi Nehemia Polen*

# Sensitization to Holiness: The Life and Works of Rabbi Kalonymos Kalmish Shapiro

ONE OF THE LUMINOUS FIGURES OF TWENTIETH-CENTURY *Hassidim* in Poland, that world that is no more, was Rabbi Kalonymos Kalmish Shapiro. Known as the Piaseczner Rebbe, he was a multifaceted personality who served as *Hassidic* master to an intellectual elite as well as to the desperately poor common folk of interbellum Poland. Famed as a pedagogue, educational theorist, and founder of a yeshiva, he was also sought after for medical advice and referrals. In the Warsaw Ghetto, as Polish Jewry went through its death agony, Rabbi Shapiro continued to teach, to encourage, to give material and spiritual support, and finally to show how it is possible to maintain a radiant faith in the midst of profound darkness and despair. His book *Esh Kodesh*, written after most of his family had already died in the war, is the last work of *Hassidism* written in Poland.

Born in 1889, R. Shapiro was a descendant of many of the most famous masters of Polish *Hassidism*, including Rabbi Elimelekh of Lyzhansk, the Seer of Lublin, and the Maggid of Kozienice. His father, Rabbi Elimelekh of Grodzisk, passed away when Kalonymos was but three years old, and the young boy was raised by his mother, Hannah Berakhah, as well as by the man who was to become his father-in-law, Rabbi Yerahmiel Moshe Hapstein of Kozienice (1860-1909). Soon after the passing of his father-in-law, he became Rebbe and then community

Rabbi in Piaseczno, a town just outside of Warsaw. In 1923, he founded the yeshiva Da-as Moshe, named after his father-in-law. In the pre-war period, it was one of the largest *Hassidic* yeshivot in Warsaw.

The period between the two World Wars was a time of revolutionary change for Jewish family life in Poland. The generation gap was perhaps even more pronounced than it was in America. The processes of Polonization and secularization were affecting the youth in particular, so that parents steeped in tradition were often viewed by their children as being hopelessly backward. In addition, the shift of population to the large cities brought new pressures and tensions to the *Hassidic* movement. Crammed into the teeming streets, alleys, and tenements of Warsaw, Lodz and other large cities, the *Hassidic* milieu was quite different from the largely rural setting of the movement's pristine youth. Warsaw, for example, was known as the "Paris of Eastern Europe"; it boasted a vibrant cultural life, including theater, art, music, and moving pictures, not to mentioned cafes and other less attractive elements of city life. Even for those youngsters who could not or did not wish to assimilate into Polish society, the many active Jewish youth movements provided an avenue for political activity as well a nurturing environment, a surrogate home. These socialist, Zionist, Yiddishist, and other youth movements were largely secular in nature and served as a vehicle of escape for those who wished to leave the bonds of traditional society and Jewish observance. For these reasons, defections were becoming increasingly commonly even in *Hassidic* circles. Finally, when we recall the extreme poverty which prevailed in the Jewish community as a whole (largely as a result of government-fostered discrimination), we get some glimpse at the problems which faced the *Hassidic* educator.

It must also be noted that the *Hassidic* movement had undergone changes since its early days. The freshness, vitality, and boldness which had once characterized the movement had inevitably dissipated somewhat with the passage of time. A movement which was once daring and innovative in its spirituality had become to some extent predictable, even conservative. While reformers had periodically made efforts to breathe new life into the movement from within, it was nevertheless true that by the twentieth century, the appellation *"Hassid"* often had more to do with attachment to a specific community, adherence to its modes of dress and loyalty to its leader, than with the fostering of inner spirituality as taught by the Ba'al Shem Tov and his disciples.

Rabbi Shapiro's goals for his yeshiva were more far reaching. He wished to develop a core group of students of "sublime stature" (*b'nai aliyah*) who might revitalize the *Hassidic* movement. But if the original Beshtian vision was to be recovered, it would now require a systematically presented, developmental approach to *Hassidic* spirituality. This was the task which R. Shapiro set for himself.

The outline of his approach were presented in his first book, *Hovat ha-Talmidim* ("The Students' Responsibility"), first published in 5962 (1932) in Warsaw. The introduction, directed to teachers and parents, addresses the failure of traditional educational methods to stem the rising tide of defections from the observant community. The answer, says R. Shapiro, is not more authoritarian discipline and rote learning, but to imbue the child with a vision of his own potential greatness and to enlist him as an active participant in his own development. The teacher must learn to speak the language of the student, and to graphically convey the delights of a life of closeness to God. In earlier times it was possible to teach the structure of Jewish religious practice without imparting a sense of its inner significance, in the hope that practice would lead to genius involvement and inner commitment. Now, however, writes R. Shapiro, the youngster's intellectual and emotional capabilities develop at an earlier age than previously, and the child must be presented, from the very beginning of his educational career, with a sense of the inner beauty of the life of Torah, to prevent his being captured by the far more obtrusively and blatant attractions of the big city and its culture. Talk of punishment should be avoided, for it is the surest way to alienate the student. Instead the teacher should sprinkle his teaching with touches of humor, and should also not neglect to invoke the power of imagination, in such forms as the parable and the story, while imparting his message.

The text itself constantly reminds the student of the powerful spiritual potential within him, that he is a descendant of the prophets of Israel, and must work hard to uncover the greatness inside him. Psychologically astute advice is given for character flaws: If a student feels an obsessive hatred towards a fellow, then:

"Write him a letter (but don't send it!) . . . Heap scorn on him, as much as your venomous heart desires; for several days read the letter out loud, while imagining that you are facing him and reviling him with those words of abuse. After some days of this, no doubt your anger will leave your heart, and . . . you will hasten to reconcile with him."

*Hovat ha-Talmidim* was the only work of R. Shapiro to be published in his lifetime. It established his reputation as a master of *Hassidic* educational theory. The essayist Hillel Zeitlin wrote a review of the book soon after it appeared, in which he praised the author for bringing order and method into *Hassidic* studies, for his emphasis on *simcha* — joy, and for injecting vitality and freshness in the life of the yeshiva student. Zeitlin concluded, "This book is a gateway for anyone, in particular for the modern Jew who has felt a genuine urge to return to his tradition (*niznez be-libo hirhur teshuvah amitit*), to enter into the palace of *Hassidism*."

Another work, which remained in manuscript during R. Shapiro's lifetime, but which has since been published in Israel, is *Hakhsharat ha-Avrekhim* ("The Young Men's Preparation"). This book, meant for those who had already mastered the material in *Hovat ha-Talmidim,* emphasizes the development and channeling of emotion. Nowadays, he writes, *hitlahavut* — fervor, must be taught and developed — by employing such means as song, music and dance (in common with other Rebbeim of his lineage, R. Shapiro played the violin himself, and would often lead his *Hassidim* in song on the violin). The goal is to "uncover one's soul," to "grab one's soul by the scruff of its neck," as he puts it.

There is a great emphasis on employing the imagination, in the form of *mahshavah hazakah* — "intense thought," which involves focusing on specific mental images and scenes, designed to bind one's bodily emotions to a sacred matrix. He suggests, for example, imagining oneself at the Holy Temple in Yerushalayim, going into the courtyard, past the *mizbeah* (altar), and finally standing at the Holy of Holies. There are passages where R. Shapiro takes one on a guided journey of a visit to Rebbe, a *Se'udah Shelishit* (Third Sabbath Meal), a festival, or turning to biblical motifs — he has us accompany Abraham and Isaac at the *Akedah,* or the Children of Israel at the Exodus from Egypt. The guided imagery is vivid and detailed, and is designed to awaken the spiritual sensitivity of the reader.

R. Shapiro introduces a technique of witnessing one's thoughts to correct negative habits and character traits. This is based on his notion that the examination of a thought from the outside tends to dampen it. He advises not to dwell in the negative thought pattern, but scrutinize the negative thought while remaining aloof from it. This technique of witnessing the stream of one's thoughts without being caught up in them eventually crystallized into a meditation practice which he called *hashkatah*[1] — silencing the conscious mind. Once the mind is silenced or stilled, it is fully receptive to *mahshavah ahat shel kedushah* — the focusing on one holy thought (a brief phrase of Torah) — to fill the mind with holiness. The next stage in the meditation is to ask God, in a quiet yet articulated manner, for help in attaining a spiritual gift, such as faith, love of God, or liveliness in His service. The meditation session ends in a *niggun*. R. Shapiro intimated that those who practice this meditation for several weeks would come to know the meaning of the verse "This is my God" (*Exodus* 15:2) in a most tangible way.

One proposal discussed in *Hakhsharat ha-Avrekhim* was the formation of a spiritual fellowship, with membership dependent on sincere dedication to the group's spiritual and fraternal goals. Taken as a whole, his approach might be called "Sensitization to Holiness," the goal of which was to arouse and sensitize the individual to the holiness within him; once the person was sensitized to the holiness within, he would be awakened to the holiness in the Torah, in the mitzvot, and in those extraordinary individuals called *tzaddikim*, and would be well on his way to becoming a *Hassid* in reality as well as in name.

R. Shapiro was more than just a theoretician of *Hassidic* pedagogy. As an active Rebbe, he daily came into contact with people from all over Poland who sought his help. In particular, he was famed for his knowledge of medicine. It is said that he acquired his medical knowledge, which seems to have included clinical practice, from physicians such as Dr. Aharon Soloveitchik, Chief of Surgery at the Jewish Hospital in Warsaw. Through the good offices of Dr. Soloveitchik, R. Shapiro's prescriptions, written in Latin, were accepted and filled in Warsaw pharmacies.

One of his *Hassidim* tells the following story. Once a *Hassid*, an old-timer of pure and simple faith, came to the Rebbe, complaining that his headaches had returned ever since the Rebbe's prescriptions had faded. The *Hassidim* who were present were puzzled by the notion of a "faded" prescription, but in any event the Rebbe took pen in hand and wrote a new prescription for the man. The man took the piece of paper and placed it firmly in the band of his hat, breathing a sigh of relief: "Thanks to the Rebbe, I feel so much better — my headache is gone!" The *Hassidim* could barely control their laughter, but the Rebbe turned

---

1. This meditation practice was described to the author by a close disciple of Rabbi Shapiro.

to them and gently explained that "The modern world classify this as 'suggestion,' but we who hold fast to the way of the Besht call it *emunah peshutah* — simple faith." The Rebbe further explained that the blessing of any person who maintains purity of speech and thought is effective for healing, but "in order to cover this effect in the garb of natural causation, I write prescriptions."

R. Shapiro was very striking in his appearance. He is universally recalled as being handsome and well groomed, distinguished and elegant — though not "modern" in his dress. He radiated an aura of dignity and nobility. His eyes were penetrating, his manner thoughtful and deliberate. As one person put it, "He was the most impressive man I ever met in my life. You could not be indifferent to him."

Those who knew his family well and who were often present at his home recall the atmosphere of love and respect which prevailed in the household. The mutual devotion and admiration between the Rebbe and his wife, Rahel Hayyah Miriam Hapstein, were evident to all. Like her three sisters, all daughters of the previous Kozienicer Rebbe, Rahel Hayyah Miriam was very learned; she would avidly follow her husband's discourses. In one passage of *Hakhsharat ha-Avrekhim,* he notes that his wife reviewed his writings, making comments and posing questions. When she passed away in 1937, he wrote a poignant and moving letter to his *Hassidim* in *Eretz Israel* eulogizing her.

The following took place soon after her passing: The Rebbe led one of his close *Hassidim* to a cabinet in his home, opened up the drawer and took out a piece of paper. On it was written a *ma'amar* — Hassidic discourse of the Rebbe, but, as the *Hassid* noted, the handwriting changed in the middle of the paper. The Rebbe explained that he was writing up his *ma'amar* when he was called away for a medical consultation. When he returned, he saw that his Rebbetzin had picked up the pen and finished writing the *ma'amar.* Displaying the paper in his hand like a treasure, the Rebbe looked at the *Hassid* and said, "You see, this is the true fulfillment of the verse *'And they shall be one flesh'* (*Genesis* 2:24)!"

We cannot assess what the full impact of R. Shapiro's leadership might have been, for nearly everything was swept away in the years of catastrophe. In the very first weeks of the war, during the bombing of Warsaw, he already lost his son and much of his immediate family; yet instead of being broken, he continued teaching, leading clandestine services, counseling and consoling, as well as providing material assistance to others. Time and again he was offered opportunities to escape to the relative safety of the East, behind the Russian lines, but he refused them all, saying, "I am not going to desert my *Hassidim* at this difficult time! Wherever my *Hassidim* are, that's where I must be. I will not consent to saving myself while leaving my *Hassidim* abandoned!" He risked his life to keep *mikvaot* open, to perform circumcisions (he was an expert *mohel*), and to celebrate the holidays in the proper manner.

But the most lasting legacy of those days in the Warsaw Ghetto was the book he wrote, based on his Sabbath talks from September 1939 until July 1942, the time of the Great Deportation. Here emerges the true greatness of this *Hassidic* master: the profound faith in God, the attempt to provide a measure of comfort and hope to his flock, the ability to transcend the horrific events of the moment and to transport himself and his listeners to a realm of peace and sanctity — all this and much more is evident on each page of *Esh Kodesh*. R. Shapiro never mentions the evil ones, the perpetrators, by name. The struggle is depicted entirely on the spiritual plane. There are passages which give no trace of their provenance, passages of great lyrical splendor and compositional grace, where the author totally transcends his personal situation, expressing a lofty vision in which all events of the mundane world, as well as the words of Torah, are seen as harmonious aspects of one Divine revelation, so that: "one hears the Torah's voice from the world as a whole; from the chirping of the birds, the mooing of the cows, from the voices and tumult of human beings — from all these one hears the voice of God in the Torah . . . " (*Esh Kodesh,* p.163).

Other passages explore the meaning of evil from a kabbalistic and *Hassidic* perspective and the nature of *emunah* — faith. Finally, drawing upon talmudic and midrashic sources, R. Shapiro develops a most daring conception of the meaning of *hester panim* — "the eclipse of God." For R. Shapiro, this biblical formulation does not mean that God hides His face, indifferent to the fate of His people. To the contrary, His pain, as it were, at Israel's suffering is so great that the world would explode were it to manifest; hence God turns aside and weeps, as it were, in His "inner chambers." But by means of a profound communion in suffering, the Jew may find God even there.

Rabbi Shapiro did not survive the war. His life was taken on 4 Heshvan, 5704 (November 1943). Shortly before he was taken away, he buried the manuscript of his writings, along with some last minute addenda, one of which acknowledges that, although the Jewish people had known many persecutions in the past, what they were undergoing at that time was simply without parallel. The manuscript was discovered after the war and eventually published by his nephew in Tel Aviv. As mentioned above, *Esh Kodesh* remains, in effect, the last testament of *Hassidism* in Poland. In a profoundly moving cover letter appended to the manuscript, R. Shapiro begs "every Jew to study my works; surely the merit of my holy ancestors will stand him and his household in good stead, both in this world and the world to come . . . ".

It is the belief of this writer that the life and works of Rabbis Shapiro are not only a monument to an illustrious past, but may yet serve as a beacon and guide for the future, for those thirsting for an authentic and profound Jewish spirituality. May his merit indeed guide us.

*Marvin Schick*

# Rav Aharon Lo Meit:
# The Legacy of Rav Aharon Kotler

IN A SPIRITUALLY IMPOVERISHED AGE WHEN THE PURSUIT OF THE "good life" envelops so many of us, it is nearly impossible to experience the essence and grandeur of the giants of our faith whose example inspires us and whose leadership elevates the community. We must rely on external evidence — on stories of their good deeds, for example — which while useful may not give us a satisfactory appreciation of what it was which impelled such men to greatness, what it was which lifted them above the masses of Torah-abiding Jews and invested them with the authority of leadership which has been handed down from Sinai to the present.

Thus it is with Rav Aharon Kotler, *zt'l,* the great Lakewood Rosh Yeshiva who is widely regarded as the outstanding figure in the growth of religious Jewry in this country. The *yahrzeit* gives us reason to reflect on his teachings and legacy and to consider especially the elements which made him one of the towering personalities in Jewish life in this century.

We begin with the external evidence of photographs of Rav Aharon, most of them taken in the last, unbelievably busy, decade of his life when he was in his sixties. So many of them convey a fierce determination. They show a man who looks much older than he was — he was about seventy-one when he passed away — and yet there emanates from his face an eagerness to go on, a commitment to devote all of his energy and talent to the *K'lal,* irrespective of how spent he was. It is not an exaggeration to say that his face appeared to be encased in flames, that a fire — a fire of Torah — surrounded him.

That is how he appeared to those who were in his presence and that is how he is remembered.

By some rare spiritual chemistry which can only be explained in terms of the ultimate in *mesiras nefesh* which Rav Aharon constantly attained, his very being defied the ordinary laws governing physical and intellectual activity. For rather than existing in an antithetical relationship, with the exhaustion acting as a barrier to further activity, in Rav Aharon's case the exhaustion and the determination to face new challenges reinforced each other. The flame of extreme devotion, of maximum commitment, of total *mesiras nefesh* which burned strongly inside Rav Aharon was fed by the experience of total exhaustion.

The result of this symbiosis of exhaustion and action were two decades of daily exertion and communal and spiritual achievements which cannot be understood through any logical calculation of what can be done in a 24-hour day. In range and intensity, Rav Aharon's twenty years in the United States were in the realm of the incredible.

There were the *shiurim* and preparation for *shiurim,* including those given at other yeshivas and those given during his memorable visits to *Eretz Yisroel.* There was the individual learning in the *beis medrash* and in offices, as well as in cars and subways during the precious moments that he could snatch during lulls in community activity. There was study with *talmidim* and the need to respond to their questions. There was the correspondence with religious leaders around the globe, answering their queries and importuning them toward greater *K'lal* responsibility. There were his own Talmudic and homiletic writings. There was the travel to and from Lakewood, at least once a week and often more frequently, usually arduously by bus and subway, and to meetings, dinners and conferences. There were the meetings themselves — literally thousands of them — with Rav Aharon invariably serving as the chairman and as the key participant, always inspiring with the greatness of his passion and with the piety which radiated constantly from him. There were the tens of thousands of telephone calls, to raise money and to direct the religious community. There was the constant pressure of fund-raising for Lakewood, for Chinuch Atzmai, for communal causes such as Peylim and Tashbar, and for individual *chessed* needs. There were the countless other details of communal work, the larger and small tasks and obligations which Rav Aharon assumed as this exhausted and inspired man went about the herculean challenge of elevating the Torah community.

*Ashrei ayin re'itah kol eleh* ... and yet those who stood awestruck before this living embodiment of Har Sinai did not and maybe could not provide even a fraction of the help that was required of them, for Rav Aharon was, in a sense, of a different species. He had two hands and two feet and his organs were our organs and he also had but a 24-hour day. From the external evidence he was like the rest of us; even so, there was something which separated him.

As one contemplates Rav Aharon's activity during these twenty years and the toll which it exacted, there comes to mind the Rambam's famous letter to Rabbi Shmuel B. Judah Ibn Tibbon, in which he writes: "When night falls, I am so exhausted that I can scarcely speak."

※ ※ ※

Rav Aharon settled in the United States in 1941. A fanciful tale has been told about his relying on a mystical formula to determine where to live. Such musings, in addition to being wildly inaccurate, trivialize and distort the lives of our *Gedolei Torah* who are motivated by an intense, inescapable sense of communal obligation. Rav Aharon came here, after all, as a refugee during the *Churban* of European Jewry and he came from Japan, with the remnants of the great European yeshivas continuing on to Shanghai. He was, unquestionably, the leader, of this precious flock of scholar-refugees — the modern-day equivalent to Yavneh and its sages led by Rabbi Yochonon ben Zakkai at the time of the destruction of the Second Temple — and he had responsibility for the welfare of these Jews which could best be fulfilled in this country. That is the principal reason why he came to the United States.

He was motivated, as well, by a determination to build Torah in this country, thereby fulfilling the prophetic words of Rav Chaim Volozhin who foresaw early in the nineteenth century that one day the United States would be a place of Torah greatness. This determination grew in intensity and importance as the enormity of the destruction of European Jewry became known. The urgent task in 1941, however, was rescue work.

Immediately, he was engaged in this work as a leader of Vaad Hatzala which had been established by the Agudas Horabbonim (Union of Orthodox Rabbis). During the war years, the primary, though not exclusive, aim was assistance to scholars, for what could be done in Europe was, sadly, limited. When the war ended, Vaad Hatzala was reorganized and expanded, with Rav Aharon and Rav Eliezer Silver, *zt'l,* as its foremost figures, and maximum attention was given to European refugees, though the organization continued to assist the scholars and their institutions.

Vaad Hatzala, Rav Aharon's first American leadership experience, revealed two somewhat related qualities which characterized all of his later activity. He had the confidence — of course, the respect, as well — of religious and lay leaders across the spectrum of Orthodoxy and he worked closely and well with them. Although an Agudist commitment was central to his outlook and while he often opposed Mizrachi and, at times, Neturei Karta, he was able to enlist persons from these camps into his communal work. In Vaad Hatzala, for instance, he served, when necessary, as a peacemeaker between Mizrachi persons and those to the right.

There was an explosive aspect to Rav Aharon's activity, arising inevitably from the burden which he carried and the constant pressure which he faced, as well as from the intensity which he brought to all that he did. He was at the same time the gentlest and kindest of persons whose modesty and piety constantly inspired others to respond affirmatively to his plea that they shoulder *K'lal* responsibilities.

Linked to this was the great warmth which developed quickly between him and Orthodox lay leaders, almost all of whom could be said to have been modern in their orientation and not particularly learned. Rav Aharon had a genuine respect for lay persons, a point which perhaps should be underscored. He liked them and he was sincerely appreciative of the help which they gave. This gratitude was not merely the appreciation of the fund-raiser for the donor, but was predicated on a sincere caring for those lay persons who were involved in what he did. He was interested in them and their families and he was kind to them and their families.

※ ※ ※

In 1943, Beth Medrash Govoha was opened. Different persons have claimed credit for the decision to establish the yeshiva in Lakewood and for helping Rav Aharon in the early years. All who played a role have abundant reason to be proud of their participation and yet Lakewood — the greatest of our yeshivas — was the creation of Rav Aharon. He imbued it with his genius, with his vision and with his spirit and Beth Medrash Govoha exists today, enlarged and given additional strength by his noble successor and son, Rav Shneuer Kotler, zt'l, as the embodiment of his aspirations for Torah greatness in America.

The advanced yeshiva which Rav Aharon established was patterned after Volozhin and other outstanding European yeshivas of the preceding 150 years. It was not to be located in a major city, students were to dorm, and the program of study was devoted entirely to Torah study for its own sake, the ideal of *Torah Lishmoh*. That had been the lifeline of our people throughout the ages and through it alone could American religious Jewry be made secure and elevated.

In this mission, Rav Aharon faced formidable difficulties. Orthodox Jewry in the 1940's was an enfeebled community. Few religious Jews shared a commitment to *Torah Lishmoh* and few cared about the notion of young men in their twenties devoting themselves entirely to Talmudic study, without much, if any, apparent concern about making a livelihood.

Perhaps more problematically, American yeshiva students lacked the background — cultural and familial — which had been crucial to the emergence of Torah scholarship in eastern Europe and they obviously lagged considerably behind the level of knowledge and intensity in study that had been achieved in the advanced European yeshivas. Boys who just shortly before while in their late teens had been adept in baseball statistics were now to emerge as scholars who would become fully immersed in Torah study.

Some of this deficit was made up by the close bond which grew between Rav Aharon and his *talmidim*. He had visited here in the 1930's on behalf of the yeshiva in Kletzk — it was the predecessor to Lakewood — and he had given *shiurim* in American yeshivas. Possibly even then and surely later on he was moved by the "eidelkeit" (sweet and gentle disposition) of American yeshiva students.

Despite the considerable age difference between Rav Aharon and Lakewood's students and despite the perhaps even greater cultural gap — they were, with some exceptions, typical American boys — he related to them and there was deepfelt affection from the Rosh Yeshiva for his *talmidim*. This was particularly apparent on Shabbos when Rav Aharon took his meals in the yeshiva dining room. Then he would relax, usually for the first time in the week, and he would be strengthened by the company of the young students and enjoy the small bits of *zmiros* and the camaraderie which emerged as he spoke of *gedolim* and yeshivas in pre-*churban* Europe.

Many of his students — who can say how many? — could not grasp the Rosh Yeshiva's brilliant *shiurim* or even conduct a lucid conversation with him. His rapid-fire speech, springing from a prodigious mind which outpaced the organs of speech, was just too fast for a goodly number of those who listened to him. Besides, the students spoke an Americanized Yiddish, that was quite different in vocabulary and diction from his Yiddish. Yet, there was communication, born from warmth and love and the students learned and grew. Even as they stood trembling in his presence, even as the Torah flame that enveloped his sacred face instilled in them a feeling of awe, that flame gave them confidence and strength and out of the Torah foundry that was Lakewood, there was forged greatness in Torah. As Rav Aharon had foreseen when he named his yeshiva, Beth Medrash Govoha has attained the heights.

A generation after his passing, his vision and flame live in the growing number of yeshivas established by his students and already by his students' students who follow in the path that he laid out.

※ ※ ※

Rescue and Lakewood occupied the lion's share of Rav Aharon's time during his early years here. Though physically and emotionally taxed by these obligations — the fund-raising burden alone was enormous — and by the daily responsibility of advising and guiding on a host of community issues, he eagerly accepted additional challenges.

In the main, organizations have become instrumental in responding to the needs of the religious community. Corresponding to what has happened in this century throughout Western society and, more specifically, in Jewish life, Orthodox activity has been increasingly reflected through the medium of formal organizations. This is a significant development which distinguishes recent decades from the prior experiences of our people and about which Rav Chaim Soloveitchik, *zt'l*, was apparently deeply concerned, for there is the prospect that with the passage of time the organizational bureaucracy will capture full control of the group and that the organization will lose its original mission.

The problem is a serious one for *Gedolei Torah* when they participate in organizations for which they are presumed to make policy. They have their intrinsic responsibilities and demands — to study and teach, to write and counsel, and to lead those over whom they have influence — and they also obviously have much else to do. The point is that they are very busy men without the additional business of organizational life. As they enter the organizational world, they face the choice of whether to be involved in a limited fashion, in which case the organization can be beyond their control, or whether to commit themselves fully to the work and processes of the group, in which case they will become even busier and more burdened.

The choice, therefore, is not merely one style or preference. Rather, it entails a willingness to muster the psychological and physical strength to carry an additional burden.

With the possible exception of Rav Chaim Ozer Grodzienski, *zt'l*, no *gadol* of the past several generations has matched Rav Aharon's involvement in organizational life and it is probable that the burden in this respect on Rav Chaim Ozer was significantly less than it was on Rav Aharon.

By 1951 at the latest — a decade after his arrival — he was the pre-eminent figure in Agudath Israel, which he helped recast, in this country and, in fact, world-wide. He was the chairman, of course, of the Moetzes Gedolei HaTorah in America and the vital force linking *gedolim* in *Eretz Yisroel,* Europe and America in the post-*Churban* years.

Like most busy people — maybe like most people, busy or not — our religious leaders are reactive people in the sense that they respond mostly to matters which are brought to them by others. A *tshuva* or responsum, for example, is usually a reaction to a question that has been asked specifically of the respondent. If any of us would spend some time during the week in the home or office of a *gadol*, we would likely be struck by the number of incoming telephone calls. Indeed, the telephone and the car have added enormously to the physical drain on *gedolim* because they add enormously to the instances when *gedolim* must respond to what others want of them.

Because *gedolim* are overwhelmed by such reactive pressures and because they want time to learn and for other personal needs, as a rule, they have very little contact with one another. The appearance of frequent interaction and a collegial relationship does not correspond with the reality. In the very busy world in which they function, our Torah leaders more often than not act independently in their own spheres of concern. In Rav Aharon's time — and only then — the situation was different because he made it different by serving as a one-man Torah network, using the telephone and the car to maintain contact with other leaders. He was on the telephone constantly, forwarding information, giving and asking for advice, seeking support and, yes, pressuring. If a meeting or visit would advance his cause, it would be arranged quickly. At one time or another and in one way or another, Rav Aharon interacted closely with just about every one of the important Torah figures of the post-Churban period. In this respect, as well as others, he had no peer. One example of this networking was the prohibition issued in 1956 against Orthodox participation in joint rabbinical bodies with Reform and Conservative clergy. Ten Torah leaders joined Rav Aharon in promulgating the *issur.*

Rav Aharon's Agudist orientation had deep ideological roots, extending far beyond formal organizational activity and Agudah and Zeirei Agudah conventions, where he always was the major figure, at dinners and meetings. He had been involved in Agudah matters in Europe, playing an important role in the 1937 Knessiah Gadola, his relative youth notwithstanding. It is a measure of his authority that after the war he exerted enormous influence over Agudist policy in Israel, initially regarding attitudes toward the *Medinah* and then on such vital issues as electoral coalitions and participation in the government. Some of his visits to Israel purposely coincided with Knesset election campaigns. He may have been the party's most potent campaign weapon, as he made numerous speeches and worked feverishly to rally support among religious voters for the Agudist cause.

While his direct involvement in Israeli Agudah affairs may have resulted in part from the necessity to fill the leadership vacuum caused by the relative aloofness to the Agudah of the Chazon Ish and Brisker Rav, they being the foremost Torah luminaries of the time in *Eretz Yisroel,* it arose in greater measure from his transcendent stature and authority. Six thousand miles away and at a time when there surely were individuals of great Torah distinction in Israel, he was able to determine or influence so much of what happened in the religious camp.

※ ※ ※

When Rav Iser Zalman Meltzer, *zt'l,* his father-in-law, passed away in 1953, Rav Aharon succeeded him as Rosh Yeshiva of Etz Chaim in Jerusalem. At an Agudah convention some time later, Rav Eliezer Silver noted — somewhat in jest, but with much respect — that world Jewry now had a new kind of leader, "a transatlantic Rosh Yeshiva."

At the meeting of the Moetzes Gedolei HaTorah which chose Rav Moshe Feinstein as Rav Aharon's successor, the body also decided that the Lakewood Rosh Yeshiva was *chad b'dora* — alone in the generation — and that he alone had the authority to rule on Israeli questions. Henceforth, the American Moetzes would rely on its Israeli counterpart, to which it would defer.

The momentum of Rav Aharon's activity and the strength of his Agudist conviction carried some leading Roshei Yeshiva and rabbis who had been involved in Mizrachi work into the Agudah camp. He also directly influenced the Agudas Horabbonim, which, too, had long been Mizrachist in its outlook, toward an Agudist orientation. However, he never became active in that group and certainly never gave it the intense commitment which characterized his important communal undertakings.

By the 1950's it was already apparent that yeshivas and their deans or Roshei Yeshiva were emerging as the crucial creative force in American Orthodoxy. Accompanying this development was the parallel loss in role and status of pulpit rabbis and their synagogues. Some rabbis responded to this deterioration in their position by charging that the Roshei Yeshiva had usurped their authority and deliberately undermined the prestige and function of the Rabbinate. Yeshiva deans, they said, were hostile to synagogues and their spiritual leaders and they had induced their students not to pursue or consider rabbinical careers, to avoid active participation in synagogues, and, generally, not to have respect for pulpit rabbis.

As the leading Rosh Yeshiva of the era, Rav Aharon was the focal point of this criticism, even when his name was not specifically mentioned. Any effort to analyze the growth of Orthodoxy during this formative period must come to grips with this issue.

On a personal level, the notion that Rav Aharon was hostile to rabbis is extremely wide off the mark. He was not, in the least, a negative person and did not engage in disparaging comments about others. Overwhelmed as he was by communal obligations, he had no time for pettiness. Furthermore, as in his relationship with lay persons, Rav Aharon was a genuinely caring and warm person. Yeshiva-oriented individuals were often surprised by his friendliness toward synagogue rabbis, including some whose views diverged considerably from his and who pointedly did not accept the authority of Agudah-affiliated *gedolim*.

What gives the rabbis' charge of usurpation an aura of plausibility is that when their role in this country is compared with what it had been in Europe, it is obvious that the American Rabbinate is a pale shadow in prestige and function of its European predecessor. On the other hand, the fact that American rabbis have not enjoyed the respect or authority accorded to rabbis in other places of Jewish settlement is hardly proof that the Roshei Yeshiva are responsible for this predicament. A far more likely explanation is that in the first half of this century American rabbis functioned under conditions which insured that once Orthodoxy got its bearings and confidence, either the rabbis would have to alter how they viewed their role or they would experience a decline in status. A weakened Orthodoxy in which all kinds of compromises were made and Torah *chinuch* was all but ignored was a fragile basis on which to establish rabbinical authority.

Indeed during the past generation, in many communities there has been a notable enhancement in rabbinical authority and function as rabbis have integrated their activity into the workings of a more self-reliant community. It is of note that this reversal of the downturn in rabbinical status has paralleled the continued growth in the yeshiva world.

Rav Aharon foresaw that Torah education at all levels was the only reliable path to religious Jewish survival and strength. Rabbis who coupled meaningful yeshiva or day school education with their synagogue activity — and more than a few did, notably among the American Rabbinate, rather than those who were European-born or educated — were Rav Aharon's allies and he gave them great encouragement. In too many instances, however, pulpit rabbis were removed and isolated from the world of *chinuch.*

The same factor — Torah *chinuch* as a priority — impelled Rav Aharon to greater involvement in Torah Umesorah. Established in 1944 by Rav Shraga Feivel Mendelowitz, *zt'l,* who was greatly admired by Rav Aharon and who worked closely with him, Torah Umesorah quickly gained acceptance as the representative agency for yeshivas and day schools in the United States and Canada. With Rav Mendelowitz's untimely death just four years later, spiritual leadership of the organization became Rav Aharon's responsibility.

As in all else, he did not regard this as an honorific or occasional obligation. The post-war years saw a rapid expansion in the number of Torah institutions across the continent. This growth was accompanied by vexatious issues concerning curriculum and *chinuch* matters. There would be questions relating to co-education and to the involvement of non-Orthodox elements. The Lakewood Rosh Yeshiva who was the foremost proponent of the ideal *Torah lishmoh,* who had been educated and virtually raised in the *beis medrash,* who had been a prodigy in the great yeshiva of Slobodka, who had given brilliant *shiurim* in the advanced yeshivas of Slutsk and Kletzk, and who served before the *Churban* alongside the spiritual giants of that period, would now have to decide on *aleph-beis* questions for schools located in cities with just a relative handful of observant Jews.

Rav Aharon met the challenge and he did so by being consistent — and by a remarkable understanding of the nuances of American Jewish life. He knew that a modern day school was not a Slobodka or a *cheder* and he knew what could be achieved. The question to him was whether a Jewish educational institution was sincere and serious in aspiring to the goal of elevating its students in Torah knowledge and observance — that, too, is an aspect of *Torah lishmoh* — and if it was serious and sincere it would be proper, at the time, to countenance practices which would not be acceptable in other settings.

So the day school movement grew, in quantity and quality, with Torah Umesorah in the vanguard. In dozens and then hundreds of schools, seedlings of Torah were planted and they took root in the minds and hearts of students. Though remote in place and attitude from full Torah commitment, some of these students continued on to *Mesivta,* even to *Beis Medrash* and *Kollel,* and today they are *bnei Torah.*

The establishment of Chinuch Atzmai — the network of Torah schools in Israel — in which Rav Aharon played a decisive role — may have been the Rosh Yeshiva's most heroic undertaking. It came at a time when he was already exhausted and it required him to fund-raise from contributors who were the mainstay of support for Lakewood. This concern did not cause a moment's hesitation on his part; he would do what was necessary without worrying about any possible harm to the institution that was dearest to him.

※ ※ ※

When the *Medina* was established in 1948, there were a number of separate school systems sponsored by various political parties, including Zerem Revi-i (Fourth Stream) which was under Agudah auspices. About two years later, the Israeli government decided to consolidate elementary school education under its control. Given the secularist bent of the Labor Government, if the consolidation plan would go through unchanged, then except for the most determined religious families, the opportunity for meaningful Torah education would be lost to Israeli youth. The consequences for the Jewish people were frightening, for already there were at work in Israel powerful forces, backed by the government, which were weaning Jews, especially those who were Sephardic, away from Judaism.

Although the danger was clear, it was not clear whether anything could be done to resist what was being advanced. The financial strain of sustaining a religious school system would be staggering. While all agreed that an independent *chinuch* was necessary, few had the courage or the confidence to implement this conviction. Still, Chinuch Atzmai was created with the assistance of Agudah activists and the blessings of *Gedolei Torah*. It came into being because Rav Aharon insisted that this be done and it was this determination and the constancy of his activity on its behalf which sustained the Torah network. He relied heavily on Rav Zalman Sorotzkin, *zt'l,* who worked with great *mesiras nefesh,* but it was Rav Aharon who was the de facto head of Chinuch Atzmai, raising the necessary funds and determining policy.

Rav Aharon's influence on the Torah community in Israel and its acceptance of his authority was itself remarkable given the distance separating America and Israel and given the fact that there were outstanding Torah personalities in Israel who could decide major questions. What Rav Aharon achieved through Chinuch Atzmai was far more remarkable and that is why this was his most heroic effort. To serve as an accepted Torah authority from a great distance is a matter of stature and communication. Chinuch Atzmai entailed much more. From a distance of six thousand miles an organization of independent yeshiva *ketanos* was brought into being and nourished and guided through the superhuman efforts of a man who carried *K'lal Yisroel.*

To strengthen Chinuch Atzmai, specifically for the crucial registration of students which occurred each spring prior to the next school year and for other activity which fortified the Torah camp in the ongoing struggle against the powerful forces of anti-religion in Israel, Peylim was formed under the direction of Rav Aharon. This, too, was an American-inspired endeavor and in large measure it operated out of this country, which is another indication of the reach of Rav Aharon's influence and of his impact on the religious *yishuv.*

In a figurative sense, though almost in a literal way as well, he carried and nourished *K'lal Yisroel, ka-asher yisa ha-omein es hayonek.*

The roots or sources of such a heightened sense of responsibility for *K'lal* are hard to discover, partly because we do not know enough about Rav Aharon's formative years and about his early communal activity and partly because it is difficult to account for a degree of exertion and *mesiras nefesh* that exceeded the devotion of other dedicated and outstanding community leaders.

Much of his correspondence with other *Gedolei Torah* and other important writings of the crucial inter-war period were apparently lost in Vilna after he and his yeshiva fled there or later on in the course of the frightful trek and ordeal which culminated in Shanghai. The YIVO archives in New York, however, may have material of value concerning Rav Aharon's pre-*Churban* activity, as well as more general aspects of religious Jewish life in Russia and Poland about which we need to learn more. It may well be worth the investments and effort to undertake a systematic examination of YIVO's archives.

※ ※ ※

Born into a most distinguished Torah family, Rav Aharon was orphaned from both parents at a very young age. As a boy, long before his bar mitzvah, he was totally immersed in Torah study. At thirteen, he was sent to Slobodka, where he quickly developed a special attachment with the Alter of Slobodka, Rav Nosson Zvi Finkel, *zt'l*, who loved him dearly. While the Alter surely influenced him, it was not necessarily in the direction of the intense *K'lal* activity that occupied the Rosh Yeshiva's later life.

A turning point came after he married Rav Iser Zalman Meltzer's daughter and moved to Slutsk where he played a major role in all aspects of his father-in-law's yeshiva. In Slutsk he was also engaged in communal matters, as well as with the government. We know that in 1917, when Russia was wracked by successive revolutions which resulted in the Communist takeover, he led the religious Jewish forces in Minsk against the Bundists in the struggle to determine who would represent Russian Jews in parliament. Subsequently, when the Soviet authorities arrested Rav Iser Zalman and increasingly put pressure on Slutsk, as well as other yeshivas, as part of their anti-religious campaign, Rav Aharon became convinced that the yeshiva must relocate. It was moved to the Polish town of Kletzk where it flourished under Rav Aharon's leadership, Rav Iser Zalman having settled in *Eretz Yisroel* in 1925.

As the Kletzker Rosh Yeshiva, Rav Aharon was much involved in local matters in what was a largely Jewish town. As his fame — and perhaps also his confidence — grew, with top students flocking to his yeshiva from throughout east Europe and more distant places, the sphere of his activity also spread. In the last decade of the life of the Chafetz Chaim, *zt'l,* Rav Aharon became close to this most revered leader of the Jewish people and he also earned the respect of Rav Chaim Ozer and Rav Elchanan Wasserman, *zt'l,* with whom he developed a close relationship. Although but in his thirties, he became an important leader in Agudath Israel and Vaad Hayeshivos, demonstrating a strong willingness to accept responsibility and also to shoulder more than his share of the burden of *K'lal* work. Obviously, as well, he demonstrated a knack for fund-raising.

These contacts and experiences — a form of *shimush* or apprenticeship, though a good deal more than that — influenced Rav Aharon's approach to communal matters and, likely, in other ways. His activity and the respect accorded to him in the 1920's and the 1930's explain the wide acceptance of his authority in the Vilna-Shanghai period and then after the *Churban.* Since Rav Aharon was recognized as one of the *Gedolei Torah* in an era of great Torah leaders, his stature was unquestioned.

Still, none of this illuminates sufficiently the emergence of so powerful a leader whose conviction and determination energized our people, gave strength to all of *K'lal Yisroel,* and profoundly affected the course of religious Jewish life. It is convenient to search for influences, to say that this or that outstanding Torah leader directed Rav Aharon toward *K'lal* activities. A more likely view is that he was born with a rare sense of obligation and a companion sense of sacrifice, that what was acquired by others was instinctive for him, so that the impulse to give of himself so magnanimously was the essence of his nature and it sprung from spiritual resources which were given in great measure to one who was equally great in mind.

Rav Aharon was a prodigy and he was prodigious both in intellect and the ideal of service to the *K'lal.*

One person, however, did have a great influence on Rav Aharon's life, giving him inspiration and establishing the environment which enabled him to devote himself entirely to the *K'lal.* That person was the Rebbitzin, herself a remarkable individual who on her own merits was one of the greatest personages in recent Jewish history. Because the pain of her more recent passing is still felt so sharply and because it is difficult to write about a woman from whom *kedusha* radiated, words do not now come easily. We felt the *Shechinah* when we were in her presence.

※ ※ ※

Born into one of the noblest Jewish families, the daughter of a renowned giant in Torah and of a mother who was brilliant and learned, the wife of the *Gadol Hador,* and herself a most learned woman, the great Rebbitzin remained throughout her more than ninety years a woman for whom humility and modesty were as integral a part of her being as Torah study and *mesiras nefesh* were the essence of her husband's.

The modesty of the home which she created was in harmony with the home which Rav Aharon conceived for Torah in America. The great Rosh Yeshiva desired to restore the crown of the Jewish people to its former glory by making for Torah a glorious home in the *beis medrash* and yeshiva. As Rav Aharon's home in the yeshiva was patterned after Volozhin and Slobodka and Kletzk, so, too, the home of the great Rebbitzin was faithful to the glory that had once been the Jewish home. It could not be tainted in the slightest by the spirit of materialism, yet the paucity of material possessions did not mean that this was a poor home. Neither Rav Aharon nor the Rebbitzin wanted anything: They did not want in the sense of desiring material things and they did not want in the sense of lacking material things. Their home was as they wanted it to be.

They showed us that the *beis medrash* and the Jewish home are not dependent for their sanctity on physical splendor. More than ever, this lesson is important for both the *beis medrash* and the home as our community and people become more indulgent and more intoxicated with wealth, splendor and ostentation.

One aspect of Rav Aharon's humility teaches an important lesson about the nature of Torah leadership. It is customary to think of those who are modest as deliberately remaining in the background, as trying as best they can to avoid anything which calls attention to themselves or their activity. This is sufficient for ordinary persons and ordinary situations. Torah leaders are in a different situation precisely because they are our leaders. It is their obligation to direct the community, to counsel and instruct and, at times, to rule and command. They must be forthright and they must not avoid responsibility, even if the acceptance of responsibility means that they will be in the public eye. For them, the requirement that they walk humbly is not a license to abdicate the exercise of authority. Moshe Rabbenu, the greatest leader that our people have known and the humblest of men, was determined, at times fierce, in his leadership of *K'lal Yisroel.*

No one understood this better than Rav Aharon or better exemplified in his own life the affinity of exalted leadership and exalted modesty. He, too, was the most modest of men, for while he asked nothing for himself — neither deference nor honor — he was insistent on *kovod haTorah* and he knew what it was to lead.

At the first dinner of Chinuch Atzmai, the featured speaker was Rav Joseph B. Soloveitchik, His magnificent oration was largely devoted to the Lakewood Rosh Yeshiva, whom he recognized as the *Gadol Hador.* "When I see Rav Aharon, I see the Vilna Gaon.... When I see Rav Aharon, I see Rav Akiva Eiger.... When I see Rav Aharon, I see my Zeide, Rav Chaim." As the names of these transcendent Torah giants were mentioned, Rav Aharon was tugging at Rav Soloveitchik, imploring him to stop. With tears in his eyes, he intoned repeatedly, *"Dos is nisht emes, dos is nisht emes."*

It was the truth.

A generation of religious Jews, many of them *bnei Torah* and *kollel* families, born after Rav Aharon's passing, look at the photographs of the great Rosh Yeshiva and experience the awe which those who knew him always experienced. They feel the fire of his Torah and they are warmed by it and given strength.

What is this fire?

"This is the law of the burnt offering which shall remain on the firewood upon the altar all night until the morning, and the fire of the altar shall be kept burning in it" (*Leviticus* 6:2).

Thus were Aharon and his sons commanded, as Rashi teaches, "for the present and for future generations." Rav Aharon was devoted entirely to service to *Hashem.* His sacrifice was brought on the altar of Torah and the fire which arose from this sacrifice continues to burn. In this long night of *golus* we continue to be guided by Rav Aharon's fire and it shall burn until the morning of the redemption of the Jewish people.

More than a quarter-century has gone by since his passing, and Rav Aharon continues to live in the *neshama* of *K'lal Yisroel* wherever Torah is studied, wherever there is *mesiras nefesh,* wherever there is *kedusha.* Yaakov Aveinu *lo meit.* Rav Aharon *lo meit.*

Dr. David Shatz

# The Rav's Philosophical Legacy

## In Tribute to Joseph B. Soloveitchik

FOR HIS THOUSANDS OF *TALMIDIM*, THE MOST VIVID AND faithful characterization of the Rav *zt"l* will always be that of a *gadol ha-dor*. His main vehicle of communication was the *shiur*; his natural idiom the *shakla ve-tarya* of a *sugya* and the complexities of a Rambam or Milchamos; his dominant intellectual pedigree, Brisk and not Berlin. Efforts to portray the Rav as a philosopher first and foremost, or as wavering between two allegiances and two worlds, will inevitably ring false to those who experienced him directly. Certainly in terms of sheer impact, the number of *musmakhim* and *lamdanim* whom the Rav produced utterly dwarfs the number of students who sought to mine and expand his thought along more straightforwardly philosophical lines.

Even so, while the need to keep this perspective is essential, no tribute to the Rav can ignore his place as a *ba'al machshavah* and as — in a perfectly pure sense of the term — a major Jewish philosopher. That one person was both a towering *gadol* and a preeminent thinker who commanded respect far outside the *yeshivah's* walls is remarkable.[1]

---

1. A prominent philosopher who several decades ago was in the Rav's *shiur* made a remark to me that is impossible to forget. This philosopher had made controversial but truly original contributions to his field of specialization. Although at the time of our conversation he was only marginally involved in Orthodoxy, he explained to me why he had felt so free to pursue original and sure-to-be contested paths. "It's because I had Rav Soloveitchik," he explained. "You see, after encountering him, I could not be intimidated by anyone else's intellect. Everyone else fell short."

Most theologians, after all, belong to academic departments. They dedicate their full professional lives to philosophizing, and so productivity and high quality are entirely expected of them. By contrast, the Rav seemed to do it all as an avocation, to be pursued in scant leftover time. Moreover, it is not just that we fail to appreciate his genius if we blind ourselves to its full scope; no less unfairly, we miss the breadth of his spirituality and sensitivity. Only by seeing the Rav as a whole can we fully grasp the implications of our loss.

Two questions are therefore apt: What has the Rav bequeathed to Orthodox Jewish philosophy in the modern world? And what can Orthodox thinkers do to carry on his legacy?

Time and again in his writings, the Rav highlights conflict, tension, discord, dialectic and paradox.[1] Yet beyond the puzzles and anomalies that he himself so brilliantly delineates, we ourselves confront anomalies when we reflect upon his pursuit of philosophy and when we assess the impact of his ideas on Jewish life.

First, as to his pursuit of philosophy. The Rav sets out a wide array of personality types: Adam the First and Adam the Second, *Ish ha-Da'at* and *Ish ha-Dat, Ish ha-Halakhah, Ish Rosh Chodesh,* and more. Yet it is a challenge to locate in this panoply the exact fusion of *geonut* in Talmud with genius in philosophy that he — and he alone — embodied.[2] Halakhic man, for example, would not have written the essay, *"Ish ha-Halakhah."* The whole point of that essay, after all, is that halakhic

---

1. As others have remarked, the stress he places on antitheses and dialectical swings is distinctive and represents a turn in Jewish thought. Cf. Rabbi Jonathan Sacks's essay, "Alienation and Faith," Tradition 13-14 (Spring-Summer 1973): 137-62.

2. As Matis Greenblatt noted to me, the force of this point depends on the familiar question of whether the ideal types which the Rav depicts have an instantiation in real life. If they are "pure" types only, and are not necessarily exemplified in reality, then in actual life particular individuals — like the Rav — might combine various types, but the union would not itself be represented as a separate type in the Rav's panoply. In *"Ish ha-Halakhah"* the Rav on the one hand affirms that the types are abstractions but on the other hand refers to real-life "halakhic men," leaving us unsure of his position. But in any case the Rav never in *"Ish ha-Halakhah"* explains why a phenomenological treatment of a halakhic personality, such as that he undertakes, might be of value; he refers only to other sorts of non-halakhic inquiries. In other words there is no type which engages in exactly the sort of investigation he undertakes in the essay, so the paradox stands. As I indicate below, *"U-Bikashtem mi-Sham"* might provide materials for a solution.

man finds the world of Halakhah entirely sufficient for his spirituality, discovering therein his freedom and his creativity. An *ish ha'Halakhah*, so described, would see no point indulging in a psychological or philosophical reconstruction of a halakhic personality, let alone one cast in neoKantian categories. But that is exactly what the essay is.[1]

Turning next to "The Lonely Man of Faith," (*Tradition* 7[1965]) the categories of Adam the First and Adam the Second fall short of representing the Rav with precision. The "man of faith" does not combine philosophical and literary reflection with Talmudic greatness, but rather scientific and technological activity with covenantal existence. As Professor Gerald Blidstein frames the paradox:

> " 'Majestic' first Adam realizes his potential and fulfills a godly mandate by subduing the physical world and perfecting it. But the positive appropriation of this major characteristic of Western civilization is not accompanied by a corresponding imperative to appropriate Western culture, its philosophical or literary achievements. This assertion seems improbable, or at least paradoxical, with regard to the Rav, whose major writings are suffused with modern Western philosophy and literature, and whose very intellectual world is constructed, in part at least, with materials provided by modern culture. Yet the paradox is fact: The Rav is a paradigm of the synthesis of Jewish and Western culture, but he nowhere prescribes this move or urges its legitimacy. The Rav constructs his thought within the categories of Western culture, but nowhere explicitly assigns a specific role to this culture."[2]

Not only do we fail to grasp *how* one individual could have so integrated the worlds of *Halakhah* and *Aggadah* on the one hand with the world of general culture on the other, but the *why* eludes us as well.

---

1. See also Rabbi Jonathan Sacks, "Rabbi J.B. Soloveitchik's Early Epistemology: A Review of *The Halakhic Mind,*" *Tradition* 23,3 (Spring 1988); 86, note 10.

2. Gerald Bildstein, "On the Jewish People in the Writings of Rabbi Joseph B. Soloveitchik," *Tradition* 24,3 (Spring 1989):21-43, p. 24. A contrast to Rav Kook springs to mind. Rav Kook spoke in exalted terms of the value of general culture in a total religious life, and developed a broad framework within which to motivate such a warm embrace of culture. But Rav Kook was not himself an expert in any secular discipline. The Rav, on the other hand, mastered secular disciplines — science, literature and philosophy — but nowhere extolled their pursuit expressly.

One might argue that these paradoxes are mitigated by the essay, *"U-Bikashtem mi-Sham"*[1]; for there the Rav portrays the religious odyssey of a personality that seems closer to his own, thereby also perhaps providing a justification for his own pursuits.[2] Even if this is so, our sense of paradox grows when we look next at the influence and impact of the Rav's philosophy.

The Rav was most revered by the community of "Modern Orthodoxy," a community that he built and for over half a century has ceaselessly inspired. Yet his philosophical thought is curiously removed from some of the chief concerns and positions of that constituency. For instance, we have already seen, the protagonist of *"Ish ha-Halakhah"* is not a "modern" Jew, albeit he finds (in *Halakhah*) the freedom and creativity which the "modern" Jew craves. More significantly, the early pages of "Lonely Man of Faith" make the boundaries of the Rav's inquiry there sharp and clear:

> *"I have never been seriously troubled by the problem of the Biblical doctrine of creation vis-a-vis the scientific story of evolution. . ., nor have I been perturbed by the confrontation of the mechanistic interpretation of the human mind with the Biblical spiritual concept of man. I have not been perplexed by the impossibility of fitting the mystery of revelation into the framework of historical empiricism. Moreover, I have not even been troubled by the theories of Biblical criticism. However, while theoretical oppositions and dichotomies have never tormented my thoughts, I could not shake off the disquieting feeling that the practical role of the man of faith within modern society is a very difficult, indeed, a paradoxical one"* ("Lonely Man of Faith," 9).

※ ※ ※

Almost consistently in his writings, the great cognitive conflicts of our day — evolution and creation, history and Bible, history and

---

1. Published in *Hadorom* 47 (5739):1-83, but apparently first drafted in the 1940's.

2. Other responses are possible. For example, the achievements of Adam the First might be read broadly, as including all cultural productivity ("Lonely Man of Faith," 14); and Blidstein goes on to advance an interesting resolution of his own.

*halakhah*, philosophy and religion — are dismissed entirely.[1] In fact, the Rav maintains that "[faith] does not lend itself completely to the act of cultural translation. There are simply no cognitive categories in which the total commitment of the man of faith could be spelled out" ("Lonely Man of Faith," 60).[2] This emphasis on the unrationalized dimension of faith gives rise to another paradox. The Rav is often seen as a contemporary exemplar of the Rambam's orientation. Yet the synthesis of faith and reason so avidly sought by the Rambam is no part of the Rav's objectives. "It is not the plan of this paper," reads the opening line of "Lonely Man," "to discuss the millennium-old problem of faith and reason." What Rambam and Saadya labored strenuously to produce — a set of cognitive claims about the nature of God and the world that would stand up to scientific and philosophical scrutiny — is given short shrift in his analysis. In fact, the closing pages of *The Halakhic Mind* constitute a frontal assault on the entire program of medieval Jewish philosophy. And yet what is the most popular model for Modern Orthodox thought if not the Maimonidean synthesis?[3]

The Rav's justification for involvement in the secular world is also crucially different from both the Rambam's and those commonly championed today. He does not contend that such involvement will generate a richer, more accurate body of philosophical, historical, and scientific claims and hence a more sophisticated and durable faith. Nor does he base his position on the idea that exposure to secular disciples produces a refinement of spiritual sensibilities. Rather, his endorsement of culture is founded on a principle rooted in *sefer bereshit,* one we might describe as moral. Human beings fulfill their divine charge and actualize their divinely ordained nature only by aggressively striving to improve human existence in concrete, material ways. They must

---

1. This point is also made by Rabbi Jonathan Sacks in the excerpt from *Tradition in an Untraditional Age* reprinted in this issue. One should note (as Shalom Carmy has pointed out) that "Lonely Man of Faith" implicitly contains a powerful response to a problem seized upon by biblical criticism, viz., the ostensible conflict between the "two" accounts of creation. Of course, this *"da ma she-tashiv"* is an incidental byproduct of the Rav's theorizing; he is occupied with a whole other set of problems.

2. *The Halakhic Man* offers a rather different perspective, however, Compare also *"U-Bikashtem mi-Sham."*

3. See also David Singer and Moshe Sokol, "Joseph Soloveitchik: Lonely Man of Faith," *Modern Judaism* 2 (1982): 227-72, p. 249.

"harness the elemental forces of nature" to conquer disease and to subdue the threats that nature poses to human life and security. Only by doing so do they imitate God's creativity, fulfill the responsibilities imposed by the mandate *"mil-u et ha-aretz ve-kivshuha,"* and attain dignity. Remarkably, this powerful and visceral argument, that secular disciples make *yishuv olam* possible, has relatively little resonance in Orthodox writing on the subject of secular studies.[1]

Likewise, the Rav offered a trenchant critique of Western culture, but one finds little of that in recent "modern" Jewish theology. His repeated claim that the only authentic source of Jewish philosophical teaching is the *Halakhah* is much in need of explication,[2] but this vision of a *halakhah*-based Jewish philosophy has not been significantly extended by others beyond paradigm cases like *teshuvah* and *tefillah* — much less elevated to a methodological principle.

If on some issues, the Rav's positions were more restrained and "conservative" than those of his constituency, in other respects, some of his constituency seems narrow and parochial by comparison to him. In "Confrontation," the Rav put forth an eloquent, philosophically based opposition to theological dialogue. His stance exerted tremendous impact. Yet in that same essay he spoke of the need for Jews to join and cooperate with non-Jews in redressing social ills and creating a better society: "we stand with civilized society shoulder to shoulder against an order which defies us all."[3] Few have expanded on that theme, and it has not found a translation into our communal life. Often the universal thrust of the Rav's writing is lost or underappreciated. When Doubleday Press chose to issue "Lonely Man of Faith" as a book, it did so because the essay was perceived as what it in fact is: a profound characterization of the place of religion in the modern world, an articulation of a predicament felt universally, a portrait of a condition belonging to what the Rav persistently calls

---

1. Lest it be thought that the imperative of *"ve-kivshuha"* is but a narrow one confined to the development of medicine and technology, we should note that economics and politics, for example, no less than science, can play a vital role in the transformation of human life. The Rav himself describes the achievements of Adam the First broadly ("Lonely Man of Faith," 14).

2. On the importance and centrality of this claim, see Marvin Fox, "The Unity and Structure of Rabbi Joseph B. Soloveitchik's Thought," *Tradition* 24:2 (Winter 1989): 44-65.

3. "Confrontation," *Tradition* 6,2 (Spring-Summer 1964): 5-29, p. 17.

"man." Thus, it is not a work of import to Jews alone.[1] Yet strangely, even some of the Rav's admirers are uncomfortable with the suggestion that "religion" is here an operative category. It is as if we adulterate his message to us if we concede that it speaks to others as well.[2]

The Rav's philosophy, then, as distinct from "the Rav's Torah," is less in evidence on the Orthodox landscape than one would expect. Why is this so?

❦ ❦ ❦

Several explanations suggest themselves. Surely in some cases we are dealing with respectful, reasoned and informed disagreement (though not necessarily made explicit). After all, disciples may emulate the Rav without submissively accepting all that he says on hashkafic matters. They emulate him by replicating the process of creative thought — this in consonance with the Rav's well-known mandate to *talmidim* to think for themselves.[3]

There is another reason that people might invoke for not following the Rav's philosophy, namely, uncertainty about exactly what views to attribute to him. The Rav's ideas diverge from work to work; based on this, one might contend that his philosophical disquisitions were tailored to specific audiences, social contexts, and personal circumstances. Because of the acutely personal and highly contextual character of the philosophical writings, readers — however greatly

---

1. Note that, whereas the text of "Lonely Man of Faith" draws frequently on Bible, the Rav confines sources from *halakhah, aggadah* and *parshanut* almost totally to the footnotes, creating, to some degree, a separate track of discussion. The first eighty-one pages of *The Halakhic Mind* are also almost exclusively universal in thrust, but those universal reflections ultimately lead to a "particularist" conclusion in the final section.

2. For example, the argument which the Rav constructs against dialogue (in "Confrontation") — viz. that the faith act is incommunicable and dialogue therefore impossible — logically should apply to all faiths.

3. Dr. Norman Lamm relates a story from his days in the Rav's *shiur*. The Rav asked him to explain a Tosafos that had been covered the day before. Dr. Lamm replied obligingly by repeating exactly what the Rav had said in the previous day's *shiur*. "Your problem is," chided the Rav, "that you come in here with your *yetzer ha-tov,* and you leave your *yetzer ha-ra* at the door."

inspired and affected — may yet hesitate to build a definite, abiding outlook upon what the Rav says in particular places.[1]

While in some cases reasoned disagreement and methodological caution may account for why the Rav's philosophical work has not had more influence, we need to consider another hypothesis: neglect.

This should not necessarily be said with a critical edge. Whereas a *yeshivah* training makes halakhic discourse familiar (if never easy!), philosophical writings are daunting and difficult in the absence of a comparable educational background. The Rav in particular utilizes a vocabulary and thought structure which have to be explained in terms of a vast cultural context and which, at many points, show a dated quality. For *talmidim* there is a real question whether the time investment needed to gain the background is worth the potential loss of growth in *lomdus*. Aggravating the problem of comprehension, the Rav's extraordinary powers of oral pedagogy and *hasbarah,* which navigated *talmidim* through the most demanding of *sugyos,* were not often available as a means of clarifying and disseminating his philosophical ideas publicly. Also, because the Rav seldom referred to the philosophic writings in *shiur,* and it was plain that they occupied a relatively small portion of his time, it became easy to assume that they were not essential to his outlook and spiritual quest. As more and more of the Rav's *chiddushei Torah* appear in written form, the philosophic works will face a still stiffer competition for attention, and some people may quite legitimately argue that they ought to be made secondary in the hierarchy. Our lives are not long enough, nor our minds capacious and quick enough, to absorb even a significant fraction of what the Rav's mind had both absorbed and created by early middle age; so we must make choices.

To these more understandable reasons for neglect of the philosophical writings I feel compelled to add a less honorable one. Some people perhaps harbored a fear that the concerns, contents and methods of those writings were sensitive — and should therefore be shut out.

---

1. Another, admittedly speculative explanation of divergences is the following. Just as in *shiurim* and *derashot,* the Rav on different occasions might construct varying approaches to a single text, problem or position, so too in philosophy he furnished a multiplicity of perspectives on particular problems. In other words, the Rav may have approached each philosophical "assignment" as a self-contained unit; the inquiry would begin afresh.

Whatever the reasons for neglect, whether benign or otherwise, in all likelihood the Rav would have been driven to ever greater levels of philosophical expression had he found a regular forum for discussing theology with others of a similar bent and expertise. Question and criticism in the context of a larger community inevitably force a thinker, particularly a great one, to sharpen his formulations, fill in lacunae, and expand his agenda. It is striking that a classic like "Lonely Man of Faith" was invited by a group other than the Rav's base constituency.

I am not in a position to say how deeply the Rav sensed that his broader concerns were not being widely discussed and assimilated, nor to comment directly on whether, if so, that disappointed him. Anecdotal evidence from reliable sources suggests he *did* know it and *was* disappointed.[1] Be that as it may, we must beware the potential cost of perpetrating such neglect. The Rav's thought would be appropriated, analyzed and disseminated by individuals who may not be in a position to place the philosophical dimension of the Rav in the context of his total persona. Admirers of the Rav need to preserve and protect that total persona, and accordingly ought to construct their own informed representations of his philosophy and its context.

In closing, I would suggest one final hypothesis to account for the phenomenon I have dealt with. The explanation, basically, is that to accept the Rav's philosophy requires a breadth and depth of spirit and commitment that lies far beyond the reach of most people. Let me elaborate.[2]

※ ※ ※

When I was first exposed to "Lonely Man of Faith" as a college student, I, with others, was deeply disappointed by the paragraph quoted earlier in which the Rav dismissed the problem of synthesizing secular disciples and religion. Isn't he sidestepping the real problem, we asked? Yet over the years, I, like many who spend their careers in academia, have come to realize the immaturity of that criticism. The

---

1. Rav Aharon Lichtenstein touched on this question in an inspiring address to the OU at its 1992 convention; he noted both private and published remarks by the Rav.
2. With regard to the theme I will now broach, I also refer the reader to Shalom Carmy's moving and perceptive essay, "Of Eagle's Flight and Snail's Pace," written for the *Orthodox Forum* in March 1993 and forthcoming in *Tradition*.

more I studied philosophy — and others will say much the same thing — the more I came to realize the limits of the contemporary stress on "rigor," the poverty of intellectual gymnastics. Philosophical problems are first and foremost *human* problems. The ones that really matter are those that engage the soul in its entirety, and the solutions that really last in the minds of people are those that anchor themselves im emotion. As Yehudah Halevi would have asked, how often does an elaborate proof of God's existence create religious fervor?[1] How often does an "'intellectual" solution to the problem of evil really do anything for humans who confront evil's stark reality? Significantly, the problem that the Rav chose to deal with in "Lonely Man" — the sense of loneliness and alienation — is psychological; it issues from the whole being and not from cognition alone. Correspondingly, he opted for visceral resolutions, those that could take hold in the deepest recesses of personality, while eschewing philosophical *pilpul*.[2] But to hold on to the visceral resolutions is extraordinary hard — even for those who, soured on "rationalist" approaches, realize that this is where the true resolution is to be found. The Rav had the needed spiritual depth. We as a rule do not.[3]

Thus it is that in *"Kol Dodi Dofek"* the Rav denigrates the value of theoretical solutions to the problems of evil, supplanting the quest for understanding God's ways with an emphasis on concrete empathy and initiative, a response that calls for powers of spirit and not mind alone. In this connection we should recall the unusually intimate bond between autobiography and philosophy in the Rav's thought, which further testifies to the remarkable interaction between personality and intellect. This nexus is plain as day in *Ish ha-Halakhah* — in the prefatory citation about Yosef seeing his father's visage, in the explicit reminiscences, in the overall subject and purpose. We meet it as well in the intensely

---

1. Cf. "Lonely Man of Faith," 32: "The trouble with all rational demonstrations of the existence of God consists in their being . . . abstract logical demonstrations divorced from the living primal experiences in which these demonstrations are rooted."

2. "This commitment is rooted not in one dimension, such as the rational one, but in the whole personality of the man of faith" ("Lonely Man of Faith," 60).

3. Medieval Jewish thinkers undoubtedly had the same depth of spirit, but the religious character of their intellectual environment made it unnecessary for them to actualize that potential fully. The Rav, by contrast, lived in a climate that forced him to make the potential actual.

personal statement that opens "Lonely Man of Faith": "What I am going to say here has been derived not from philosophical dialectics, abstract speculation, or detached impersonal reflections, but from actual situations and experiences with which I have been confronted. [The lecture] is a tale of a personal dilemma." Personal elements are also detectable in the rousing, often poetic drama of *"U-Bikashtem mi-Sham,"* the galvanizing Zionist passion of *"Kol Dodi Dofek,"* and much more.

The Rav, then, placed his intellectual quest in an emotional frame and his emotional existence in an intellectual one. If we will never fully understand how he integrated the worlds of Halakhah and philosophy, still less will we understand how he was able to deal with the deepest and most affecting feelings of human life, both private feelings and universal ones, in intellectual categories; categories which, for all their rigor and high level of abstraction, never robbed the emotions of their richness and authenticity.

Some of the Rav's most stunning intellectual explorations were conceived as *hespeidim*. *Hespeidim* can go to two extremes — cold, dry intellectualism on the one hand; gushes of inchoate, unstructured, and hence ultimately communicated feeling on the other. Armed with a perfect *makor* and a breathtaking conceptual apparatus, the Rav took hold of emotions, shaped them, ordered them, structured them; thereby he made them shareable, communicable, comprehensible.[1] Recall, too, that much of the Rav's *halakhah* and *hashkafah* were prepared to mark occasions, from *yahrzeits* to *siyumim*. For the community, the intellectual rhythm of the year was set by personal occasions in the Rav's life. Likewise, much was delivered at especially evocative times such as Aseres Yemei Teshuvah and Tish'ah be-Av. *Halakhah* objectifies emotions according to the Rav, and so too can a halakhic or philosophical discourse enable Jews to deal with highly charged moments. The act of learning produces a *"kiyyum ha-mitzvah"* — of remembering, of mourning, of rejoicing, or whatever the occasion called for.

To return now to our puzzle: Why hasn't the Rav's philosophy taken full hold? We must appreciate the gulf between the Rav's personal spiritual powers and our own. His idea that faith is untranslatable and unrationalizable is not easily internalized. Resigning oneself to incessantly

---

1. See the opening sections of his *sheloshim* eulogy for the Rebbetzin of Talne in *Tradition* 17,2 (Spring 1978): 73-83.

moving between opposing poles — from aggressiveness to submissiveness and back — is an arduous task, and we also have trouble handling the "defeat" inherent in submissiveness, of which the Rav often speaks. We find it demanding to see ourselves as charged with responsibility as both "majestic" and "convenantal" beings, and we have difficulties integrating membership in a particular community with membership in the human community as a whole. A "man of faith" achieves these states; but he is lonely indeed.

I suggest that we think of the challenge ahead, of appropriating the Rav's philosophy, not as the intellectual mastery of ideas *per se,* but as the summoning of spiritual reserves; not as the task of learning from a text but rather that of being inspired by a model. The Rav taught us by example that it is no intellectual embarrassment to be a person of faith in the contemporary world, to affirm belief in the face of powerful cultural challenge. What we require to follow his lead is not more intellectual insight alone but more emotional and spiritual depth. To adapt the final words of "Lonely Man of Faith," are we "entitled to a more privileged position and a less exacting and sacrificial role"?

*Herman Wouk*

# A Word of Thanks

THE SYNAGOGUE WAS CROWDED. I HAD BOUGHT NO SEAT. THE usher sent me upstairs with scant ceremony to a tiny hot balcony, perhaps first designed as a choir loft. It was crowded too, but I managed to wedge myself into a corner of a bench. I could not see the synagogue floor or the *bimah,* only the top of the ark, but I did not consider myself ill-treated. Anyone showing up on Yom Kippur at the Jewish Center, the most fashionable and elegant Orthodox shul in New York, without having a place for himself in advance, was lucky to gain admittance.

My parents were worshipping in the Bronx at my grandfather's shul. Being an overburdened radio writer at the time — it was 1937 — I had preferred to stay in my Manhattan apartment, hence my last-minute invasion of the Jewish Center. I had heard of Rabbi Leo Jung, but I had never met him or heard him speak.

Sermon time came. I settled back, my mind closed, to enjoy my own meditations. The voice surprised me: warm, cultured, curiously blending solemnity and ironic humor. The words surprised me: clear, literate, striking words, neither pompous nor affected. I began to pay attention, and then the ideas surprised me: religious ideas, articulated in the light of the secular wisdom I had learned, and some secular wisdom that I hadn't learned. Spoken in this manner, viewed in this fresh — and I had thought inevitably unkind — light, the Judaic commitments of my Hassidic grandfather seemed not naive, but wise beyond secular

---

*Editor's Note:* Much of this article was originally included in the volume published on the occasion of Rabbi Leo Jung's seventieth birthday.

wisdom. Some instinct had always told me that Judaism held the deep truths, despite the skeptical criticism I had absorbed, but my instinct thus far had been little more than a guess. I got on my feet, craned my neck to catch a glimpse of the speaker, and saw an unusually handsome man with commanding eyes, a neat beard faintly tinged with gray, and spare controlled gestures.

I do not remember what Rabbi Leo Jung said in that sermon. I do remember that I listened and that the sermon was a turning point for me: the discovery that a modern mind could hold to Judaism and possibly persuade others that the faith could maintain itself in this most doubting age.

※ ※ ※

Naturally, I made it my business to become friendly with this man. I found him quite approachable, busy as he was. He had a custom of walking around the Central Park reservoir every day. It soon became a settled thing that I accompany him on these walks. Through hot days and cold, through sunshine, fog, snow and rain — he liked his walk in all weathers — we marched around the oval cinder path, enjoying the air and the view of the skyscrapers, and thrashing out one by one the classic theological conundrums. We talked at length, too, about the ideas and commitments of the Jewish faith. This pleasant and informing ambulatory friendship went on for several years, interrupted by his travels or mine and then resumed.

During my service in World War II as a naval officer I kept up a steady correspondence with him. I came back after three years in the Pacific and settled in the New York suburbs, a newly married man. Dr. Jung and I still managed an occasional Central Park walk. His stride was as springy, his pace as brisk, and his controversial wit as swift as ever. By then I was not arguing against him very much. The years at sea had allowed me time to think things through. Give or take a few idiosyncrasies of viewpoint, I had arrived at the general Orthodox position I hold now. We began to dream, to talk, and to plan of propagating that view. I published my first novel, and Dr. Jung said that I should turn my pen to the service of Judaism.

He formed a discussion group of young men with traditional views. Our meetings went on for a year, until my first child was born and I had to drop out. During that year Dr. Jung bore down hard on my duty to write on behalf of the Jewish faith. Once he gave me a book by Samson Raphael Hirsch, *The Nineteen Letters of Ben Uziel,* and told me that that should be my model. I read the work and was overawed by its learning and zeal, neither of which, I felt, I could possibly match. It seemed the height of presumption for me to think of following in the path of Hirsch.

All the same, Dr. Jung had planted a thought in my mind. The thought grew in time to be the book called *This Is My God.* I was thirteen years bringing off the task. In that stretch of time I did not manage to transform myself from a layman to a Talmudic scholar. I tried, but the world was too much with me, and anyway it appears I was destined to be a story-teller, not a philosopher. I learned a great deal, but the more I learned the more the margins of mastery seemed to recede. At last I despaired of learning enough, and sat down to execute the assignment, hoping to contribute clarity and writing skill to the undertaking, without aspiring to be another Hirsch.

I submitted the finished manuscript to Dr. Jung, and had the benefit of a detailed and wise critique, which made the work much better. When the volume was published in 1959 I sent him one of the first copies off the press, and I also returned to him the copy of *The Nineteen Letters of Ben Uziel,* by now somewhat battered. The task was done.

※ ※ ※

So I owe an eternal debt to my late teacher and friend, Dr. Leo Jung, not only for a long process of education, and for an invaluable editorial review, but for the original suggestion for *This Is My God,* which has stayed in print ever since. In my case, Dr. Jung's influence on a young man had a public result. But he had an equally powerful effect on the lives of thousands of other people, this effect being expressed in their daily private actions.

Through some of the most desperate decades that the Jewish people have ever endured, Rabbi Leo Jung held the fort for the Mosaic faith by his writings, his speeches, his teaching, and his editorial work, all infused with his charming and forceful intelligence. He worked himself into physical exhaustion in welfare and rescue missions, but always came back with new vigor and amazing endurance.

If thirty Leo Jungs had been effectively placed all over the United States at the time he began his ministry, I believe American Jewry today would be largely Orthodox in outlook; but there was only one Leo Jung. While he was with us we regarded him as a beloved leader, and we looked to him for strength and light in the struggle that never ends to honor the Torah of Moses. And now that he is gone, that remains his legacy to us — strength and light to battle on in his spirit.

*Chaval al daavdin v'lo mishtakchin*
"Alas for those who are gone, and whose like is not to be found!" — *Sanhedrin*, 111a

## ☙ Contemporary Issues

- ☐ *The Truth About Homosexuality*
- ☐ *Orthodox Soul-Searching After Goldstein*
- ☐ *Of Patting (and Breaking) Backs*
- ☐ *Why There Was No Gabbai at the Regency Theater*

Dr. Joseph Berger

# The Truth About Homosexuality

*Don't believe everything you see in the media, warns psychiatrist Dr. Joseph Berger in a cogent rejoinder to popular current myths*

BECAUSE MOST PEOPLE DO NOT HAVE A DETAILED KNOWLedge of the scientific literature on homosexuality, they are vulnerable to the vast amount of incorrect and often deliberately misleading information that receives disproportionate publicity in the media. There is widespread ignorance even among physicians and most psychiatrists.

The claims of the homosexual activists can be summarized in the following assertion: "that homosexuality is an innate, irreversible, normal, healthy, alternative lifestyle (or sexual orientation, or form of sexual expression)."

This assertion has profound implications for our community. We owe it to ourselves to diminish gullibility to false propaganda.* Let us examine the latest scientific positions on these claims.

---

*A good outline for the lay reader is "The Mainstreaming of Homosexuality." Ward and Swarts. *The World and I.* Washington. 1993. 8.365-381.

## ☙ What Are the Genetic Claims?

"Innate" means inborn, and thus primarily genetic. There have been many claims over the years for a genetic basis for homosexuality. None have been satisfactorily substantiated.

There have been problems with the methodology of the studies, such as dissatisfaction with the methods used to choose subjects, with the criteria that were used to define whether relatives were or were not homosexual, and with the quality of the results.

A good example of a paper that is very problematic but has been quoted by other, later researchers as having demonstrated a *significant* genetic contribution to homosexuality was a 1986 paper from the University of Minnesota,[1] based on their extremely unusual collection of identical twins who were adopted by different families and brought up apart. Theoretically, this ought to be the ideal testing ground to demonstrate whether any characteristic — physical, intellectual or emotional — is produced by genes, or is a product of the environment one grew up in.

In this particular study, out of 55 twin pairs, there were six — four female and two male — where at least one twin was known to be homosexual. Of the four female twin pairs, in none of them was the other twin homosexual. That is strongly *against* a genetic inheritance.

But of the two male twin pairs, in one pair both were homosexual. However, the histories of both these men were highly unusual. They had major problems going back to childhood, with learning disabilities, speech impediments, hyperactivity, and episodes of depression. At the time they were assessed, their homosexual activity was with each other.

A very small sample of one out of two, and that one being very unusual, is extremely weak support for a genetic inheritance theory. But this is the material that subsequent researchers describe as being "consistent with the possibility of strong genetic influence"[2] or that homosexuality has a "substantial hereditary component."[3]

---

1. Eckert et al. *British Journal of Psychiatry*. 1986. 148. 421-425.
2. Buchrich et al. *Behavior Genetics*. 1991. 21.1. 75-96.
3. Bailey and Pillard. *Archives of General Psychiatry*. 1991. 48. 1089-1096.

Another study that was published (on the same day that an article by its authors appeared on the Op-Ed page of *The New York Times*) was based on telephone interviews with homosexual men who answered advertisements in homosexual publications, and whose brothers were sent questionnaires. Neither of these methods can be taken seriously by psychodynamic psychiatrists who would want to interview someone personally, at length, to make a serious assessment of his/her sexuality.

In addition, the results did not show anywhere near the strong support for a genetic inheritance that the authors claimed. When almost half of the identical twins in even such a biased study did not show concordance (the same characteristic) for homosexuality, this casts serious doubt on a true genetic inheritance.

## ~§ Is There a Gene for Homosexuality?

The other main genetic claim that has hit the headlines recently has been the claim that a certain region on the X chromosome is responsible for homosexuality.[1] It is far too early to jump to any conclusions about this one study. The sample size — the numbers of people tested — is far too small, and the study has not yet been replicated by others.

Again, the general public that sees articles about such claims on the front pages of the newspapers rarely understands how much caution real scientists must apply in evaluating such claims. The truth of the matter is that when such very preliminary material appears on the front pages of newspapers, it is likely that political, rather than truly scientific issues are at stake. And there are very few areas where this is more true than in the minefield of homosexuality.

There have been more technical criticisms of the data from the chromosome study. It is also interesting to note that in spite of studies from numerous centers done over many years, in some physical diseases that do seem to run in certain families (such as certain breast cancers and intestinal polyps), scientists have not yet reached definite agreement on precisely which portions of which chromosomes are responsible for the disease.

---

1. Hamer et al. *Science*. 1993. 261. 321-327.

## ❧ Are There Differences in Brain Anatomy?

First, there was much publicity given to a claim by a researcher named Simon LeVay that he had discovered a portion of the brain that was different in homosexuals.[1]

This is a claim based on anatomy, but LeVay's work remains unconfirmed by anyone else and there have been numerous criticisms of the quality of the research and of the significance of the findings. LeVay used postmortem material from people who had died of AIDS, but there was considerable uncertainty about the actual sex lives of the people. The sort of brain cell study that LeVay undertook is usually done in collaboration with at least one other researcher to check whether they are seeing the same cells, but LeVay had *no* collaborators. In addition to numerous other criticisms, it must be noted that no one has demonstrated that the small brain area examined by LeVay has anything to do with sexual orientation.

## ❧ Are There Abnormal Hormones?

The other main area studied for a possible "inborn" cause of homosexuality has been that of hormones.[2] Put very simply, do male homosexuals have less — or perhaps more — of either male or female sex hormones, and do women homosexuals have more or less male or female sex hormones?

In summary, the results have never consistently demonstrated any significant differences. There have been various claims over the years, but none have stood the tests of time and retesting.

Some researchers then raised the possibility that perhaps hormones affected the developing fetus. This was supported to a certain extent by some evidence from animal studies on guinea pigs, rats and monkeys showing that interfering with the sex hormones in the developing fetus did seem to cause some changes in sexual behavior in later life.

But there has been no confirmatory evidence that this is true for human beings. So the results from all the latest scientific research so far

---

1. LeVay. *Science.* 1991. 253. 1034.
2. A good review is that of Friedman and Downey. *Journal of Neuropsychiatry and Clinical Neurosciences.* 1993. 5.131-153.

demonstrate no support for the notion that homosexuality is hereditary, genetic, or based on brain differences, prenatal or later hormonal influences. In other words, there is no evidence that homosexuality is "innate" or "inborn."

## Is Homosexuality Reversible?

The next claim was that "homosexuality is irreversible." This is probably the greatest myth of all. There is overwhelming evidence from numerous studies by different researchers, that homosexuality is treatable and reversible[1] for a certain proportion of people who are sufficiently well-motivated and sufficiently flexible in their personalities.

Readers might like to know that over 15 years ago, two of the leading workers in this field noted that, in spite of all the evidence of successful treatment that was available even then, absolutely nothing would convince homosexual activists that successful treatment exists.[2] This has been an *article of religious-political faith* for many homosexual activists who argue that homosexuality is not an illness or a disease, therefore it doesn't require treatment and there is nothing to treat.

The observation that there are a considerable number of people who were treated successfully has led some extremists, such as psychoanalyst Richard Isay, to suggest that psychotherapy treatment of a homosexual patient may be a "flagrant abuse," to extremist groups attempting to censor the publication of work demonstrating successful treatment of homosexuals. Such groups have even attempted to pressure the American Psychiatric Association to ban any treatment of homosexuality, even if freely and voluntarily requested or desired by a homosexual patient.

## Who Defines Normal or Abnormal?

The question of "normality" leads to discussion of how that term is defined. If "normal" is defined in statistical terms, referring to what is by far the commonest; and therefore what is very uncommon or rare is

---

1. Some references may be found in my paper, "Psychotherapeutic Treatment of Male Homosexuality," in *American Journal of Psychotherapy*. Spring 1994. 48. 251-261.

2. Bieber I. and Bieber T. *Canadian Journal of Psychiatry*. 1979. 24. 409-421.

"abnormal," then there is absolutely no doubt that heterosexuality is the norm or "normal" and homosexuality is abnormal, deviating from the norm.

For a number of years following the famous Kinsey surveys published in the late 1940's, claims were made that homosexuals constituted 10% or more of adults in North America. Homosexual activists even today place considerable emphasis on that obsolete data, because they wish to claim that in the United States alone there are perhaps 25 million or more homosexuals.

The truth of the matter is that the Kinsey studies have been shown to be quite unsound methodologically, and every major study of recent years using much more reliable techniques has consistently shown a vastly lower rate of homosexuality — barely 1% in women, and somewhere between 1-2% in men.

The significance of these results for the question of normality is that it becomes very hard to argue against the proposition that at 98%, heterosexuality is the norm, and at 1-2%, homosexuality is abnormal. Obviously, the use of the term "deviant" carries other implications, and therefore, though it might be true in statistical terms, its pejorative connotations have led to its being banished from discussion in this context.

There are, however, other uses of the word normal, and in the medical-scientific context, probably the most important meaning or implication is "free of disease or pathology."

This is one of the most controversial aspects of this problem. For many years, psychodynamic theory held that homosexuality was the outcome of abnormal psychosexual development, and that there had been some interference with the normal psychological development that should have led to comfortable heterosexuality. In some way, therefore, homosexuals were emotionally disturbed.

Some people took this to mean disease or illness, and when a psychologist came along and ran a series of psychological tests that seemed to demonstrate no psychological differences between homosexuals and heterosexuals, this work was seized upon by homosexual activists who believed that they now had proof that they were as "normal" as everyone else. They claimed that they did not suffer from a disease, but had been unfairly persecuted and stigmatized by a biased and ignorant world.

As with so many things in life, the truth lies somewhere between the extremes. There is no doubt that homosexuals have been persecuted and stigmatized by ignorant and fearful people, but there is also no doubt that the psychological tests that showed no differences between homosexuals and heterosexuals were not very good tests.[1]

On the other hand, the biological facts of human life point so overwhelmingly to a recognition of the biological normality of heterosexuality and the biological abnormality of homosexuality as to suggest that it is a perverse abdication of common sense and reality to think otherwise.

What psychodynamic psychiatry then did was to attempt to explain, based on work with hundreds and thousands of patients, why people who had no *physical* cause for this difference might *psychologically* have developed homosexual thoughts, fantasies and desires.

Phrasing the issue in this way takes us away from the concept of illness or disease, and moves us more into a framework of explanation of difference. What we are left with then is not a characterization of homosexuality as a sickness *per se,* but as an interference with — or a failure to reach — full psychosexual development. By that term we mean the ability to develop comfortable, intimate — including sexual — loving, healthy, non-abusive, long-lasting relationships with adults of the opposite sex.

Those people who say that they can only develop such relationships with their own sex, that they dislike the opposite sex, that they cannot be intimately comfortable with the opposite sex, or that they have no interest in or desire for the opposite sex, are usually not abnormal physically. Their bodies and all their organs are biologically equipped for heterosexuality, not homosexuality.

Furthermore, the basic, most fundamental principle of all in biology has traditionally been that everything is directed towards the preservation and integrity of the cell and the organism and to its eventual reproduction, which in higher forms of life means the reproduction that can only come about through heterosexual unions. That our more liberated, liberal and tolerant societies "allow" two adults of the same sex to live together and even bring up children together cannot obliterate the biological facts of life.

---

1. This area is not well known. There are excellent summaries by Fine and by T. Bieber in the study, "Homosexuality in the Male: A report of a Psychiatric Study Group." Socarides, Bieber, et al. *International Journal of Psychiatry.* 1973. 2. 471-478.

As a patient recently said to me, "You don't have to be a rocket scientist to know that male and female organs were designed for heterosexual, not homosexual, relations." That is biological reality, whatever facade may be presented to the world.

It is these realities that leave some psychiatrists still convinced that those homosexuals who deny such realities are therefore psychologically unhealthy. They may not be "sick" in the conventional sense of the word. They may function very well, they may be able to hold down the most demanding jobs, professions, or positions of public office, and they may indeed be able to sustain loving relationships with a partner of the same sex. The *majority* probably don't, but most clinicians and researchers would accept nowadays that there is at least a significant minority that might fulfill all these criteria.

But from the biological point of view, they remain in a state of denial of their biological heritage, and the best explanations of why that might have happened in any particular individual remain psychological explanations. Therefore, in some scholars' eyes, the state of denial, and the psychological explanation that there has been a failure or interference in psychosexual development, identify the outcome as unhealthy, even though the words "illness" or "disease" are probably inappropriate or outmoded terms for this state.

What some critics point out with justification, though, is that the sexual activities and behavior of many homosexuals are *unhealthy*, with high risks of contracting and transmitting serious and even fatal diseases.[1]

There is no doubt that the same applies to heterosexuality; careless promiscuity carries similar risks. But the same degree of compulsive, furtive, utterly impersonal homosexual promiscuity that has nothing whatsoever to do with external community acceptance or rejection — that is to say that this behavior takes place even in large metropolitan areas where homosexuals can openly meet in bars, dance clubs, advertise, and mix freely and openly — appears to be a much more frequent manifestation of homosexual, rather than heterosexual, fantasy and desire.

---

1. Statistics from the Center for Disease Control published in the journal AIDS show that in the United States, for all groups except Black and Hispanic, approximately 80% or more of AIDS in men was transmitted by homosexual contact.

# ✺ Is Homosexuality a Matter of Choice?

The last claim is that homosexuality is an "alternative," an alternative sexual orientation, expression, or lifestyle. Again, the manner in which discussion is conducted affects the outcome of any debate.

If, for example, by "alternative," one speaks of murdering another person as being an alternative to loving someone, or that an apple and an orange are alternative fruits to eat, then science may have little to contribute. Homosexual propaganda has therefore claimed that homosexuality is an "alternative" variation in just the same way as left-handedness or blue eyes are alternatives.

Furthermore, if that notion were valid, and if in addition, homosexuality were definitely proven to be biological in origin and an orientation over which the individual has absolutely no choice, then it would indeed pose a serious challenge to traditional Jewish belief and practice.

Not that such a challenge cannot be met. Similar challenges in the scientific arenas of physics and biology have received highly competent responses from such scholars as Dr. Aviezer and Dr. Schroeder from the world of physics, and Dr. Feit[1] from the realm of immunobiology, and Rabbi Goldberg's superb presentation of the traditional Jewish moral-religious perspective on homosexuality in *Tradition* last year.[2]

The scientific contribution to this portion of the debate lies — in my opinion — in the area of choice. Is homosexuality something that is innate and fixed, over which an individual has no choice, or is it not innate and fixed, and therefore there is choice?

As we have seen earlier, the scientific evidence does not support a notion of homosexuality as being inborn, genetic, arising from a brain or hormonal abnormality in pre- or post-natal life, as innate. However, that does not mean that homosexuality is something that is freely chosen as an adult by someone who could easily and freely choose to become heterosexual.

The best scientific evidence from our knowledge of psychiatric development and behavior is that the situation is similar to many other emotional behaviors and problems, in that there are different levels of severity.

---

1. See Dr. Feit's thoughtful article "Darwin and Drash," in *The Torah U-Madda Journal*. 1990. 2.25-36.
2. Rabbi Hillel Goldberg. *Tradition*. 1993. 27.28-35.

These different levels or degrees of severity have probably resulted from different degrees of harm and interference in early childhood and adolescent development. In some conditions, there possibly may also be a small genetic contribution.

The practical outcome, though, is that the greater degree of severity, which usually means the earlier and the greater the harm and interference that was done, the less likely will it be that the situation can be much changed or reversed, or that treatment will have much chance of success.

The truth of the matter is that for a number of homosexuals, they may indeed have very little choice in terms of their orientation. (For the religious Jew the matter of *behavior* is a whole other story that Rabbi Hillel Goldberg, among others, has discussed in a brilliant and exemplary manner.)

However, for a great many others, there is choice. There is the choice to at least enter a psychodynamic therapy with a well-trained therapist and begin to explore the nature of the patient's desires for the same sex and fear or discomfort with the opposite sex. This is especially true of the many previously married women who may have been in unhappy or abusive marriages and who, in a widely used contemporary phrase may have turned to a "trendy lesbianism," looking for a warmth and comfort that is not truly homosexual desire, but is really a very profound wish for a maternal nurturing.

The scientific literature on homosexuality is not easy reading. It is highly polarized and has become heavily political and polemical. There is often a vehemence and name-calling that is unusual in the worlds of science and medicine. There are many gross distortions of science and of recent scientific history. There are many quite unjustified claims and enormous bias. Even scholars have to approach this material very carefully. The lay reader, often restricted to snippets submitted from, or selected by, highly biased sources, has to be even more careful not to succumb to one of the most powerful propaganda exercises of modern times.[1]

---

1. See E.T. Rueda. *The Homosexual Network.* 1982. An excellent reference source detailing the platform, aims and methods of the National Gay Caucus and various subsequent homosexual organizations.

*Rabbi Hillel Goldberg*

# Orthodox Soul-Searching After Goldstein

I F ONLY.

If only it were possible to condemn unequivocally, unqualifiedly, Dr. Baruch Goldstein's massacre, to grieve for the dead and the deadly consequences, and then be exempt from further responsibility. If only this massacre were an isolated deed, related to no other developments in the Orthodox Jewish community. If only simple, sincere condemnation were enough. Indeed, this massacre is to be condemned unequivocally, unqualifiedly, sincerely. But, alas, there is obfuscation about this killing — obfuscation that reduces or eliminates the sense of responsibility for soul-searching.

There is, first of all, temptation to put Dr. Goldstein's massacre in context. The contexts, to be sure, are many:

- ☐ the hypocrisy of the world in condemning the Jewish, terrorist killing of Arabs while downplaying or even ignoring the Arab, terrorist killing of Jews;
- ☐ the fact that the State of Israel condemned the act of Dr. Baruch Goldstein while some Arab states not only do not condemn parallel attacks on Israel but actually sponsor them;
- ☐ the asymmetry between massive Arab terrorism and rare Jewish terrorism;
- ☐ the Rabin government's delegitimation of a segment of Israeli citizenry — West Bank settlers — an attitude sensed by Arab terrorists and thus directly contributory to the deaths of innocent Jews;
- ☐ the Rabin government's rejection of debate on the peace accord with the PLO;

- ☐ the sycophantic need of some Jews to apologize specifically to the modern inventor of terrorism, Yassir Arafat, for Baruch Goldstein, in the absence of parallel apologies from Arafat for the numberless, nameless Arab mass murders and murderers under his command;
- ☐ the discussion of the Hebron massacre of 1994 without reference to post-September 13, 1993 Arab terrorist killings of Jews, such as the Palestinian ambush and murder of five-month pregnant Zippora Sasson, shot in the head and abdomen on Feb. 18, 1994;
- ☐ the discussion of the Hebron massacre of 1994 without reference to the Hebron massacre of 1929;
- ☐ the hypocrisy of the UN, "silent after synagogue attacks in Istanbul, Paris, Vienna, Antwerp, Copenhagen and Rome" (as Charles Krauthammer observed) but livid over Israel for the attack in a mosque;
- ☐ the spiritual bankruptcy of those secular Zionists who regard *any part* of the Land of Israel (not just Judea or Samaria) as simple real estate, the Jewish right to which is merely historical;
- ☐ the perverse glee of the enemies of Israel in exploiting the death of innocents as a propaganda bonanza;
- ☐ the fact that the otherwise compassionate Dr. Goldstein may have had one too many innocent Jews die in his arms, or in his sight, and become deranged.

These (and other) contexts of the Hebron massacre of 1994 are damning — of others. However, it is necessary for the Orthodox Jewish community to put aside these contexts just now, not because they are unimportant or illegitimate, but because they have overwhelmed parts of our community at the expense of our own perception of and allegiance to the Torah. Symptomatic of a divergence from the Torah by some Orthodox Jews — their numbers, however small, are too large to ignore — is the impossibility of talking about Dr. Goldstein's murder of innocents without reference to these contexts. The time has come to take stock, to do *cheshbon hanefesh,* if the Torah of God cannot be heard other than through polemical, psychological or political filters. It is time to take stock if an Orthodox Jew — no different from a Conservative, Reform, Humanist, Secular Zionist, Reconstructionist, atheist or other Jew — puts conditions on the Torah, specifically on its proscription against murder and on its authority-structure for the adjudication of life-and-death matters. For Torah Jews there is always a transcendent source of judgment that must color context — not the other way around. On the murder of innocents at the very least, the Torah's judgment stands absolutely alone, unaffected by any context. If some retrospectively praise Dr. Baruch Goldstein, or justify his actions in light of political or psychological conditions, the Torah of God becomes the Torah of the relativists. Perhaps God in His judgment of Baruch Goldstein takes context into account. But we are not God. Ours is not to be God. Ours is not to presume on God, to judge for Him, or to presume to know how He judges us.

Ours is to obey the Torah.

And the Torah is "not in Heaven." As understood by Torah's authoritative interpreters — the Talmudic sages — the phrase "it [the Torah] is not in Heaven" connotes an authority-structure under which the decisions of the majority of the most learned halachic sages in each era are binding; and these decisions, if not yet rendered due to the newness of a given situation, must be sought out. On the murder of innocents at the very least, a Torah Jew does not take the law into his own hands, or praise someone who does.

If all this sounds elementary — unnecessary to reiterate to Orthodox Jews — Dr. Goldstein proves otherwise. He was educated in Orthodox institutions and was an observant Jew himself; and his act, whether calculated or deranged, has met with approval by a few in our community. If, at the very least, the mutuality at the heart of *Klal Yisrael* encompasses Orthodox Jewry, it is time to take stock; specifically, in three areas. No doubt, on a personal level, many and perhaps most Orthodox Jews have no connection to these three problematic areas. But on a communal basis, we all face them: if we were not implicated in the act of Dr. Goldstein on any level, it would not have shocked us (or delighted us, as the sad case may be) as utterly as it did.

❦ ❦ ❦

## ৵ Kahanism

Parts of our community have tolerated the ideas of the late Rabbi Meir Kahane. Whatever else they may stand for, these ideas are predicated upon Rabbi Kahane's, and Rabbi Kahane's right alone, to legitimate them. If he ever accepted the authority of universally recognized halachic authorities like Rabbis Joseph B. Soloveitchik, Moshe Feinstein or Yosef S. Eliashiv, it was a well-kept secret. What is well known is that no universally recognized halachic authority approved of his methods or program. Learned though Rabbi Kahane was, he was not, and he knew he was not, learned enough to make decisions on matters of life-and-death, indeed, on matters of murder. Yet he made them. Gone from his lexicon and activity was obeisance to an appropriately high-level halachic, Orthodox authority-structure. He arrogated to himself the decision-making right reserved to our sages. He thus relativized the Torah, *and he was listened to by some Orthodox Jews.* Logically, even perhaps directly, he lead to Dr. Baruch Goldstein, who took the law into his own hands.

## ✺ Westernization

For some time now, segments throughout the Orthodox community have subtly but incessantly undercut the idea of supreme rabbinic authority, which is indispensable to the integrity of the Torah that is not in Heaven. Some have become too Westernized in the absorption of secular axioms by which society in general, and religious authority in particular, are supposed to operate. Some have become wiser than the Torah scholars when it comes to contemporary issues about which, supposedly, some know better. It has become fashionable to attack the concept of *emunat chachamim*; or extrapolate from the Western premise that all men are created equal the halachically spurious approach that all Orthodox Jews are created equal in their understanding of the Torah; or to condition the acceptance of rabbinic authority on the Western axiom of personal autonomy. However, when the "I" becomes the authority, there can be no "Thou." When the ability of the halachic authority-structure's learned sages to rule on matters of contemporary import is impugned, so is their ability to rule on matters of murder. For the learned sages to be respected as such, they must be respected in all areas. The end result of this subtle undercutting of Torah authority is to compartmentalize — to separate judgments on nationalist, ethical, or professional matters from the Torah. The end result of compartmentalization is to decide matters for oneself; alas, a few even follow the logic to include the matter of murder.

## ✺ "Charismaticism"

On the one hand, some in our community have derogated genuine Torah authority; on the other hand, some have taken people of talent to be way above their merit. Case in point: Dr. Goldstein. One comment made after his act was this: "From what he [Dr. Goldstein] did can only come good because that's what they say of a *tzaddik* [righteous person]." Under the Torah, a person's acts are not righteous because of who he is; a person's acts are righteous because they accord with the Torah's standards of righteousness. The person is not the measure of the standard; the standard is the measure of the person — and murder is not a Torah standard! Nor is the hyperbolic elevation of persons who, whatever their merits, are glorified as if they were above the standards of the Torah, above the stricture of the Torah sages. Present in our community is "charismaticism," a condition of exaggeration that tolerates, before or after the fact, a variety of distortions it is not now the place to delineate, except one: murder.

※ ※ ※

What are the faithful of Israel, the guardians of Torah, to do? We live in a dark exile (notwithstanding bright miracles in the Land of Israel and elsewhere). We do not always have access to Torah authority; we are children of the Holocaust, riven by historical burden; we suffer political, economic, or spiritual impositions by the nations. We are, after all, pursued by assimilation or by armies. Communal soul-searching is hardly congenial just now. But this mass murder, committed by one of our own, is unprecedented. So must be the urgency of our soul-searching.

Our soul-searching must be public as well as private, as a statement by 44 Orthodox rabbis and *roshei yeshivah* in Israel noted: "There is no understanding and no forgiveness for the murder of people while they are praying to the Creator of the Universe. As people and as Jews, we grieve the blood spilled, and protest against this horrible desecration of God's name. We call on everyone who is able to denounce and eradicate the phenomenon of any understanding of and agreement with these types of acts."

It may be tempting to put soul-searching over the Hebron massacre of 1994 in context: no Arab leader, anywhere, urged soul-searching in the aftermath of Munich, Maalot, the Achille Lauro, the hijackings of planes, buses and cars. But we are the people of the Torah, the holy congregation of *teshuvah, tefillah,* and *tzedakah.* Of stretching beyond self-satisfaction. Of being part of a chosen nation, and loving humankind at the same time. We are the people of *middos, kavanah,* and intellectual honesty — of soul-searching.

*Rabbi Yaakov D. Homnick*

# Of Patting (and Breaking) Backs

AN ANECDOTE RESONATES IN MY MIND: RAPHAEL WALDMAN, who had been a journalist at *The Baltimore Sun* before accepting Torah observance, described an early experience as a guest at an Orthodox home. He had been asked by his hosts, in the breathless and conspiratorial tones reserved for such forays, to describe the existential conditions of life outside the Pale. "I gave them what they wanted," he concluded. "I told them that there was nothing out there!"

This small conceit of the insular crowd, the idea that outside of our little circle the world is a de-ideologized zone of corruption and permissiveness, generally seems a harmless enough foible. Its impact on the *kiruv* system has revealed a far more pernicious aspect.

The process of correcting our behavior, as practiced by us daily, is aptly called *teshuvah,* Hebrew for "return." Clearly, the place of goodness that we seek is one that we have known, even if only for fleeting instants in our lives. It is the space that we occupy when we are at our best, where our education and our identification mesh, where ideology embraces reality, where good will meets good deed. It is somewhere that we have been before and, more meaningfully, it is where we feel most natural.

Yet, we would deny to the new initiate that luxury. We too often insist on belittling, even negating, all the attainments which have characterized the earlier periods of their lives. The family life is hollow; the education shallow; the society degenerate; the relationships unhealthy; the character unformed; the views uninformed. Our new friends cannot "return" to that place in the soul unless we grant them access.

It is the view of my more sensitive colleagues that by this self-indulgent way of drumming home our exclusive custody over the moral high ground, we inflict undeserved damage upon our charges. If we pat ourselves on the back long enough, we eventually become spineless.

The people of the Western world, and more so the Jews among them, are fundamentally decent people, inculcated with most of the virtues of good character. Our job is to point out to our students those qualities which are best in their basic orientation and to build upon those foundations with the prescriptions, the wisdom and the values of the Torah serving as the enriching context.

When this is not done, a portion of our clientele gets lost, unable to face the stark test of self-negation we are imposing. Another portion stumbles over the line into commitment, but then sinks into a profound abyss. If he cannot take pride in his education and his career, if his family is only the instrument of betrayal which denied him his birthright, if his hobbies and interests were empty pastimes, if his friends were pulling him down, if his loves were illusions and his ideas were propaganda and his instincts were subverted by a decadent society, then he has nothing that is worthwhile; he is bankrupt. His head cannot be respected and his heart cannot be trusted, his ego cannot be consulted nor can his conscience be heeded.

In an essay written some years ago, I gave a name to this phenomenon. It is called LEST, Lost Ego Syndrome of Transition. Consigning people to such a limbo, even for a brief period, can have catastrophic effects on their personalities and states of mental health. Unfortunately, I have witnessed variations on this theme all too often.

Rabbi Yitzchok Hutner (1906-1979), my great teacher, was still alive during the initial stages of the *teshuvah* movement. Laibel Kruger, who served as his personal valet at that time, reported that Rav Hutner, when introduced to those early students, would ask, "Are you keeping up with your career? Are you keeping up with your hobbies? Are you keeping up with your family?"

That wisdom is no less timely now. We are not inviting people to go from bad to good; rather, to give their goodness a rootedness, a system, a permanence —to go from good to better.

*Chava Willig Levy*

# Why There Was No Gabbai at the Regency Theater

MANHATTAN'S UPPER WEST SIDE BOASTS MANY WONDERful houses of worship. Back in 1979, I belonged to two of them. One was Lincoln Square Synagogue — where I worshiped God. The other was the now-defunct Regency Theater, specializing in film classics — where I adored Katherine Hepburn, James Stewart and, of course, Woody Allen.

These two places had a lot in common. They both played to packed houses; it was practically impossible to get a seat in either hall, although your chances were slightly better at the Regency. And, like Lincoln Square, the movie house even had a "Beginners' *Minyan*" of sorts — like the time I brought ten of my uninitiated friends there to see *Casablanca* for the first time.

But there the similarities end. Over the years, I noticed one striking difference between these two houses of worship: At the Regency, you never saw a *gabbai*.

Apparently, Regency-goers rarely needed a *gabbai* or usher to escort them to their seats. Perhaps that's because they always came on time, if not early. What's more, if anyone had the audacity to talk — or even whisper — during the Regency's services, everyone around the culprit became, in effect, a *gabbai*.

Regency-goers were so devout that they would help you to do *teshuvah* at the drop of a popcorn box. Occasionally, I needed to whisper a bit of narrative to my husband Michael, who is blind. I did so with trepidation, knowing that someone more religious than I would tap me on the shoulder and remind me that I was to refrain from personal conversations in this sacred place. And interestingly, I and anyone else confronted with this transgression meekly submitted to the reprimand, apologizing for our effrontery, our evil inclination.

And it was understood: These were the house rules. If you broke them, you'd better believe the peer pressure could get pretty intense! If you were unrepentant, they practically ran you out of the theater.

I have been to many synagogues since 1979, where the scenario is quite uniform, yet altogether different from the Regency. As a rule, no matter what *shul* you are in, if you ask people near you to stop talking, explaining that their conversation is interfering with your experience of the service, you do so at your own risk. Whereas the Regency perpetrator inevitably would apologize for his or her transgression, the synagogue culprit may be puzzled, if not incensed, by the confrontation.

I guess there isn't much peer pressure in a *shul*. Perhaps those disturbed by the talking don't feel they have a right — as they do at a movie theater — to ask those around them to follow the house rules. And that's why my *shul* has a *gabbai* and the Regency didn't.

Well, I think the time has come for life to imitate art. Here is a modest proposal:

Why don't we divest the *gabbai* of his role as keeper of synagogue silence and play that role ourselves, just as we would during our favorite movie? For the "frummies" at the Regency, silence was deemed a prerequisite, a matter of life and death. And those buffs usually knew the film's outcome! Couldn't we set the same standard at our houses of worship, where our prayers really *are* a matter of life and death — and where we are *not* privileged to know their outcome?

# ⋄§ Education

☐ *Teaching Thinking Skills in the Judaic Studies Curriculum*
☐ *Nobody's Business*

*Rabbi Aharon Hersh Fried*

# Teaching Thinking Skills in the Judaic Studies Curriculum

THE MAJOR SUBJECT AREAS WE TEACH IN OUR *LIMUDEI KODESH* classes, *Chumash* with Rashi, *Mishna,* and Gemara, probably require more analysis and synthesis of complex ideas than do any other subjects our students will ever meet in school. These subjects require not only basic skills in reasoning, but also skills of textual analyses and linguistic skills. The student of a *pasuk* of *Chumash* with Rashi must be able to recognize anomalies and inconsistencies in the text, infer special meaning from them, and reason logically to arrive at an understanding of what the Torah is coming to teach him.[1]

It is somewhat surprising in light of all this how little emphasis is placed on the DIRECT teaching of thinking skills in our day schools and *chadorim.*

Our approach to teaching children how to think has been to expose them to the thinking of Rashi and of Chazal with the expectation that by hearing and understanding the thinking of these great men our students too will learn how to think. This is an INDIRECT approach, one which may work for only the very brightest in our classrooms, those who least need our help.

Hearing and being able to repeat what somebody else has said is no guarantee of one's having understood it. It is certainly no guarantee of one's having acquired and internalized the thinking processes involved.

---

1. If the reader at this point finds himself protesting, "The child doesn't have to do all that. He merely has to understand what Chazal and Rashi say!" then he has proven my point before I've even tried to make it. There is no way to fully appreciate what Chazal derive from a *pasuk* without being able to go through the thinking process which led to it.

Learning to do something requires opportunities to try out what one has learned and to receive clear feedback on where one has gone wrong so that one can correct one's errors. As Chazal tell us, *"Ein odom omed al dvar Halacha elo im ken nichshal bo t'chila"* — "A person does not fully acquire mastery of any *Halacha* unless he has first stumbled over it." To properly learn thinking, our students must be given opportunities to practice thinking.

Unfortunately, we do very little of this. What we tend to do most of the time is feed our students information which they are required to assimilate and at some later date to recite or reproduce from memory on assignments, tests, and examinations. Thus we tend to exercise the faculty of memory (important) and ignore the (equally important) faculty of thinking.[1]

There are those who would take issue and contend that we do in fact teach thinking — witness all of the *targillim* (exercises) which are done in *Chumash,* such as *"mi amar el mi"* and *"al me ne'emar"* etc. These exercises do have potential use as teaching materials for basic comprehension skills. In fact they would work if students would be required to search the texts and work out the answers for themselves. Unfortunately, in most classrooms the teacher goes over all of the questions in class and often even puts all of the answers on the board for the students to copy. The students are then required only to memorize the answers and to spit them back on homework assignments or on tests. Again, an exercise in memory only.

Now it is true that at least some of the skills involved in learning *Chumash* with Rashi and Gemara can be taught only to students at higher elementary or high school levels. Still, if our students are to attain these higher order skills at any level in their school careers, then they should be taught preparatory thinking skills at younger ages. These skills can be taught without great difficulty. We need only abandon our

---

1. I should perhaps make it clear that when I speak of thinking skills, I am not speaking of "pie-in-the-sky" questions of the nature of, "If you were Moses in Egypt, how would you have approached Pharaoh?" or of questions of "mah l'malah uma l'matah." I am speaking of simply (or not so simply) understanding what Rashi says and why, what it is about the *pasuk* that forced Rashi to seek an interpretation, what brought him to the particular interpretation he gives, how could the *pasuk* have been written differently, and how would we then have understood if differently. Similar questions for understanding could be raised for a *blatt* Gemara.

tendency to spoon-feed information to our students. Instead, we should make them think and seek out some of the information for themselves.

Having spent a number of years in *chinuch*, I have met some of the misconceptions and positions which mitigate against an active approach to the teaching of thinking.

Many of those involved in *chinuch* believe that:

☐ *Thinking is not something you can teach;* "either you have it or you don't."[1]
☐ *"Real thinking is something that doesn't come to children until they are older* and there is therefore no point in straining children's minds at an early age to do something which will emerge naturally and spontaneously at a later age.[2] Although thinking might be a teachable skill, educators do not feel they know how to teach it.
☐ If they were to spend time teaching children how to think they would be forced to cover less ground, something the administration and the parents would never stand for.
☐ Since *thinking is taught in the General Studies curriculum,* shouldn't that suffice??!!

---

1. They confuse the controversy which exists in psychology about the extent to which intelligence can be modified with our ability to improve thinking skills. While it is certainly true that some students come to school with certain inherent limitations, it is an extremely small minority who are so limited that they cannot learn to MASTER and receive good grades in all that's required in the elementary and high school curricula. The current practice of not directly teaching children how to think cripples many more than this minute minority.

What is particularly disheartening is meeting up with the many children whose very real thinking problems remain undiagnosed and even unnoticed for years because they do well in the rote skill areas of reading and translating. Many of these children go unnoticed until age 10, 12 or even later (depending on the age at which comprehension in Gemara becomes a real issue) before receiving any help. Even then, it is only the most problematic children who are noticed. Many "just average" children are ignored and allowed to struggle on without any help. This is accepted as normal because they "just don't have it." These children are thus robbed of many years during which they might have received help and been taught how to think.

2. Besides which, it is so much more important in the earlier years to teach the child to read and translate the texts properly. (This is true; witness all of the children who reach high school and beyond and still struggle with reading basic *Chumash,* Rashi and Gemara texts. Compare these students with the *cheder* students' fluency in these basically rote skills.) However, the need to concentrate on rote skills need not exclude all concentration on thinking skills.

Without getting into a long theoretical discussion of the psychology of thinking, allow me to outline an approach which I have found enables me to think productively about the Teaching of Thinking. I hope it may do the same for others and allow thinking to actively enter our curriculum.

☐ Firstly, I *characterize thinking skills as habits,* habits of thought.

For a small demonstration of this, complete the following statement:

The name of a President of the U.S. is James Polk and the white of the egg is called the _____ .

If like most people you completed the statement with "yolk" rather than with the correct "albumen," you have demonstrated the workings of a habit of thought — rhyming. Because of the way the task was set up, this habit led you to the wrong answer. Most of the time we hope to learn those habits which lead us to correct answers.

☐ Secondly, *thinking is not one undefined ability.* It is made up of many small and distinct "habits" of thought which when combined allow us to do some very complex thinking tasks — some "real" thinking.

Thus to properly teach thinking we need to build on some fundamental, individual thinking skills. Once these have been mastered we are able to build on the next level of thinking skills. This process of *teaching successive thinking skills needs to be continued* until complex operations become possible.

☐ Thirdly, *although some children will pick up these habits seemingly spontaneously* through incidental learning, very much in the way they picked up speech and language, *many will not.* Many children need to be taught thinking skills directly, just as many children need to be taught how to use language.

☐ Because most research has shown that *there is precious little generalization of thinking skills across subject areas* and across situations, it is important that thinking be taught in each subject area with specific problems culled from that subject area.[1]

---

1. Not only is the content in different subject areas different, but often even the types of thinking skills required are different. A listing of the specific skills required at each level for the study of Judaic studies is beyond the scope of this paper. Still, as is true for all subjects, children must learn to classify and organize information into appropriate categories according to some defined attributes (be they concrete or abstract), they must learn to serialize objects, events or information (that is, they must learn to order them along some continuum, such as size, or time, or degree of severity or importance etc.), and they must

☐ Furthermore, I believe that these skills can be taught without sacrificing too much of the material a teacher is meant to cover. Really *only minor but very meaningful modifications in a teacher's approach are necessary.*

If age-appropriate questions are given to the child in the early grades, if appropriate and constructive feedback is provided, the child can develop proper "habits of thought" without great difficulty.

Let us now look at some ways in which teachers at the earliest grades can begin to teach their children how to think.

For example, at the very earliest level, when the "Alef-Bais" is taught, why must the teacher tell the child the name of each letter? Why not give the child three letters (such as alef, bais and gimel), two of which he's already learned (alef and bais) and ask him to "find" the gimel — a simple inference task.

Why, also, is it necessary for children learning how to read to be faced always with reading what we place in front of then? Why not exercise their brains by giving them the opportunity to create words on their own (by writing them or by using rubber stamps or stickers)? Having the child create his own words (in whatever language) and giving him feedback on whether they are phonetically correct can be a great way to involve the child's mind.

When we get to translating *Chumash,* instead of then giving the child matching tasks in which he has to use his memory only to match Hebrew words with their translations, why not also give him words which he has not yet met, but whose precise meaning he can figure out from the information we do give him? Thus, for example, a child who has learned the first two *p'sukim* of *Beraishis* might be given the following matching task:

| | |
|---|---|
| the heavens | *v'ha'aretz* |
| the earth | *hashomayim* |
| and the earth | *v'hashomayim* |
| and the heaven | *sha'aretz* |

---

learn to make deductions and inferences. Because much of what they will be dealing with in Judaic studies is textual, our students must learn how to extract information from text, make inferences from text, understand the structure of the text, pick up on anomalies in the text, and make inferences from those anomalies. They also need to learn to deal with questions of "What if the *pasuk* had said . . . then what would it have meant. . .?" an often very difficult task for children, albeit a very basic one for learning *Chumash* with Rashi and Gemara.

Now although he has met and learned by rote to translate three of these words, he has never met "v'hashomayim." He does not, however, need to be the world's greatest genius to figure out its translation. He might use a process of elimination, or he might pay attention to the relative lengths of the two words which contain "shomayim." It doesn't matter, so long as he finds the answer for himself.

We spend much time teaching children the rules of basic *dikduk* and the structure of the Hebrew language. We present this to them for memorization. Why not allow them to discover this information for themselves? Why not present them with a number of words which they have learned to translate by rote and ask them to find the Hebrew equivalent of some English translation? Thus we might ask them, "Given the following words and their translations, which letters in Hebrew mean 'my' and which mean 'your'?"

| | | |
|---|---|---|
| my house | — | *baysee* |
| your house | — | *bayscha* |
| my field | — | *sadee* |
| your field | — | *sadcha* |
| my brother | — | *achee* |
| your brother | — | *achicha* |

When it comes to translating *p'sukim,* we often mistakenly assume that if a child can translate a *pasuk* he also understands it. We sometimes test this by asking the child to tell us what the *pasuk* is saying in "his own words." What generally follows is an awkward paraphrase of the *pasuk* which so closely parallels the translation that we are left unsure as to what the child really understands and what he is merely miming. Worse still, the child is left unsure and unaided by our questioning. More precise questions requiring less verbalization and more thinking on the child's part would serve us both better. Thus, for a simple example, take the following *pasuk*:

*Vayomer Elokim yehi ohr va'yehi ohr.* After the child has learned to translate this by rote, why not ask him simply, "Which words in this *pasuk* did *Hashem* say? Which words tell us what happened after *Hashem* spoke?"

We could get a bit more complex, and ask, "If *Hashem* only said, '*yehi ohr,*' who said, '*Vayomer Elokim*' and '*vayehi ohr*?'"

Or, we might take the *pasuk* in *Parshas Noach; Tzohar taase lateyvah u'el ama techalena milemala upesach hateva betzida tasim tachtiyim shniyim ushlishim taaseha,* and ask the child, "How many different commandments was Noach given in this *pasuk*?"

To teach the child to pick up on seemingly superfluous words in *p'sukim,* I might present him with the following *pasuk*: *Vayoled Noach shlosha bonim es Shem es Chom v'es Yofes,* and ask: "Which two words in this *pasuk* could the Torah have left out without our losing any information? (Not the "es"s.)" If the child has difficulty answering, I might restructure the way I present the *pasuk* to him, thus I might write: Vayoled Noach — Shlosha bonim — es Shem — es Chom — v'es Yofes — in the hope that this will make it easier for him to find the answer. I might also lead him through a trial and error search for the answer, whereby he would choose an answer and then check back to see whether he has indeed not lost any information. I might construct exercises (using other *p'sukim,* but perhaps with sentences in his own language first) which will give him an opportunity to learn the specific skill required by a particular question (e.g. how to spot the quote in a *pasuk*). I might do any or all of these things, but the one thing I would not do is to give him the answer. That would be robbing him of the opportunity to think.

The exercises I have presented are very basic and simple ones. They can gradually be made much more complex. Thus students may be asked to find the "main idea" in a group of *p'sukim,* or to break up and organize an entire *Parsha* into a number of topics. Similarly for Gemara, questions can be asked along the lines of: "Which words in the Gemara make the proof to the question, and which make up the answer?" These too can gradually be made more complex. Thus the student might be given an out-of-sequence list of discreet logical statements which cover all of the "shakla v'taryeh" of a section of Gemara, and be asked to (a) rearrange the statements to correspond to the sequence of the Gemara, (b) identify the Gemara text which corresponds to each statement, and (c) answer some very precise and well-thought-out questions which test the student's understanding of the relevance and importance of each step in the Gemara's argument. Space does not allow for more examples in this article. I will have to leave further examples to the imagination and creativity of the reader.

Suffice it to say that children need and can be taught to think. It is we parents and teachers, however, who need to change our thinking first.

*Charlotte Friedland*

# Nobody's Business\*

DEBBY HAD BEGUN HER CAREER AS A TERRORIST EARLY IN life. The talk of the teachers' lounge, the bully of the playground, she had achieved a notoriety seldom earned by a ten-year-old. So, it was not surprising when I chanced to enter the principal's office one nippy day in November and overheard Debby's teacher resigning once again. The woman was gesturing frantically, raving about the antics of the devil in pigtails. This time, she insisted resolutely, either she or the child would have to go. The principal could take his choice.

As I stood in the doorway listening to the tirade, punctuated by the principal's soft monosyllables of sympathy, a strange suspicion swept over me. It intrigued me that teachers in the school had targeted Debby for all disruptions. If lunch went sour, it was probably Debby's fault. "What is it about this child that invites blame?" I wondered.

Without another thought, I volunteered to try my hand with her. The answer was a flat "no."

"Don't do it," muttered the other teacher. "You'll ruin your reputation."

"It's not your business to save every wayward child." counseled the principal. "I'll find some other school to take her off our hands . . . ."

---

\*Based on a story by "Morah Blanca" Rosenfeld. "Morah Blanca," a teacher for many years, is the creator of the "Mitzvah Tree" concept used in kindergartens around the world. She has produced numerous recordings of her original songs and stories including: "The Mitzvah Tree," Stories Under the Mitzvah Tree," "I hear a Mitzvah," "It's Mitzvah Time!" "Shabbos with the Mitzvah Tree Triplets," and "Free to do Mitzvos."

". . . . where she will be kicked from class to class," I countered. "Look, she's none of my business and none of yours. Next year she'll be nobody's business again. What will happen to such a child?" I badgered, I argued and I nagged until I had won Debby. At the time, I thought it was a victory.

As it was, this year's group had only recently reached a shaky cohesiveness. Instinctively, I knew that bringing Debby into my class would be like throwing a shark into a goldfish pond. The very least I should do is consult first with the goldfish.

It pays to be direct, especially with children: they see through euphemisms and double-talk. The whole school knew about Debby. Why mince words? I asked the class if they could find it in their hearts to do this special mitzvah, the mitzvah of giving someone a new start in life. I made no secret of the fact that it might be rough at times, but that I felt it would be worth the trouble. I promised not to bring her in if they didn't want her. Then I waited.

It is rare for children to be given any true power, and some educators might say I was risking an instant veto. But I knew my girls. I felt they would rise to the challenge, and they did.

My next step was to find Debby. Banished from class once again, she had retreated to her own private corner of the hallway. This was her domain, a place to weave fantasies and plan revenge. I came upon her leaning into her niche, her arms crossed in defiance, her toe kicking an imaginary object.

Putting my arm around her shoulders, I whispered, "I hear you're having some trouble with your teacher. Would you like to join my class?" Debby stiffened at first, then stared at me in surprise.

"Yes," she mumbled, "yes, I would." She quickly ran to gather her things and I triumphantly led her into my room. Suddenly, we heard loud clapping and hooting from Debby's previous class: they were celebrating her departure. As I showed Debby in, my class broke out in spontaneous applause and cheers. With lowered eyes she grinned shyly at them and they smiled back.

That night, it was time to do some detective work. I itched to find out her story, the whole story of what made her the spiteful child of horrid repute. I dialed her phone number.

Debby's mother answered and, upon learning that I was from the school, snapped, "Don't talk to me about Debby. I've heard it all." I explained that Debby had been transferred to my class and that I merely wanted to become acquainted. There was silence at the other end of the wire. "Debby told me," she finally said, her voice suspicious, but softer. "She seemed excited about it. She said, 'Morah Blanca put her arm around me.' She mentioned that the class clapped for her, too. I guess they don't know her yet."

I told her that we were happy to have her daughter in our class. She didn't seem to hear me.

"Yeah, well let me know when she gives you any trouble. She'll get a good spanking." She yawned wearily.

Five words from that conversation bounded through my brain over and over: "...put her arm around me...." Why would the child report in such detail? From her guarded manner, I never would have guessed that Debby had been so elated by my gesture. I mused over the "good spanking" too. The violence Debby inflicted on others in the schoolyard was probably only a fraction of what she suffered at home.

There was more to her story, I sensed, but for the moment this information would suffice. Clearly, Debby was deeply troubled, her behavior in school only a symptom of the complex emotions barreling through her. It was then that doubts first began to pierce my armor of idealism. Wouldn't it be better to refer her to a psychologist? Could my efforts with her drain my ability to cope with the others? After all, is it any mitzvah to destroy my class for the sake of one child? I spent a sleepless night.

When I returned to school in the morning, I found that these same fears had been circulating among the class parents. In a chain-call ricochet, a frantic crescendo of antagonism had culminated in a petition to remove the troublemaker from our class. I was stunned, but the block was enough to strengthen my resolve to keep Debby. That evening, with the help of two mothers who shared my determination, I started a telephone campaign of my own. We made it clear to the parents that the child will remain in my class, but anyone who cared to, could switch her child to another teacher.

Ultimately, it was the children themselves who resolved the showdown. Though their parents urged them to take refuge in another class, not a single child would leave me. It was settled then. Debby was ours, and we were hers.

※ ※ ※

In the days and months that followed, I observed Debby in all of her phases: the time she giggled uncontrollably; the time she spread glue all over her face and hands; the time she bit another girl. But through it all, I noted with pride that the other children treated her with care and tenderness. The knowledge that they were participating in a mitzvah of enormous magnitude brought out a *chesed* and maturity far beyond their years.

Day after frustrating day, I asked myself, "Why am I drawn to this impossible child?" As I reflected on my teaching career, I noticed that I have always been touched by the child who is most rejected.

I remembered five-year-old Suri, who burned with self-hatred for the most absurd reason: her bright red hair had triggered a bigoted antipathy in her old-world grandparents. Shamefully nicknamed and teased by her family, she had developed a disgust for her hair and everything else about herself. Naturally, other students shunned this child whose tough exterior shielded a shattered ego.

How I yearned to counteract this terrible influence on her life! I would tell her each day how pretty she looked. I took her on my lap to brush her long, truly lovely tresses. On the last day of school, I brought her a blue satin ribbon and braided it into her hair. She wore it as though it were a medal of honor.

What about the obese child, the gawky child, the shy child? There are many with noticeable impediments, others just carry it in their hearts. All you have to do is look. A caring teacher can make all the difference in such a child's life. By simply showing that you recognize his problem and respect his struggle, you can help a child jump the hurdles barring his way. As far as I'm concerned, that's what being a teacher is all about.

But a simple word of encouragement would never be enough for my Debby. Her pain was too deep for a smile to cure. I was determined to find out more about her now. On the excuse of giving a daily behavior report, I called her home each day, alternately speaking to her mother and father, I strained to catch any clues in their conversation that would explain her agony. Slowly, the puzzle pieces fit together, forming a terrifying picture of an emotionally tortured child.

Born second after their son, Debby had been treated like an intruder by her parents since the day she was brought home from the hospital. In order to prevent jealousy in their favored older child, Debby had been systematically ignored. She was never hugged or kissed, never played with, rarely picked up at all. She was followed by two younger siblings in rapid succession and quickly was made responsible for their care. If there was a complaint from school, she was severely punished.

No wonder she wanted to give the whole world a black eye. It was incredible to me that after her horrible days at school, she could drag herself home to help cook supper and bathe the little ones.

The first step, of course, was to stop the beatings. I implored her parents to overlook her failures, to treat their daughter more kindly. Apparently touched by my concern, they even agreed to accompany me to a psychologist. He listened to them carefully and discussed my observations. Surmising that they would not return to see him, the psychologist pointed to me and told them, "Trust everything this woman tells you. She knows your daughter well and she can accomplish things you never dared to dream." We knew it would be a struggle. After ten years, a father must learn to think twice before striking his child. A mother must lower her demands and defuse her anger. I prayed each day that the parents' resolution to salvage their little girl would not melt in the heat of a rash moment.

Debby noticed the change in her parents' actions, and she realized I was behind it. Though I was stern with her at times, Debby's affection and gratitude grew. Yet there was still a look in her eye, a look that I recognized but could not place.

The more I thought about it, distant echoes began to ring through the recesses of my mind. My emotions fight the oncoming memories. My brain labors desperately to snuff them out, but I cannot. In my mind's eye I can now clearly picture myself at just about Debby's age.

※ ※ ※

I am standing behind my little suitcase at the railway station in Vienna. My mother and brothers are there too. The year is 1938, and I am to board the "kinder transport," a train bound for safety and freedom in England. My mother kisses me and tells me to be a good girl. There are other parents putting children on the train too. Some of them are crying. But my mother smiles one of her grand smiles as she gently lifts me onto the train. She whispers that she will see me soon. Then the train begins to move. Something enormous wells up inside me. I want to scream, "Mama! Please, Mama, let me stay with you!" But it is too late. All I can see in the distance is her white handkerchief, covering her eyes.

Did I sense then that I would never see her again? I can't remember. But I fondly recall the solid, impressive demeanor of Rabbi Dr. Solomon Schonfeld, the man who risked his life time and again to take children out of that cauldron of terror to safety in Great Britain. Jewish families there had promised to take the children, but scores of religious youngsters wound up placed in non-religious homes or with gentiles. I too found myself in a cottage in the English countryside, the bewildered guest of the village butcher. Separated from my family, my language, even my fellow Jews, my world turned upside-down in a flash.

When war with Germany became inevitable, an event occurred which would change my life forever. The evacuation of thousands of schoolchildren from the cities out to the countryside created a bizarre situation in a little town called Shefford. The townsfolk there had turned out in the market square to do their patriotic duty by accepting London children into their homes. To their consternation, 500 Jewish youngsters, many of them refugees from Nazi Germany, tumbled off the buses.

Wearing strange clothes, speaking a foreign language, and clutching paper bags with their special food, these children were not what the Sheffordians had expected. They had hoped to host proper British kin who could fill out their church choir and bring fresh vitality to the village. Instead, many of them found themselves seated at dinner opposite incomprehensible children who smiled pleasantly, but could only stammer the one English line rehearsed with them by Rabbi Schonfeld, "We are fish-eating vegetarians!"

Through diplomacy, and boundless dedication to her children, the principal of the transplanted Jewish school, Dr. Judith Grunfeld, succeeded in silencing the angry mutterings of the community. What's more, she and her staff labored with devotion to reconstitute the school in this alien setting. Drawing upon her own deep *emunah,* she encouraged her wards, who had been flung like chaff across five towns, to be strong in their Yiddishkeit. The Shefford Jewish school became a symbol of the eternity of the Jewish people and a testimony to their unremitting devotion to Torah, at precisely the same moment as the barbaric destruction of Jewish life on the mainland was taking place.

I had not been a part of this rescue enterprise and knew nothing of its existence. But one Spring day, a shiny black car pulled up in front of our house and a tall, majestic woman stepped out of it. She approached in a regal, yet gentle manner and asked me my name. It was Dr. Grunfeld herself, acting upon direction of the Chief Rabbi. He had been asked to find me by my brothers, who had been sent to Canada.

She explained that she had a school for Jewish children just like me and invited me to join her there. I refused. Torn from my family for over three years, alienated from everything I ever loved, I now wanted nothing more than the stability of a quiet English life. Judaism was no longer meaningful to me. It was one of those tender, distant recollections, like my mother at the station. The principal's jaw tightened slightly and her eyes swept downward as she told me to think it over. I thought I was rid of her.

I had not reckoned upon the persistence of this woman whose entire life was committed to saving every living spark of Judaism. Tenaciously, she returned some weeks later, this time bringing with her two girls of my age. They took me by my hands and told me about their wonderful school. They begged me to come, pulling me toward them. Suddenly, resentment and shame overtook me. "Leave me here," I cried. "I can't go with you anymore!" How I remember my tears as they turned and left.

It was no accident that Dr. Grunfeld was known as "The Queen" by all who knew her. No obstacle was too great for her to conquer. She understood my turmoil and never reprimanded me. She visited again, and this time a yearning to return to my people engulfed me. I went with her to learn, to grow, to begin living again. To this day, she is a part of me, my spiritual mother. To this day, I silently thank her every time I say another *brocha,* do another mitzvah. They are her *brochos,* her mitzvos.

How had she reached this frightened, lonely child? At the time, I thought that I hid it all so well! I never went out before I straightened my shoulders and wiped away the tears. How did she see them?

Could it be that she caught the hollow longing in my eyes that I see in Debby's? Slowly, the realization crept over me that I find myself in every child that I teach. I became aware that without my knowing it, the dark loneliness of my own childhood had united with Debby's. Without being told, I knew all of her secrets.

At the same moment, I understood how Dr. Grunfeld could treat every Jewish child as her own child. At Shefford, I learned the healing power of love. It isn't enough to love your children, your pupils. You must tell them you love them. Maybe that is why I prefer teaching the very young. You can love them and be unashamed.

Even in the older grades the instructor who adores her subject and ignores the personalities of her students will fail. Think back to your most memorable teachers. Weren't they the ones who genuinely cared about you?

I suspect that our human capacity to love others, and receive love, is so tremendous that most of us are somewhat deprived. That is why a moment of caring can reach the soul where hours of reason fall short.

But even well-meaning parents and teachers blunder, sometimes habitually. If the impact of every nasty look, every cutting word could be visibly imprinted on our children's faces, our thoughtless behavior would abruptly stop. Like Debby's parents, we all have the choice of continuing our destructive actions or taking steps to correct them.

✻ ✻ ✻

Little by little, I convinced Debby that she had the ability to choose her mode of behavior. She could be cooperative or churlish; helpful or hostile. It was all up to her. In the warmth of our "mitzvah classroom" her true characteristics gradually began to blossom. It was thrilling for me to see her included in the children's games, or chosen as a partner for a class trip. I was proud to watch her react sharply when another girl was banned from a jumprope game. As though it were the most natural thing in the world for her, Debby brought her own jumprope the next day, insisting that the other child lead the game. We discovered that the flip side of Debby's demonstrative conduct was a true quality of leadership.

I don't want to leave you with the impression that a caring educator will change the life of every student she meets. Nor should you imagine that everyone you help will appreciate your efforts. Many of the children who left my class would pass me on the street today without a second glance. They don't remember, or care to remember, the countless times I picked them up, dried their tears and urged them to try again.

But now and then, a young adult will rush to me, excited and joyful to find "Morah Blanca" once again. Eyes sparkling, she will tell me that she still recalls the songs I taught her. Another will introduce me to her little son or daughter: "This was my Mitzvah Tree Morah . . ."

Debby is one of those. Today she is the congenial mother of three treasured children, and she makes it her business to regularly share her life with me. There are times, I admit, while she is gaily describing the latest of her children's capers, that my mind wanders. I recollect the sullen little girl in the hallway, her deep burning eyes, her tight little fist. She remembers too, and though neither of us ever says it, we both know we were lost children, adrift in a senseless world until someone decided that we were too precious to be abandoned. We belonged to nobody back then, but we each had a teacher who cared enough to tear away the veil of confusion and save a world.

# ❧ Halachah and Talmudic Interpretation

- ☐ *The Brain Death Controversy in Jewish Law*
- ☐ *From What Point Should the Megillah Be Read?*

*Rabbi Yitzchak Breitowitz*

# The Brain Death Controversy in Jewish Law

HISTORICALLY, DEATH WAS NOT PARTICULARLY DIFFICULT TO define from either a legal or halachic standpoint. Generally, all vital systems of the body — respiratory, neurological and circulatory — would fail at the same time and none of these functions could be prolonged without the maintenance of the others. Today, with major technological advances in life support, particularly the development of respirators and heart-lung machines, it is entirely possible to keep some bodily systems "functioning" long after others have ceased. Since we no longer face the inevitable simultaneity of systematic failures, it has become necessary to define with greater precision and specificity which physiological systems are indicators of life and which (if any) are not, especially in light of the scarcity of medical resources and the pressing need for organs for transplantation purposes. In recent years, the concept of "neurological death," commonly called "brain death," "whole brain death" or "brain-stem death" (and, sometimes, inaccurately termed "cerebral death"), has gained increasing acceptance within the medical profession and among the vast majority of state legislatures and courts in the United States. Whether this standard comports with *halachah* is a matter of

---

*Editor's Note:* As Rabbi Marc Angel notes, the more accurate term for this phenomenon is "brain-stem death." Rabbi Breitowitz chose to employ "brain death," the term commonly used in the popular press, to enable the readers of his article to relate its contents to reports that appear in the media.

great controversy among rabbinic authorities.[1] The purpose of this article is not to take sides nor in any way resolve the halachic debate. Its purpose is more modest. This article will attempt to explain to the general reader: (1) what is "brain death" and how it is clinically determined; (2) some (not all) of the major sources on whether it is an acceptable criterion of death from the standpoint of *halachah*; (3) the viewpoints of contemporary authorities and (4) the halachic and legal ramifications of one view or the other.

## ◆§ What Is "Brain Death" And How Is It Diagnosed?

The concept of total "brain death" as an alternative to the older definition of irreversible circulatory-respiratory failure was first introduced in a 1968 report authored by a special committee of the Harvard Medical School[2] and was later adopted, with some modifications, by the President's Commission for the Study of Ethical Problems in Medicine and Biomedical Research, as a recommendation for state legislatures and courts.[3] The "brain death" standard was also employed in the model legislation, known as the Uniform Determination of Death Act, which has been enacted by a large number of jurisdictions and the standard has been endorsed by the influential American Bar Association.

---

1. The literature on brain death — medical, legal, halachic — is huge and only selective citations can be given here. The best nonhalachic survey of the legal and medical issues can be found in a report of the President's Commission for the Study of Ethical Problems in Medicine and Biomedical and Behavioral Research, *Defining Death* (1981). Halachic treatment (as well as good discussion of related legal and medical approaches) can be found in a book of Rabbi J. David Bleich, *Time Of Death In Jewish Law* (Z. Berman, 1991) which is a compendium of Bleich's previously published Hebrew and English articles expounding his well-known opposition to "brain death" criteria. An excellent symposium (which also presents R. Tendler's opposing view) appears in volume 17 of the *Journal Of Halacha And Contemporary Society* (Spring 1989). Finally, the October 1991 *Jewish Observer* contains an interesting exchange of correspondence between Rabbi Tendler and Chaim Zweibel, General Counsel of Agudath Israel of America.
2. *A Definition of Irreversible Coma* — Report of the Ad Hoc Committee of the Harvard Medical School to Examine the Definition of Brain Death, 205JAMA 337-350 (1968).
3. President's Commission for the Study of Ethical Problems in Medicine and Biomedical and Behavioral Research, *Defining Death: Medical, Legal, and Ethical Issues in the Determination of Death* (Government Printing Office, 1981).

While New York is one of the few jurisdictions that does not have a "brain death" statute, it has adopted the identical rule through the binding decisions of its highest court.[1]

The rapid, and near universal, acceptance of neurological criteria of death is probably attributable to three factors. First, moving the time of death to an earlier point facilitates organ transplants, and indeed makes such transplants possible. Organs, especially the heart and liver, are suitable for transplantation only if they are removed at a time when blood is still circulating. Once cardiac arrest stops circulation, rapid tissue degeneration makes the organ unsuitable for such use. Given the increasing success of these operations and the relative uselessness (from a secular standpoint!) of sustaining "brain dead" patients on respirators, there is a natural temptation to redefine death so that organs become available to serve higher ends. It is no coincidence that the movement towards acceptance of "brain death" coincided with the development of cyclosporine and other anti-rejection drugs.

Additional considerations involve triage and allocation of scarce medical resources. It is extraordinary expensive (in terms of equipment and labor) to maintain patients on respirators and other life support and using these resources for "brain death" patients prevents their deployment for those who stand a better chance of recovery. Yet a third impetus towards redefinition is an understandable desire to spare families the agony and anguish of watching a loved one experience a protracted death.

For whatever the reason, the current definition of "death" is now a composite one: death is deemed to occur when there is either irreversible cessation of circulatory and respiratory functions (the "old" definition) or *irreversible cessation of all functions of the entire brain including the brain-stem.*[2] The principal utility of this second standard permits declaring as dead a comatose, ventilator-dependent patient, incapable of spontaneous respiration but whose heart is still beating due to the provision of oxygen via an artificial breathing apparatus.

---

1. See *People v. Eulo,* 63 N.Y. 2d 341 (1984).
2. Brain stem death occurs when, due to trauma, the brain swells and the pressure in the skull rises to exceed blood pressure. The brain is deprived of blood and oxygen and the brain tissue begins to liquefy [lyse]. While total dysfunction occurs minutes after deprivation of oxygen, total liquefication does not take place until some time after cardiac death, indeed sometimes several days after interment.

At the outset, two points must be made absolutely clear. First, contrary to the misperceptions of many lay people, "brain death" is not synonymous with merely being comatose or unresponsive to stimuli. Indeed, even a flat EEG (electroencephalogram) does not indicate brain-stem destruction. The human brain consists of three basic anatomic regions: (1) the cerebrum; (2) the cerebellum; and (3) the brain-stem consisting of the midbrain, the pons, and the medulla, which extends downwards to become the spinal cord. The cerebrum controls memory, consciousness, and higher mental functioning. The cerebellum controls various muscle functions while the brain-stem controls respiration and various reflexes (e.g., swallow and gag). A patient may be in a deep coma and nonresponsive to most external stimuli but still very much alive. At most, such patients may have a dysfunctional cerebrum but, by virtue of the brain stem remaining intact, are capable of spontaneous respiration and heartbeat. Indeed, the most famous of these cases, Karen Ann Quinlan, was able to live off a respirator for almost a decade. While such persons may be popularly referred to as brain dead, they are more accurately described as being in a persistent vegetative state [PVS] and are very much alive under both secular and Jewish law. Removal of organs from such a donor would indisputably be homicide. This is even more true for the phenomenon known as being "locked-in" where the patient is fully conscious but unable to respond.

A second point to keep in mind is the relationship among respiration, circulation, and the brain. The heart, like any organ, or indeed cell, needs oxygen to survive and without oxygen will simply stop beating. Respiration, in turn, is controlled by the vagus nerve whose nucleus is located in the medulla of the brain-stem. The primary stimulant for the operation of the nerve is the presence of excess carbon dioxide in the blood. When stimulated, the nerve causes the diaphragm and chest muscles to expand, allowing the lungs to fill with air. Spontaneous respiratory activity can therefore not continue once there is brain stem destruction or dysfunction. The heart, on the other hand, is not controlled by the brain but is autonomous. It is obvious, of course, that unless the patient is hooked up to a breathing apparatus, destruction of the brain-stem will inevitably lead to cardiac cessation not because of any direct control the brain stem exercises over the heart but simply because the heart muscle is deprived of oxygen. Where, however, the patient's intake of oxygen is being artificially maintained, the heart may continue to beat and blood circulate for a considerable time after total brain-stem destruction.[1] The time lag between brain death and circulatory death is on the average only two to ten days, though there is at least one case on record where a woman's heart continued to beat for 63 days after a diagnosis of brain death.[2] (Indeed, she delivered a live baby through a Caesarean section.) It is this crucial gap between cessation of spontaneous respiration and cessation of heart beat that defines the parameters of the phenomenon called "brain-stem death."

The steps taken in a clinical diagnosis of "brain death" vary from medical center to medical center and those differences may have significant halachic repercussions but will typically involve the following:[3] (1) a determination that the patient is in a deep coma and is profoundly unresponsive to external stimuli; (2) absences of elicitable brain-stem reflexes such as swallowing, gag, cough, sigh, hiccup, corneal, and vestibulo-ocular (ear); (3) absence of spontaneous respiration as determined by an apnea test;[4] and (4) performance of tests for evoked potentials testing the brain-stem's responsiveness to a variety of external stimuli. These tests are to be repeated between 6-24 hours later to insure irreversibility — with life support supplied for the interim —

---

1. A good description of the scientific aspects of brain death can be found in 24 *Tradition* I, 8-14 (Summer 1989) (Dr. Jakobovitz's annotations to the Chief Rabbinate's ruling) and in Kielson, "Determining the Time of Death-Medical Aspects," 17 *Journal of Halacha and Contemporary Society* 7-13 (Spring 1989).

2. See sources cited in Bleich, "Of Cerebral Cardiac Death", 24 *Tradition* 44, 61n.5 (Spring 1989), reprinted in *Time Of Death In Jewish Law*, pp. 129-160.

3. Much of this information was derived from the articles cited in note 1 above and a communication of Rabbi Moshe Tendler to the members of the RCA dated Summer 1991.

4. Apnea testing takes many forms. One standard test may involve providing the patient with 100% oxygen for 20-30 minutes through the respirator and then shutting off the machine, thereby allowing the carbon dioxide in the blood to rise but at the same time allowing for passive gaseous diffusion of oxygen through the tubes of the machine or through a tube inserted directly into the trachea. This allows the $CO^2$ in the blood to rise, enabling a test of the respiratory response without depriving the patient of necessary oxygen in the interim. While a normally functioning brain-stem would induce respiration at a fairly low pressure of $CO^2$, a diagnosis of death will not be confirmed until the $CO^2$ pressure is considerably above the normal triggering point but nevertheless fails to elicit a respiratory response.

and a specific cause for brain dysfunction must be identified before the patient will be declared dead.[1]

An additional test that is sometimes employed (when other clinical tests are deemed inconclusive) is radionuclide cerebral angiography [nuclide or radioisotope scanning]. A harmless radioactive dye is injected into the patient's blood-stem, typically through the intravenous tubing already in place. In brain-dead patients, scanning will reveal an abrupt cutoff of circulation below the base of the brain with no visible fluid draining away. While many observers have described this test as nearly 100% accurate, others have claimed the brain-stem circulation, especially in the medulla, is not well visualized and absolute absence of blood flow to this region cannot be diagnosed with certainty.[2]

Note that a patient who is brain dead may theoretically continue to have muscle spasms or twitchings or even sit up. Whether this so-called Lazarus Reflex is an indicator of life will be discussed in due course; what is undisputed is that such movements are coordinated not from the brain but solely from the spinal cord. It should also be noted that there are several instances of clinically brain dead patients carrying live babies to term.[3] Again, this may or may not be significant.

---

1. Note that a flat EEG (electroencephalogram) is not a necessary condition for a brain death diagnosis. A flat EEG does not in any event insure brain-stem death but at best, indicates only absence of (perceptible) upper brain activity. Conversely, even in patients with a brain death diagnosis, sporadic, minimal EEG activity has occasionally been found. The Harvard criteria regard a flat EEG as helpful and confirmatory but not essential to a brain death diagnosis.

2. Compare letter of Rabbi Tendler printed in the October 1991 *Jewish Observer* with the degree of skepticism expressed by Dr. Keilson, *supra* note 6, at 12. Indeed, some earlier studies had indicated that angiography only measures deficit, not cessation of blood flow even to the cerebrum and that up to 24% of normal blood flow could still be present. Modern refinements in these techniques probably allow for a definitive determination of zero blood flow to the cerebrum but "persistent perfusion and survival of the brain stem" remain a distinct possibility. See studies cited in Bleich, *supra* note 7, at notes 13-21. I have no information as to the accuracy of any of those studies; I simply point them out for the edification of the reader.

3. See the sources in the medical literature cited by Bleich, *supra* note 7, at 62 n. 5 (at 133, n. 5 in the book).

## ~§ Is Brain Death an Acceptable Halachic Criterion of Death?

The question breaks down into two distinct issues. First, is irreversible dysfunction of the entire brain a valid criterion of death? Second, even if the answer is yes, are the medical tests currently utilized in establishing such a condition halachically valid indicators of its presence? One could easily subscribe to "whole brain" death as a concept and yet reject the particular diagnostic tools employed.

There are number of halachic sources that are relevant to the question of "brain death," the most important being the *Mishnah* in *Oholot 1:6*, the Talmud in *Yoma 85a,* passages in *Teshuvot Chatam Sofer* and *Teshuvot Chacham Tzvi*, and various pronouncements of R. Moshe Feinstein in his *Iggrot Moshe*.[1] This is not the forum for a detailed examination of these sources other than to note that a number of them are equivocal and subject to a variety of interpretations.

Briefly stated, the *Mishnah* in *Oholot* establishes the dual propositions that, first, physical decapitation of an animal is a conclusive indicator of death and second, some degree of subsequent movement is not incompatible with a finding of death provided that such movement qualifies as spastic in nature (*pirchus be'alma*) like the twitching of the "severed tail of a lizard." The Talmud in *Yoma 85a*, detailing with a person trapped under a building, rules that a determination of respiratory failure establishes death without the need to continue to uncover the debris to check heartbeat. Proponents of "brain death" argue that a dysfunctional brain-stem is equivalent to a decapitated one (physiological decapitation), that destruction of the brain-stem inevitably means inability to spontaneously respire (meeting the criterion in *Yoma*) and that subsequent "movement," whether the Lazarus Reflex or the heartbeat, falls into the category of *pirchus* since such movement is not coordinated from a "central root and point of origin,"[2] i.e., the brain.

The counter-arguments are: first, physiological dysfunction is not the equivalent of anatomical decapitation. The only phenomenon short of

---

1. See *Teshuvot Chatam Sofer, Yoreh Deah* no. 338; *Teshuvot Chacham Tzvi,* no. 77; and *Iggrot Moshe, Yoreh Deah* II, nos. 164,174; *Yoreh Deah* III, no. 132; *Choshen Mishpat* II, nos. 72-73.
2. See *Peirush HaMishnayot* of Rambam to *Oholot* 1:6.

actual decapitation that might similarly qualify is a total liquefaction (lysis) of the brain, something that probably does not occur until well after cardiac arrest. Second, according to Rashi in *Yoma,* cessation of respiration is a conclusive indicator of death only when the person is "comparable to a dead man who does not move his limbs." While certain forms of postmortem movement may be characterized as merely spastic and would not qualify as "movement," the rhythmic coordinated beating of a heart and the maintenance of a circulatory system can hardly be characterized as *pirchus* since such heartbeat is life-sustaining and identical to that in a normally functioning individual. Reference is also made to the *teshuvot* of *Chatam Sofer* and *Chacham Tzvi* who both write that it is only the cessation of respiration *and* pulse (heartbeat) that allows for a determination of death and the *Gemara* in *Yoma* merely creates a presumption that upon cessation of respiration and an appropriate waiting time, one is permitted to assume that heartbeat has stopped as well. Since this assumption is obviously not true in the case of "brain dead" patients hooked up to respirators whose heartbeats are monitored, such patients may not be declared as dead.

The position of R. Moshe Feinstein, whose *psak* could well have been definitive at least in the United States, is unfortunately a matter of some controversy. His son-in-law, Rabbi Dr. Moshe Tendler, a Rosh Yeshiva in RIETS and Professor of Biology, Yeshiva College, has vigorously argued that Rabbi Feinstein supported a total "brain death" standard based on the concept of decapitation in *Mishnah Oholot.*[1] His position finds strong support in *Iggrot Moshe*, *Yoreh Deah III* no. 132 which seems to validate nuclide scanning as a valid determinant of death. This is also the understanding of the Israeli Chief Rabbinate, R. David Feinstein (who admits, however, to having no inside information on the topic), and R. Shabtai Rappaport, the editor of R. Moshe's responsa.[2]

Others, however, have interpreted his *teshuvot* very differently, pointing out that R. Moshe reiterated twice (indeed, in one instance two years after the "nuclide scanning" reference) that removal of an organ

---

1. See, for example, Rabbi Tendler's letter in October 1991 *Jewish Observer.*
2. The Chief Rabbinate's ruling accepting "brain death" explicitly relies on R. Moshe for authority. See *Techumim* Vol. 7, 187-192 (5746) and Jakobovitz, "Brain Death and Heart Transplant: The Israeli Chief Rabbinate's Directives," 24 *Tradition* I-14 (Summer 1989); R. David's understanding is quoted by R. Tendler in his own October letter to *JO*; and R. Shabtai Rappaport's letter appears in 12 *Assia* no. 3-4 (Kislev 5750), pp. 10-12.

for transplantation was murder of the donor.¹ (R. Tendler's response: Both of those *teshuvot* refer to comatose patients in a persistent vegetative state who are capable of spontaneous respiration and are very much alive and not to those who are respirator-dependent.) They also cite R. Moshe's express opposition to proposed "brain death" legislation in New York unless it contained a "religious exemption."² (R. Tendler's response: Although R. Moshe accepted the concept of "brain death," his support of an exemption was simply to accommodate the view of other religious Jews who disagree.) Finally, they note that in the very *teshuvah* upholding the use of angiographic scanning, R. Moshe approvingly cites *Teshuvot Chatam Sofer,* Y.D. no. 338, who insists on absence of *dofeik*, pulse, and indeed states that one is dead only if there is an inability to breathe and no other sign of life is recognizable with them (*Vegam lo nikarim behem inynei chiyut achairim*). Their conclusion: R. Moshe merely validated nucline scanning as a criterion to verify *one* determinant of death, i.e., absence of respiration, but did not maintain that it alone was sufficient.³ This author certainly lacks both the competence and the authority to resolve this dispute but presents it to the reader so that he may see why this area has been so fraught with unresolved controversy.

## ☙ Contemporary Views

The following is a cataloguing of the major schools of thought among contemporary *poskim* and *rabanim* on the brain death issue and some of the recent events connected with this question.

> 1. As noted, Rabbi Dr. Moshe Tendler has been the most vigorous advocate for the halachic acceptability of brain death criteria. In his capacity as chairman of the RCA's Biomedical Ethics Committee, Rabbi Tendler spearheaded the preparation of a health-care proxy form that, among other innovations, would

---

1. See *Iggrot Moshe, Yoreh Deah* II, no. 174 (5728) and *Choshen Mishpat* II, no. 72 (5738). The *teshuvah* in *Yoreh Deah* III, no. 132 cited in support of brain death criteria was authored in 5736.
2. Written statement of 8 Shevat 5737.
3. It should be noted, however, that the *teshuvah* concerning nuclide scanning was addressed to R. Tendler for his own guidance, surely entitling his understanding of the responsa to great weight.

authorize the removal of vital organs from a respirator dependent, brain dead patient for transplantation purposes. Although the form was approved by the RCA's central administration, its provisions on brain death were opposed by a majority of the RCA's own *Vaad Halacha* (Rabbis Rivkin, Schachter, Wagner and Willig).[1]

2. The Israeli Chief Rabbinate Council, in an order dated Cheshvan 5747, has also approved the utilization of "brain death" criteria in authorizing Hadassah Hospital to perform heart transplants but on a somewhat different theory than Rabbi Tendler. Positing that cessation of independent respiration was the only criterion of death (based on *Yoma* 85 but somewhat inexplicably also citing *Chatam Sofer*, Y.D. no. 338), the Rabbinate ruled that brain death was confirmatory of irreversible cessation of respiration. Theoretically, this would allow for a standard far less exacting than clinical brain death, perhaps nothing more than failure of an apnea test. Indeed, Dr. Steinberg, the principal medical consultant to the Rabbinate, dismissed any requirement of nuclide scanning since destruction of the brain's respiratory center may be conclusively verified without such test.[2] Since defining "death" exclusively in terms of inability to spontaneously respire would lead to the absurdity that even a fully conscious, functioning polio patient in an iron lung is dead, a subsequent communication from R. Shaul Yisraeli, a member of the Chief Rabbinate Council, qualified the Rabbinate's ruling by imposing, as an additional requirement, that the "patient be like a stone without movement"[3] (but apparently maintaining that heartbeat does not qualify as such movement). It is probable, though not certain,

---

1. The current status of the original RCA proxy is unclear. In light of the negative *psak* of Rabbis Auerbach and Elyashiv, Rabbi Marc Angel, the President of the RCA, circulated a cover letter to the membership cautioning that the proxy form should not be used until the individual *rav* has thoroughly studied the issue and consulted experts in the field. Rabbi Tendler has similarly stated that at least portions of the proxy form were merely a first draft to be circulated to *rabanim*.

2. Dr. Steinberg's paper, originally prepared to assist the Chief Rabbinate in their deliberations, appears in *Or Hamizrach* (Tishrei 5748).

3. Quoted in Bleich, *Time Of Death* at 167-168.

that R. Tendler's test of "physiological decapitation" and the Rabbinate's newly formulated test of "respiratory failure coupled with profound nonresponsiveness" amount to the same thing though the Rabbinate has not retracted from its noninsistence on nuclide scanning.

3. Rabbi J. David Bleich, Rosh Kollel at Yeshiva University and author of many papers and a recently published book on the subject, has stated that anything short of total liquefaction (lysis) of the brain cannot constitute the equivalent of decapitation. He further maintains, relying on Rashi in *Yoma*, the *Chatam Sofer*, and the *Chacham Tzvi*, that even total lysis would be insufficient in the presence of cardiac activity but dismissed the matter as being only of theoretical importance since cessation of heartbeat inevitably occurs prior to total lysis. He also asserts that his position is not based on stringency in case of doubt but rather on the certainty that the brain dead patient is still alive, a certainty that could be relied upon even to be lenient, e.g., a Cohen may enter a "brain dead" patient's room without violating the prohibition of *tumat meit*.

4. Rabbi Aaron Soloveitchik, Rosh Yeshiva of Brisk and RIETS, has gone slightly further than Rabbi Bleich. Even if the heart has stopped and the patient is no longer breathing, the patient is alive if there is some detectable electrical activity in the brain.[1] It has been noted, however, that there is no recorded instance of this phenomenon occurring.

5. Rabbi Hershel Schachter, Rosh Yeshiva and Rosh Kollel of RIETS, has taken a more cautious view. Conceding that the concept of "brain death" may find support in the decisions of R. Moshe, he concludes that such a patient should be in the category of *safeik chai, safeik met* (doubtful life). While removal of organs would be prohibited as possible murder, one would also have to be stringent in treating the patient as *met*, e.g., a Cohen would not be allowed to enter the patient's room.[2]

---

1. His views may be found in 17 *Journal Of Halacha* at 41-50 (Spring 1989).

2. Rabbi Schachter's intermediate position may be found in the same journal at pp. 32-40.

**6.** Most contemporary *poskim* in Eretz Yisrael (other than the Chief Rabbinate) have unequivocally repudiated the concept of death based on neurological or respiratory criteria.[1] Of special significance are letters[2] signed by R. Shlomo Zalman Auerbach and R. Yosef Elyashiv, widely acknowledged as the leading *poskim* in Eretz Yisrael (if not the world), stating that removal of organs from a donor whose heart is beating and whose entire brain including the brain-stem is not functioning at all is prohibited and involves the taking of life. Unfortunately, these very brief communications do not indicate if the *psak* is based on *vadei* (certainty) or *safeik* (doubt) nor do they address what the decision would be in case of total lysis.

## ⊷§ Halachic and Legal Ramifications

Obviously, in a matter so fraught with controversy, every family confronted with the tragic situation of a brain dead patient must follow the ruling of its *posek*. To the extent the patient is halachically alive, removal of an organ even for *pikuach nefesh* would be tantamount to murder. The principle of *ain dochin nefesh mipnei nefesh* — that one life may not set aside to ensure another life — applies with full force even where the life to be terminated is of short duration and seems to lack meaning or purpose and even where the potential recipient has excellent chances for full recovery and long life. If, on the other hand, the donor is dead, the harvesting of organs to save another life becomes a *mitzvah* of the highest order. In light of the overwhelming opposition to the "brain death" concept, caution and a stance of *shev v'al taaseh* (passivity) appears to be the most prudent course. How the "brain death" problem will play out in other areas such as inheritance, capacity of a wife to contract a new marriage, or the need for *chalitzah* if a man dies leaving a brain dead child will have to await further clarification.

---

1. These include R. Elazer Schach, Rosh Yeshiva of Ponevez; R. Yitzchok Weiss, recently deceased *Rav* of the *Eida Chareidis*; R' Yitzchak Kulitz, Chief Rabbi of Jerusalem; R. Eliezer Waldenberg, author of *Tzitz Eliezer*; R. Nisim Karlitz, Chief Rabbi of Ramat Aharon; R. Shmuel Wosner, Rabbi of Zichron Meir; and R. Nosen Gestetner. References to those decisions can be found in Bleich, *Time Of Death* at 144-145.

2. Letter of 18 Menachem Av 5751. A second letter reaffirming this stance was issued during the *Aseret Yemei Teshuvah* 5752.

There are, however, two other points that need to be considered. The argument is occasionally made that if halachah rejects the concept of "brain" or "respiratory" death, Orthodox Jews would be unable to receive harvested organs on the grounds that the recipient would be an accessory to a murder. As others have noted,[1] this conclusion does not follow. To the extent the organ in question would have been removed for transplantation whether or not this specific recipient consents, i.e., there is a waiting list of several people, the Orthodox recipient is not considered to be a causative factor (gorem) in the termination of a life. There is no general principle in halachah that prohibits the use of objects obtained through sinful means. It is true that if, because of tissue typing and the like, the organ is suitable for only one recipient and if that recipient declines the transplant, the organ will not be harvested, an Orthodox recipient may indeed be compelled to decline. But this is rarely, if ever, the case.[2]

A second point: as noted, "brain death" is the legal definition of death in the vast majority of the United States. New York is the only state that requires medical personnel to make a reasonable effort to notify family members before a determination of brain death and to make "reasonable accommodation" for the patient's religious beliefs.[3] In all other jurisdictions, doctors would be empowered unilaterally to disconnect a patient from life-support mechanism once that patient meets the legal definition of death.[4] Hospital personnel may or may not defer to the wishes of the family but there is no duty on their part to do so or even to ascertain what those wishes are.[5]

---

1. See comments of R. Soloveitchik, cited in note 22.
2. According to a recently published article in the *Journal Of The American Medical Association* (Jan. 1992), the demand for hearts, kidneys, and lungs far exceeds the available supply.
3. See 10 N.Y.C.R.R., sect. 400-16 (1987). The regulation mandating religious accommodation is also reprinted in an excellent article by Zweibel, "Accommodating Religious Objections to Brain Death: Legal Considerations," 17 *Journal of Halacha* 49 (Spring 1989).
4. Of course, even in New York, only "reasonable accommodation" is required and one can well imagine triage considerations forcing patients off respirators prematurely.
5. Moreover, even where doctors defer to the family's wishes, insurance companies may refuse to pay the costs of sustaining what is legally regarded as a cadaver. This is likely not to be a problem in New York since the regulatory duty of "reasonable accommodation" prevents a determination of brain death.

Perhaps one point of consensus that may emerge in an area otherwise fraught with acrimonious controversy would be the desirability of enacting "religious accommodations" exceptions nationwide. After all, even the proponents of a "brain death" standard understand that others, in all honesty and conscience, may hold a different *halachic* view, one which they should not be compelled to violate. Hopefully, our community will be responsive to such an effort.

## ☙ Conclusion

"You preserve the soul within me and You will in the future take it from me" (Daily Prayers). Only God, Who is the source of all life, can take life away. We are enjoined to cherish and nurture life as long as it is present, no matter how fleeting or ephemeral. Yet it is precisely because each moment of life is so precious that God has imposed on man the awesome responsibility of defining the moment of death, the point after which the needs of the dead may, and indeed must, be subordinated to those of the currently living. No one has ever seen a *neshamah* leave a body and it is the unenviable task of our *gedolim* and *poskim* to tell us when this occurs. May *Hakodesh Baruch Hu* grant them the insight to truly make our Torah a *Torat Chayim*.

Rabbi Nachman Cohen

# From What Point Should the Megillah Be Read?

*A Deeper Understanding of the Roots of Talmudic Disputes and How It Explains the Controversy as to Where to Begin Reading the Megillah*

Anyone who studies the *Talmud* knows that it is replete with *halachic* disagreements. Chazal teach us that while one view might be accepted over the other for purposes of normative *Halacha*, in fact, *alu v'alu divrei Elokim Chaim* — "both views are those of the Living God" (*Eruvin* 13b). The views expressed do not contradict each other. Rather, in their totality, they serve to set forth a complete and complementary understanding of the issue at point *kol tzophyich nassu kol yachad y'rannainu*: R. Yochanan said that: "In the End of Days, all of your prophets will raise their voices complementing each other in song" (*Sanhedrin* 91b). In fact, even as regards normative law, many views which are not adopted as the *Halacha* today will become the *Halacha* in the Messianic Era. Thus, for example, we are told that in the Messianic Era, the *Halacha* will follow the rules of Beis Shammai (Ari *Hakodesh* quoted by *Likutei Torah* on *Korach* Chapter 4).

Kabbalists explain that the reason for *halachic* disputes is not that the *halachic* tradition had been lost, but rather that each individual's soul emanates from a different level in the Heavenly hierarchy and this determines the *middah* — attribute — through which he serves God. The manner in which he interprets the Torah and *Halacha* is dependent upon his *middah*. Thus, the *Zohar* (II:245) relates that the *middah* of Shammai was *g'vurah* — judgment, and that of Hillel was *chessed* — mercy.

At the beginning of *Tractate Avos* this view is reiterated by the Tosefos Chadashim when he quotes R. Levi Yitzchok of Berdichev asking the well-known question, "Why is this tractate called *Avos?*" Rav Levi Yitzchok gives the following unconventional reply: The sense in which the term "avos" is used is that of "first principles." He who studies *Tractate Avos* will be given an understanding of the *halachic* perspectives through which individual *tanna'im* generate their *halachic* positions throughout the rest of *Shas*. "For the rule is that a person's perspective in Torah follows from the manner of his *avodas Hashem* . . . [e.g. since] R. Meir's soul is on the level of the World of Thought, he obligates those who directly cause a damage to be culpable — *dan dena d'garmi.*"

With regard to the determination of the normative *Halacha*, R. Levi Yitzchok cites the head of the Nikolsburg *Beis Din*, who explains that the expression, "Beis Shammai's view in the place of Beis Hillel is invalid," means that while the spiritual level of Beis Shammai was greater than that of Beis Hillel and therefore, when *Moshiach* arrives the *Halacha* will follow the views of Beis Shammai, yet, in this world, the *Halacha* does not follow Beis Shammai. This is because "in the place of Beis Hillel," i.e. the present world, Beis Shammai's positions are not considered complete — *einam Mishna*.

In His infinite wisdom, God understood that for the world to reach its perfection, there had to be a precise balance between those granted the varying attributes. Each individual who worships God and pursues the Torah based on his *middah* is serving to fulfill the Divine scheme. (See Introduction to *Likutei Amarim*.) As God wishes that there be many approaches and understandings of Torah — *alu v'alu divrei Elokim Chaim* — it is man's obligation to study and understand all the rabbinic positions — both those that are *l'Halacha l'ma'aseh* and those which are not — for it is only by understanding the totality of these views that man can come to as complete an understanding of the Torah of the Almighty as is possible.

*From What Point Should the Megillah Be Read*

## ৺ A Specific Dispute

In this vein, I wish to investigate the Talmudic dispute regarding the point from which one must read *Megillas Esther* to fulfill one's obligation. This investigation will help clarify the positions held by each *tanna*, by providing a backdrop from which they can better be understood. This dispute is listed in the *Mishna* as follows:

From what point in the *Megillah* must a person begin his reading in order to fulfill his obligation?

   a. R. Meir: He must read it from the beginning.
   b. R. Yehuda: He must begin from *Ish Yehudi* — "There was a Jewish man in Shushan, and his name was Mordechai."
   c. R. Yosi: He must read from *Achar had'varim ha'alu* — "And it was after this occurrence that King Achashverosh elevated Haman."
   d. R. Shimon b. Yochai: He must read from *Ba-lyla hahu* — "On that night the king was unable to sleep."

R. Yochanan explains that the *tanna'im* differ over the interpretation of the verse *V'tichtov Esther . . . es kol hatokef* — "And Queen Esther and Mordechai, the Yehudi, wrote all the acts of power."

   a. R. Meir claims this refers to the power of Achashverosh:
   b. R. Yehuda that it refers to the power of Mordechai:
   c. R. Yosi that it refers to the power of Haman:
   d. R. Shimon b. Yochai that it refers to the power of the miracle.

Rav states that the *Halacha* follows R. Meir. The *Megillah* must be read in its entirety.

In the foregoing dispute there are two major questions:

   1. Given that there is Scriptural support for each of the stated positions, why does any given *tanna* — each a student of the same Rebbe, R. Akiva — choose one position over the other?
   2. Given the general rule that when R. Meir, R. Yehuda and R. Yosi argue, the *Halacha* follows R. Yosi because he was a master of logic, why in this case does the *Halacha* follow R. Meir? While according to R. Yochanan the following of R. Meir's view is only by custom, on what basis did this custom arise? (For sources

on the rules of *p'sak Halacha*, see *Talmudic Encyclopedia* IX, 279, n. 507-520.)

Given our introduction, it would be enlightening to understand the manner in which R. Meir, R. Yehuda, R. Yosi and R. Shimon b. Yochai are characterized in Chazal and kabbalistic literature vis-a-vis their *avodas haKodesh*.

## R. Meir

The *Tzemach Tzedek* (*Derech Mitzvosekha*) writes that R. Meir's soul emanates from the level "where there is no distinction between *tahor* and *tameh* (spiritually pure and profane)." This is the level that Adam was on before he sinned (*Torah Ohr* 5b). On that level, "all is good." This is the meaning of the pericope which states that in R. Meir's Torah, there was written the words *"Kosnot ohr"* (clothes of light) instead of *"Kosnot ohr"* (clothes of skin). On the level of *ohr* — light, the highest of spiritual levels, no evil exists. It is only on the level of *ohr* — skin (the mundane, physical level of Adam after the sin) that evil is manifest.

## R. Yehuda

R. Yehuda's *middah* was below that of R. Meir. The *Idra Rabbah* (127) classifies his soul as emanating from the level of *Chesed* of *Z'er Anpin*. On this level, the potential for evil exists. This explains a basic difference between the *avodah* of R. Meir and that of R. Yehuda. R. Meir, whose soul emanated from the level "all is good," sought to convert all the "evil" which exists in the world into good. R. Yehuda, whose soul emanated from a level in which the potential for evil existed, sought to abolish evil. Thus, whereas R. Meir argued that God's last and greatest blessing in *Parshas B'chukosei* to the man who had reached spiritual perfection, *"V'ohlech eschem kommeyus"* — "I will make you erect," means this man will grow to "twice the height of Adam," in that he will not only maintain all of the sanctified attributes granted to Adam — *ohr hayashar,* but will also purify all of the evil which exists in the world and elevate it to the service of God — *ohr hachozer.*

R. Yehuda maintains that the future ideal man will be but "as tall as Adam" — in that he will have quashed all of the evil that Adam brought into the world through the transgression of the *Eitz HaDa'as*.

### R. Yosi

R. Yosi is motivated by this-worldly concerns. The *Gemara* (*Gittin* 67) characterizes R. Yosi's *halachic* approach as *nimuko i'mo* — very logical and straightforward. His *middah* causes him to insist that *Halacha* has to be generated an understood solely on the basis of this-worldly factors. As the Torah does not speak in kabbalistic terms, *Halacha* need not take these into account. (*Zohar* 3:223: The numerical value of R. Yosi's name, 86, is the same as that of *Elokim* — the name of God which depicts His manifestation in the physical world.)

### R. Shimon

In *Idra Rabba* (p. 127), R. Shimon's attribute is said to be that of *Da'as*. *Likutei Levi Yitzchok* (p. 214) explains this as follows: *Da'as* is that attribute which is a prerequisite to redemption. Thus, before the Egyptian redemption was possible, it first says *"Vayadah Elokim."* The redeemer must be guided primarily by the attribute of *Da'as*. This was said to be the attribute of Moshe Rabbenu. R. Shimon's possessing the attribute of *Da'as* implies that he was preoccupied with redemption.

## ৵ The Reading of the Megillah

With this backdrop, it is possible to understand the varying rulings as to where one should commence reading the *Megillah*. R. Yosi's *middah*, as stated above, causes him to observe occurrences on the this-worldly level. When viewing the events of Purim, the plot against the Jews commences with the appointment of Haman to prime minister. Therefore, it is from this point that the *Megillah* should be read. Parenthetically, this is what is done in the *Al HaNissim* prayer. It starts with "...When Haman, the wicked, was elevated, he wished to destroy ... all of the Jews."

R. Shimon, the author of the *Zohar*, who was permeated with *Da'as* and a preoccupation with redemption, chooses that point in the *Megillah* from which the redemption of the Jews from Haman's decree begins — *Ba-lyla hahu nadadah shanat hamelech* — "On this night the king was unable to sleep."

R. Yehuda, who is preoccupied with the abolition of evil from the world, wishes to accent the significance of Mordechai to the events of Purim. R. Yehuda explains that the verse "And God will be at war with Amalek from generation to generation" (*Sh'mos* 17:16) means that the war will wage from the generation of Shmuel to the generation of Mordechai (*P'sikta d'R. Kahana* 29a). Mordechai, a descendant of Binyamin — who never bowed to Essav — is the one who had the ability to destroy every vestige of Amalek. This, to R. Yehuda, is the great significance of the Purim story. Hence, he posits that the *Megillah* must be read from *Ish Yehudi hayah b'Shushan haBirah ushmo Mordechai*.

R. Meir, a descendant of Essav (*Ki tzaid b'phiv: zeh R' Meir* [*P'ri Tzaddik* I:80]), whose soul emanates from the *Olam haTohu* — the level where "all is good," sees the importance of the *Megillah* vis-a-vis the Purim story to be from beginning to end. To R. Meir, *tikkun ha'olam* — the rectification of the entire world — is the ultimate reality. He viewed the world as pure and not-yet-pure — *Hu haya omar al hatameh tahor*. It is not enough for R. Meir that Israel reach perfection, but as a descendant of the Caesar Nero (*Gittin* 56) — the ruler who was involved with the destruction of the Second Temple, just as he was able to reach his level of perfection despite his predecessor's background, so too, inhabitants of the earth can and will come to recognize the Kingdom of God.

The whole thrust of the Purim miracle is that it came about through what appears to have been natural historical events. In fact, these events were the hidden workings of the Almighty — *derech hanistar*. The *Megillah* teaches that nothing that goes on at any point on Earth at any moment in world history is bereft of God's Hidden Hand. Thus, Jews must be mindful not only of Jewish history, but of world history as well. And R. Meir insists that one read about the ascendency of Achashverosh to the throne and the downfall of Vashti because they played an important role in the totality of the Purim story. But he also insists that one understand that at the end of the *Megillah* when we read "And King Achashverosh placed a tax on the land and islands . . ." that this, too, is Torah. For us, this thought is quite remote. We have no understanding of what the significance of this tax was and why it was placed in the

*Megillah*. Yet, at the End of Days, when man takes a retrospective view of world history, he will be able to see how this, and all events in history, helped create a beautiful tapestry, whereby the inhabitants of the world were led to proclaim God, King of the Universe.

Rambam (*Megillah* 2:18) states that in the Messianic Era, all of the books of Prophets and Scriptures will have served their purpose (*asidim le'vatail*). [According to the Ra'avad, this means they will no longer be read publicly] except for *Megillas Esther*. It will remain forever, as will the *Chumash* and the Oral Torah. The significance of the *Megillah* is that it teaches that God's presence is always manifest in the world, be it through open miracles or the "laws of nature." It furthermore teaches that God is not only the God of Israel, but also the God of the entire universe. It is for this reason that Rambam rules that the *Megillah* must be read in its entirety.

Those who apply the method outlined above to Talmudic disputes find that it in no way serves to bypass or supersede the discussions and writings of the *Rishonim*, *Achronim, Poskim* and *Tshuvot,* because for the most part the *Halachah L'maaseh* follows the views (*shanemooko emo*) to which rational *Svorah* must be applied. Also, *Halacha* follows the view that *Lo Bashamayim He* — *Halacha* should not be determined based on Kabbalistic considerations. Nevertheless, for a *ben Torah* who has achieved success in his studies by the traditional logical *halachic* process, but who seeks a more complete understanding of *daas Chazal* and *Gadlus HaBoray,* the method demonstrated above should be made part of his spiritual portfolio.

# ~§ Health

☐ *Helpful Tips to Insure an Easier Fast*

*Ira Milner, R.D.*

# Helpful Tips to Insure an Easier Fast

WHILE SOME PEOPLE FAST WITH LITTLE DIFFICULTY, MOST of us expect to feel more or less bedraggled after only a few hours. If fasting means headaches and assorted misery for you, it might be the fault of what you eat or drink beforehand. A few simple cautions in planning your pre-*taanit* menu could make all the difference.

### ᴈ Drink Plenty of Fluids

Water has been called "the indispensable nutrient" for a very good reason. Although a person can live without food for weeks, a few days without water would be fatal. Water makes up approximately 60% of the body's weight and is involved in practically every bodily function. Among its essential tasks, it transports nutrients and oxygen through the blood; maintains body temperature; lubricates the joints; cushions a developing fetus; and serves as a medium for the thousands of crucial chemical reactions taking place in the body.

Much of the discomfort commonly experienced during a fast may be due to avoidable water loss. Treat yourself to a leisurely glass of non-caffeinated beverage several times a day well before a planned fast.

Providing the body with enough fluids to function properly is a daily business. Your recommended intake is six to eight 8-ounce glasses (or their equivalent) per day, but that should be upped to eight to ten glasses the day before a fast. (Because the elderly tend to have less developed thirst sensations than younger people, they should be especially careful about getting their daily quota of water.) Don't worry about drinking too much, since the body is highly efficient at getting rid of what it doesn't need.

Beverages are not the only source of water. Even foods you might consider dry contain some water. Most fruits, for instance, are more than 80% water; bread has around 35%. Eggs consist of 75% water; meats, between 40% and 75%; vegetables, from 70% to 95%. Although coffee and tea also supply water, the diuretic properties of caffeine make those beverages inadvisable at a pre-fast meal. Diuretics produce water loss at the cell level and therefore ultimately increase the body's need for water.

## ↝ Decrease Protein

Most Americans consume far too much protein, averaging 2-3 times more than needed. A growing body of evidence suggests that high animal protein intake can be a contributing factor in heart disease, certain cancers and may pose a problem for those suffering from kidney disease.

Eating excessive amounts of protein may also be counterproductive before a fast. Since protein attracts water, too much of it may actually leach water from the tissues. In extreme cases dehydration could result, because the unneeded protein pulls out water that will later be necessary to remove the waste products of protein synthesis from the body.

## ↝ Increase Starch and Fiber

Sugars (including honey and corn syrup) are simple carbohydrates. Starch and most dietary fibers are considered complex carbohydrates because they are chemical chains of many sugar molecules. During digestion both starch and sugar break down into glucose — the simplest form of sugar. Consumption of complex carbohydrates helps to ease the pangs of a fast because they take longer to break down in the digestive process.

A diet of reduced intake is best supplemented with additional complex carbohydrates. Increasing those carbs will also help the body retain water.

Your best bet before a fast, then, is to load up on foods from the following list: breads and cereals (especially whole grain); pasta, rice, and potatoes; vegetables with edible skins, stems, and seeds; legumes; fruits (especially those with edible skins and seeds); nuts; popcorn (without the added fat and salt it makes a great, healthy snack).

## Decrease Salt

No real news here. When you eat salted foods, your blood level of sodium rises. This not only stimulates the brain's thirst receptor (which triggers the thirst sensation), it also affects the body's water requirement, because water is needed to remove salt from the body. So even if you can't live without pickles and other salted delectables on a daily basis, try to resist anything but the lightest salting of the foods you eat before a fast.

## Avoid Caffeine

If you regularly drink more than two or three cups of coffee a day — or if you are a caffeinated cola fanatic — consider tapering off several days before, so that by one or two days prior to the fast you will not be consuming any caffeine at all. Although caffeine isn't technically addictive, the body becomes accustomed to its stimulant effects. Suddenly abstaining from caffeine after an extended period of even moderate intake will probably produce the characteristic "withdrawal headache." The diuretic properties of caffeine after an extended period of even moderate intake will probably produce the characteristic "withdrawal headache." The diuretic properties of caffeine, as mentioned earlier, will aggravate you further with increased need for water. Finally, you can minimize water loss by being careful not to exert yourself too much the day before a fast. Exercise only moderately, and stay out of the sun as much as possible.

By following the suggested recommendations set forth we believe that some of the discomfort experienced on the *taanit* can be alleviated.

## The Basics

- ☐ eight to ten glasses of water (or other, non-caffeinated beverages)
- ☐ small portions of animal protein

- ☐ large portions of starch and carbohydrates (whole grain breads and cereals, pasta, potatoes, legumes, unsalted popcorn)
- ☐ vegetables and fruits with edible skins/seeds

## ܀§ Avoid

- ☐ coffee, tea, caffeinated sodas
- ☐ fried, salted, or spicy foods

## ܀§ Menu Suggestions

- ☐ liberal amounts of plain water, 100% fruit juice, seltzer, and herbal tea (Teabags rather than bulk tea are preferable)
- ☐ whole-grain challah
- ☐ chicken (broiled, baked, grilled, boiled)
- ☐ rice (preferably brown) and lentils or limas
- ☐ lightly sauteed or steamed mixed vegetables (zucchini, summer squash, snow peas, carrots) *or* tossed salad with romaine or other dark-green varieties of lettuce.
- ☐ cakes and lots of fresh fruit

# History

- *The Frankfurt Secession Controversy*
- *A Purim in Every Generation*
- *Resettlement of the Land as Viewed by the Vilna Gaon's Circle*
- *The Wrong Response to Modernity*
- *From the Caves of Qumran*

*Dr. Judith Bleich*

# The Frankfurt Secession Controversy

THAT RABBI SAMSON RAPHAEL HIRSCH WAS THE LEADING ideologue of nineteenth-century German Orthodoxy is beyond dispute. Yet Hirsch has suffered at the hands of both admirers and detractors. Some have cast aspersions on his scholarly attainments and motives that powered his communal agenda; others have done him the disservice of advancing exaggerated claims ascribing to him the role of rabbinic authority without peer and describing him as a uniquely creative philosopher. In the thicket of exaggerations, deprecations, misstatements, claims and counterclaims it becomes difficult to capture a true picture of this remarkable rabbinic leader — a picture of an individual who mastered the idiom of the day, whose finger unerringly felt the pulse of the times, and idealistic and spiritual personality with an extraordinary gift for words and a creative, imaginative flair for homiletical interpretation and, above all, a visionary with that rarest of talents — a genius for practical application.

Most surveys and analyses of Hirsch's endeavors focus upon his intellectual accomplishments as educator, philosopher, exegete and polemicist. However, these contributions should not be allowed to eclipse his achievements in the sphere of communal activity. For almost four decades, from 1851-1888, he stood at the helm of Frankfurt's autonomous Orthodox congregation, the *Israelitsche Religionsgesellschaft,* and caused it to rise to a commanding position in the forefront of Western Orthodoxy.

The *kehillah* which he nurtured and led to preeminence was sired by ideological conviction and born of controversy with governmentally legislated freedom of conscience serving as midwife. In early nineteenth-century Germany, the Jewish community in each city was organized as a *kehillah,* known as a *Gemeinde,* an umbrella organization or supercommunity, which enjoyed the patronage of the government and was supported primarily by a tax earmarked for religious purposes that was levied upon Jew and Christian alike. The governing board of the *Gemeinde* was responsible for the administration of religious, educational, social and philanthropic institutions and organizations. The increasing dominance of partisans of the Reform movement and the establishment of Reform institutions under the aegis of the *Gemeinde* led Hirsch to demand that his Orthodox correligionists withdraw from the *Gemeinde* and establish their own independent institutions.[1] Hirsch contended that membership in the communal organization constituted a form of endorsement or, at the very minimum, conferral of legitimacy upon the ideological positions espoused by all institutions sponsored by the *Gemeinde*. He asserted that *Halakhah* forbids any such endorsement or conferral of legitimacy upon deviant ideologies and accordingly rules that formal association with any organization that denies the fundamental principles of Judaism is forbidden by Jewish law.

---

1. See the valuable discussion in Robert Liberles' *Religious Conflict in Social Context: The Resurgence of Orthodox Judaism in Frankfurt am Main, 1838-1877* (Westport, Connecticut and London, England, 1985), pp. 165-226. It is commonly assumed that separatism as a policy of the Orthodox community began in the 1870's with Hirsch. In fact, the idea of autonomous religious communities, each practicing Judaism in accordance with its own dictates, dates from an earlier period and was advanced as a desideratum by exponents of Reform. Thus in the 1830's Abraham Geiger maintained that the only manner in which the Reform movement could move forward at a suitable pace was by obtaining permission to form autonomous religious organizations apart from the general community. See Abraham Geiger, *Nachgelassene Schriften,* ed. by Ludwig Geiger, V (Berlin, 1878), 54-55 and Max Wiener, *Abraham Geiger and Liberal Judaism: The Challenge of the Nineteenth Century* (Cincinnati, 1981), pp. 99-100 . . .. Subsequently, Geiger reversed his position and determined that he could best attain his goals from within the broader community and twice declined invitations to become the spiritual leader of the independent Reform congregation in Berlin. However, the Berlin congregation did function as an autonomous Reform congregation, organized on separatist lines but functioning within the general community. As Liberles, p. 169, notes, "The young Abraham Geiger contemplated schism and the Reform congregation of Berlin attemped it, but, the fact remains that separatism never fully blossomed as a strategy or as a principle in the German Reform camp." While schism presented an opportunity for a theologically consistent program, most Reform congregations displayed little interest in such autonomy and were satisfied with instituting superficial "aesthetic" changes. Since moderate changes of this type could be achieved within a communal framework, there was no motivation for schism. See Liberles, p. 170.

However, for a significant period of time, Hirsch was unable to translate those convictions into action. Under German law, registration and membership in the local *kehillah* was automatic and a Jew could renounce membership only upon conversion to Christianity or upon a declaration that he was *konfessionslos* (without religion). Such a declaration was widely regarded as tantamount to a renunciation of Judaism. Hirsch correctly considered those provisions of German law to be an interference with the fundamental principle of freedom of religious conscience. As long as the law remained in effect, the members of Hirsch's community had little choice but to retain their compulsory membership in the umbrella *Gemeinde* even after they had formed their own autonomous *Israelitsche Religionsgesellschaft.* In 1873 the Prussian Parliament promulgated a law that enabled Christians of various denominations to disassociate themselves from the established church and to form their own religious communities. To Hirsch, passage of this law served as the harbinger of a new era and beckoned Jews as well to campaign for permission to establish a civilly recognized autonomous Orthodox community.[1] For Hirsch, Orthodox secession from the *Gemeinde* was the logical and necessary culmination of the newly recognized socio-religious configurations since he he was sincerely convinced that "there is no wider gap between any of the various Christian denominations than there is between Reform Judaism and Orthodox Judaism."[2] Therefore, Hirsch immediately began to lobby for conferral of a similar right upon Jewish citizens. Eventually, with the assistance of an influential statesman, Eduard Lasker, Hirsch succeeded

---

1. Liberles, p. 225 ff., quite correctly underscores the fact that secession was not "the cause of the strengthening of Orthodoxy in Germany . . . rather it was an expression of that strength." He concludes: "All Orthodox leaders including Bamberger welcomed the law of separation, but only Hirsch approached it from a perspective of strength. For the others it was a guarantee of minority rights; for Hirsch it represented the right to be fully independent . . . for Hirsch, emancipation was an opportunity. In that he was unique, as early as 1836 and as late as 1877."

2. *Denkschrift uuber die Judenfrage in dem Gesetz betreffend den Austritt aus der Kriche* (Berlin, 1873), p. 6. The essay was published anonymously but later included in Hirsch's *Gesammelte Schriften,* IV (Frankfurt, 1908), 250-265. An English translation has been published in *The Collected Writings of Rabbi Samson Raphael Hirsch* [hereafter cited as C.W.; minor modifications in translation of citations made by this writer], volume VI, *Jewish Communal Life and Independent Orthodoxy* (New York and Jerusalem, 1990), p. 158.

in this endeavor. On July 28, 1876, the Prussian Parliament passed the Law of Secession granting Jews the right to withdraw from the organized community without a formal renunciation of Jewish identification and the concomitant right to form independent Jewish communities.

Following promulgation of the Law of Secession, Hirsch urged his congregants to secede from the established Jewish community of Frankfurt since it was now legally permissible for them to hold exclusive membership in the Orthodox community. Some congregants followed Hirsch's directive; however, a large number elected to remain within the general *kehillah* as well. To a large extent, it was the comparative newcomers to Frankfurt who followed Hirsch unquestioningly; members of many of the older Frankfurt families who had a deep attachment to the historical *kehillah* and its institutions chose to retain dual membership. Many of the latter were particularly loath to surrender their burial rights in the communal cemetery in which their forebears were interred.[1] A very tense situation developed within the Frankfurt community, a situation that became greatly exacerbated when the renowned Rabbi Seligmann Baer Bamberger of Wuurzburg issued a ruling supporting the decision for those who chose to remain within the general *kehillah*.[2]

A major contribution to the dissemination of Hirsch's literary oeuvre in English has been the translation, in 1984-1990, of six volumes of his

---

1. Of interest are analyses and reminiscences of the events in Frankfurt contained in *Historia Judaica* (October, 1948), X, no. 2. In three articles — [Saemy Japhet], "The Secession of the Frankfurt Community under Samson Raphael Hirsch" (pp. 100-122); Isaac Heinmemann, "Supplementary Remarks on the Secession from the Frankfurt Community under Samson Raphael Hirsch" (pp. 123-134); and Jacob Rosenheim, "Historical Significance of the struggle for Secession from the Frankfurt Jewish Community" (pp. 135-146) — the developments in Frankfurt are discussed by natives of the city who were intimately involved in its communal affairs. All three accounts provide intriguing background data but are highly subjective. See also Liberles, pp. 215-217. The distinctions between Hirsch and R. Ezriel Hildesheimer in their respective positions regarding secession are clarified in the exchange of correspondence in Ezriel Hildesheimer's, "Mitokh Hiluf ha-Mikhtavim bein Maran R. Ezriel Hildesheimer Zatzal ubein Maran R. Shimshon Raphael Hirsch Zatzal u-Mekoravav," *Yad Sha'ul: Sefer Zikaron al Shem haRav Dr. Sha'ul Weingort*, ed. by J.J. Weinberg and P. Biberfeld (Tel Aviv, 1952), pp. 233-251.
2. *Offene Antwort auf den an ihn gerichteten offenen Brief des Hern S. R. Hirsch* (Wuurzburg, 1877). C. W., VI, 226-253. . . The sole rabbinic personality of stature to oppose Hirsch was Bamberger. Citation of the view of R. Jacob Ettlinger as being in opposition to Hirsch by R. Zevi Yehudah Kook as recorded in *Ha-Tzofeh*,

Collected Writings, the Gesammelte Schriften.[1] Of these, the sixth volume, entitled *Jewish Communal Life and Independent Orthodoxy*, constitutes a welcome and noteworthy historical resource. That volume includes a series of essays in which Hirsch develops philosophical notions concerning the nature and status of a community as well as documents and memoranda dating from the 1870's pertaining to specific issues of communal

---

December 29, 1972, is an obvious error of fact since at the time of the dispute between Hirsch and Bamberger over secession, Ettlinger was no longer alive. The rejoinder of David Henshke, "Mahloket le-Shem Shamayim," *HaMa'ayan*, vol. XIII, no. 4, pp. 41-51, is very much to the point. Henshke also cites a similar error in Judah Leib Maimon's *HaRe'iyah* (Jerusalem, 1965), p. 123.

1. Over a hundred years after their publication, the written works of Hirsch remain a treasured resource for the student and scholar. If these works do not have the same magnetic effect upon some contemporary readers that they had in earlier decades, it is simply because of their particular potency in striking resonant chords that were uniquely nineteenth century in nature. The effectiveness of Hirsch's writings at the time of their publication is to be attributed, in part, precisely to the manner in which they captured the idiom, the mind-set, and the sensibilities of nineteenth-century Germany. Although to today's reader sections of these works may seem too forced, too heavy or too didactic in tone, it is those very qualities which contributed to their popularity at a different stage in time . . . The value of Hirsch's written works was fully appreciated by leading Torah scholars both of his own generation and of the generation that followed. Rabbi Israel Salanter sought to promote the translation of the *Nineteen Letters* into Russian. See Dov Katz, *Tenu'at ha-Mussar*, third edition (Tel Aviv, 1958), I, 223. R. Chaim Ozer Grodzinsky, *Ahiezer: Kovetz Iggerot*, II, 589-590, also commended translations of Hirsch's writings and wrote in superlative terms of "the gaon and schoolar, of blessed memory, who knew the ailments of the children of his generation and endeavored to cure them and was successful in drawing pure, living waters, waters of healing and refreshment, for those who suffer maladies of the soul." Cf. the encomium of Rav Kook, *Iggerot ha-Re'iyah*, I, 182: "The giant in knowledge, noble prince of God, the *gaon*, R. Shimshon Hirsch, who with the saving might of his right hand preserved the remnant of Western Jewry." . . . The English-speaking public has benefitted from the rendering into English of Hirsch's works in the years since 1942 when Bernard Drachman's translation of the *Nineteen Letters* was first published. Thereafter, over a period of time, there has appeared a spate of translation of Hirschiana, including the translation of the Commentaries on the Pentateuch, Psalms, Proverbs, Ethics of the Fathers, *Siddur* and *Haggadah*. Numerous essays by Hirsch as well as his seminal work, *Horeb*, were rendered into English by Dayan I. Grunfeld. The Rabbi Dr. Joseph Breuer Foundation and the Samson Raphael Hirsch Publications Society have undertaken the publication in English of *The Collected Writings*, of which volume VII of a projected eight-volume series is forthcoming.

autonomy and culminates with the exchange of views between Hirsch and Bamberger regarding the secession of the Frankfurt community. Publication of the entire text of the interchange between Hirsch and Bamberger is invaluable because that dispute has been the subject of much misunderstanding and misinformation.

Hirsch regarded the proposition that Reform and Orthodox communities could not function as part of the same *Gemeinde* as axiomatic. Such a concept, he opined, can be entertained only by people "who have come to regard all things religious as nothing more than meaningless forms and matters of individual taste."[1] Those to whom the authority of the law is paramount cannot possibly join in a single religious community with those who do not accept the validity of that Law, argued Hirsch, "For these two belief systems are as opposed to one another as yea is to nay. The question of whether the Law is outdated or eternal opens a gap between the two belief systems that divides them more sharply in principle than any two [other] religious denominations."[2]

For Jews to whom religious truths are absolute, it is intolerable to belong to a community that appears to give the impression that "Orthodox Judaism alone is ... not enough."[3] To bestow legitimacy upon deviation from Orthodoxy or to lend credence to the notion that there exist "two kinds of Judaism, each co-equal equal with the other" is unconscionable.[4] Good faith does not permit an intellectually honest person to be an adherent of a community that "cultivates Reform for the Reformers and Orthodoxy for the Orthodox" and thus "prevents Judaism, the one sole indivisible Jewish religious law, into a restaurant where meals are offered *á la carte*, with each guest consistently ordering from the menu those dishes that are to his 'taste.' "[5]

Bamberger, on the other hand, did not regard membership in the *kehillah*, as structured in the German communities of his day, as constituting a *malum per se*. Membership in an umbrella organization that sponsored various social, philanthropic and religious institutions did not, in his opinion, constitute recognition of the legitimacy of the ideologies espoused by its diverse constituent organizations and would

---

1. C.W., VI, 174.
2. Ibid., P. 81.
3. Ibid., p. 181.
4. Ibid., p. 202.
5. Ibid., p. 301.

not be perceived in that manner by any reasonable observer.

Much of the material contained in Bamberger's rebuttal of Hirsch's position, although intriguing and of weighty halakhic import, is tangential and unresponsive to the issues raised. The only salient point is a fundamental empirical disagreement with regard to whether continued participation in the *kehillah* might, or might not, be perceived as endorsement and legitimization of the views and policies espoused by institutions supported by the *kehillah*. Bamberger contended that the nature of the association with the Frankfurt *kehillah* structure was such that continued membership could not be construed as legitimization of heresy.

Contrary to the misunderstanding of Bamberger's position by some, he did not regard continued membership in the *Gemeinde* as religiously or ideologically mandated as a means of preserving the unity of the Jewish community. Quite to the contrary, were all observant Jews prepared to renounce their membership in the community, Bamberger would have offered them his unqualified support. In his "Open Reply to Rabbi Hirsch," in which he reiterated his opinion that secession was not mandatory in Frankfurt, Bamberger wrote, "Like you, dear Rabbi, I regard the Secession Law of July 28, 1876 as a great blessing for Orthodox Judaism."[1]

Bamberger's position was born of (1) the view that continued membership in the *Gemeinde* did not constitute a transgression and (2) recognition that for various and sundry reasons a significant number of individuals simply would not sever their association.[2] Under

---

1. Ibid., p. 250. Bamberger would have been appalled at the manner in which he has repeatedly been cited as an opponent of secession in principle. A representative example are the comments of Ruth Sofer, *Yisrael Kedoshim: Kovetz Sihot be-Inyanei Emunah* (Jerusalem, 1990), I, 173, whose factual account is replete with errors and simply echoes a common misconception.

2. In a communication to Bamberger urging the latter to reverse his ruling regarding the Frankfurt community, Maharam Schick (*Teshuvot Maharam Schick, Orah Hayyim,* no. 306) conceded that Hirsch had overstated the case in condemning as sinners those who did not join the secessionists since there were many devout individuals who hesitated to take that step for reasons that were entirely sociological in nature. Maharam Schick expressed his personal view, confirmed by his own experience, that, quite apart from the *halakhic* considerations involved in the question of secession, in the course of time, continued association with the non-observant in a common *kehillah* structure would prove deleterious. Furthermore, he stated that he was the recipient of a "tradition" handed down by Hatam Sofer that one should "distance oneself as much as possible from them and their cohorts and not be in one association with them."

such circumstances, he regarded secession and abandonment of the *Gemeinde* as delterious since the result would be to leave the observant members of the *Gemeinde* without properly supervised religious institutions and leadership. Bamberger was motivated by a concern for "a rather numerous group who do not subscribe to the principles of Reform but who want to conduct their lives in the spirit of Orthodoxy.... Without a doubt, there is no excuse for the conduct of those people who do not use the religious institutions of the *Religionsgesellschaft* .... However, does this give us the right to say: 'These people must remain without a *mikveh,* without kosher butchers; they must not have a synagogue in the Orthodox sense of the term'? Certainly not."[1]

Bamberger was motivated by a sense of responsibility for all members of the community. Nevertheless, he recognized that responsibility to the community at large must be balanced against responsibility to oneself. A person may not compromise his own religious observance or ignore his own spiritual needs for the sake of others. Accordingly, Bamberger insisted that there be no interference by other elements in the internal operation of institutions catering to the needs of the Orthodox. Bamberger was prepared to endorse retention of membership in the *kehillah* only in circumstance in which the Orthodox would be granted total autonomy in conducting the affairs of their own synagogues and religious organizations. As late as February 1877, he endorsed Hirsch's call for secession in Frankfurt[2] and reserved his position only when such autonomy was guaranteed by the *kehillah.* With regard to other communities in which the fundamental demands of the Orthodox were not granted, Bamberger ruled unequivocally that secession was not merely permissible, but mandatory. In a responsum concerning the issue of secession, Bamberger's son Simchah notes explicitly that only when the specified conditions were met did his father "agree that, according to his reasoning, there is no obligation to separate from the Reform congregation. However, when these conditions are lacking, his opinion has been recorded three and four times, namely in the matter of Carlsruhe, Vienna, Wiesbaden and Frankfurt, that it is incumbent upon the law-abiding to separate themselves from the Reform congregation."[3]

Only later, after concessions assuring them of autonomy in matters

---

1. *C.W.,* VI, 249.
2. Ibid., pp. 238-239.
3. *Teshuvot Zekher Simhah,* no. 230. Cf. also Liberles, p. 225.

of religious practice had been granted to the Orthodox community in Frankfurt, did Bamberger rule that *Austritt* (secession) was not mandatory in that community under the newly prevailing circumstances. Clearly, he did not view *Austritt* as either forbidden or repugnant. Bamberger simply recognized the power and cogency of the familial, social and emotional motives for remaining within the *kehillah*. Although he also fully recognized that retention of membership in the *kehillah* would minimize divisiveness within the community and provide opportunities for positive influence over others, he did not raise continued association to the level of an ideological imperative.

Not so the leaders of the Frankfurt *Gemeinde*. For them secession was an unsanctionable breach in the unity of the community; unity of the community was not only a cardinal principle but one with regard to which there could be no disagreement. Although they were prepared to tolerate diverse theological positions with regard to any and all of the fundamental principles of Jewish faith and observance, they regarded affirmation of communal unity as the one dogma to which all must subscribe. Much earlier they had argued, "There will be no end to sectarianism if every tiny faction which does not agree with the forms recognized by the majority has the right, on that account, to withdraw from the whole."[1] Later, they wrote, "The religion of the majority alone, according to the principles of Judaism, is the true and legitimate religion."[2]

A sharp split, bordering on schism, developed within the Orthodox community in Germany in the wake of the Frankfurt controversy. Following Hirsch's policy of *Trennungsorthodoxie* (separatist Orthodoxy), Jewish communities in several cities, notably those of Berlin, Wiesbaden, Darmstadt and Mainz, established separatist Orthodox communal structures. At the same time, a large segment of the Orthodox community, whose position was considerably strengthened by Bamberger's sanction, chose to administer their own Orthodox institutions under the aegis of the overall communal organization. Proponents of the latter policy, which came to be known as *Gemeindeorthodoxie* (communal Orthodoxy), entered into such arrangements with the established *Gemeinde* in many cities, notably in Berlin, Cologne, Frankfurt, Hamburg

---

1. From a memorandum of the governing body of the Frankfurt *kehillah* to the city of Senate in 1854, cited by Liberles, p. 179.

2. From a memorandum of the governing body of the Frankfurt *kehillah* to the city of Senate in 1858, cited by Liberles, p. 179.

and Breslau.[1] Frequently, the very threat of secession appears to have had a significant effect in prompting the *kehillah* to accommodate the demands of the Orthodox.[2] Certainly, this was the case in Frankfurt itself where it is palpably evident that the various concessions granted the Orthodox within the *kehillah* were the direct result of a desire to limit the number of those who would secede. Both the secessionists and loyalists regarded their respective policies as ideologically mandated rather than as merely pragmatically optimal. The result was internal factionalism and acrimony within the Orthodox community. Time did not heal or mitigate the rift within the Orthodox community. The two opposing camps remained separate and unreconciled until the advent of the Holocaust which decimated German Jewry.

---

1. Despite the wealth of analytic comment in Noah Rosenbloom's *Tradition in an Age of Reform: The Religious Philosophy of Samson Raphael Hirsch* (Philadelphia, 1976), that work is marred by a partisanship that moves the author to interpret objective data in a manner that is not compelling. In particular, Rosenbloom's account of the controversy over secession is flawed. Rosenbloom is certainly entitled to regard secession as having been an unwise policy. But labelling Hirsch's action as "heedlessness" (p. 117) is hardly an appropriate designation since Hirsch believed he was "heeding" a higher imperative. The portrayal of those in other communiities who followed Hirsch's secessionist policy as "malcontents" is also entirely unsupported and without basis in fact. Rosenbloom, p. 119, writes "As expected, Hirsch's action was emulated by malcontents in other communities in Germany, such as Baden, Karlsruhe, Darmstadt, Wiesbaden, Giessen, Cologne, Bingen and Strassburg." The implication that those who — correctly or misguidedly — followed this policy were misanthropic, dyspeptic individuals, unhappy because of petty concerns or jealousies, can only reflect an unscholarly bias.

2. Although, as noted above, note 2, Liberles maintains that the Law of Secession was a manifestation of the strength of the Orthodox, the enactment of that statute certainly served to enhance that strength. Cf. Liberles, p. 211. Although the situation in Austria was not identical to that in Germany, the threat of Austritt served to curb radical Reform tendencies in that country as well. The Austrian government rejected a petition presented by the Orthodox members of the Schiffschul in 1872 for permission to secede and form a separate community. Nevertheless, the possibility that the Orthodox might eventually obtain such permission and act upon it influenced Vienna's Jewish communal leaders to desist from introducing ideological reforms in the communal synagogues. See Marsha L. Rozenblit, "The Struggle Over Religious Reform in Nineteenth-Century Vienna," AJS Review, vol. XIV, no. 2 (Fall, 1989), pp. 209-221. It is noteworthy that Rozenblit, p. 219, demonstrates that the fear of loss of tax revenue was a significant factor in the ultimate decision.

Much has been written regarding the respective merits and failings of both approaches. The separatists have been taken to task as being responsible for a tragic waste of resources and for promoting divisiveness and disharmony. Hirsch's defenders, on the other hand, have maintained that were it not for the Law of Secession making establishment of autonomous Orthodox communities a viable option, even *Gemeindeorthodoxie* would have been unable to wrest any concession from the general communities which were dominated by adherents of the Reform movement. Very much to the point are the remarks of the Lithuanian rabbinic authority Rabbi Chaim Ozer Grodzinsky. R. Chaim Ozer hesitated to offer a definitive opinion because he regarded resolution of the dispute to be contingent upon the details of the situation in any given community. Only a rabbinic decisor familiar with the configuration of relevant factors in a specific locale could determine the wisest course of action under the circumstances. Nevertheless, he declared that, in his opinion, Hirsch's action was necessary for the preservation of German Orthodoxy:

> *"There is no doubt that the sage and saint Rabbi S. R. Hirsch, of blessed memory . . . did a great thing in founding the admirable and outstanding* Religionsgesellschaft *which became an exemplary Jewish community. Had the God-fearing not separated themselves by means of a separate* kehillah, *due to their minority status they would have become submerged within the general community — [a development] which did not occur when they separated and developed on their own. Then even the general community was forced to improve itself and to conduct the general institutions in a sacred manner."*[1]

Whatever arguments may be presented in support, or in criticism, of the wisdom and value of Hirsch's policy, several important points must be emphasized in the interest of historical accuracy:

1. Hirsch's argument against compulsory membership in, and taxation on behalf of, an overall religious superstructure was based upon considerations of freedom of conscience and infringement of basic civil liberties. Freedom of religion, argued Hirsch, entails not only freedom to desist from a form of worship which runs counter to an individual's convictions, but also freedom to

---

1. *Ahi'ezer: Kovetz Iggerot,* I, 243.

refrain from actively supporting such forms of worship and the propagation of theological tenets offensive to a person's convictions. Thus, Hirsch claimed that the legal right of secession was based upon the fundamental principle of freedom of religious conscience which includes an individual's right to join with other like-minded citizens in forming an independent community.[1]

Hirsch was keenly aware of the dangers inherent in any government entanglement in religious affairs and was categorically opposed to all forms of government intervention in the internal affairs of the Jewish community. He was aggrieved that such intervention had originally been solicited by those who initiated religious reforms[2] but he censured with equal vehemence the attempts of the Orthodox to avail themselves of governmental power in order to compel compliance with religious dictates. Hirsch deemed such policies to be fundamentally flawed and declared:

> "We cannot use sufficiently strong words to caution and plead against the exercise of such un-Jewish, unjustifiable methods of religious coercion as requesting the help of non-Jewish authorities in enforcing our religious laws . . . . Government authorities cannot, will not, and indeed must not be the instruments to turn us back into devout Torah-true Jews; they are not qualified to make us perform our religious duties as Jews."[3]

Realist that he was, Hirsch cautioned that the same governmental hand that wields power to build also wields power to destroy: "Have the past thirty years not yet taught us the consequences of such intervention?"[4]

2. It is a distortion of fact to contend that Hirsch's advocacy of separation from the larger Jewish community was indicative of a

---

1. *C.W.*, VI, 167-179. Hirsch also decried the financial support that accrued to Reform institutions as a result of taxes collected from Orthodox members and was well aware of the potential for enhancing the quality and scope of the activities of Orthodox institutions that would result from diversion of those funds to his autonomous community. Nevertheless, for him, financial considerations were secondary. He emphasized that the desire for secession was not a smokescreen for personal financial concerns on the part of individuals "using conscience to protect their money bags." Ibid., p. 179.
2. Ibid., pp. 52-53.
3. Ibid., pp. 55-56.
4. Ibid., p. 56.

lack of concern for individuals who did not accept the teachings of traditional Judaism.[1] Hirsch's *Nineteen Letters,* published in 1836, and a significant portion of his subsequent writings were explicitly addressed to the soul-searching, the ambivalent and the non-observant. Ultimately, Hirsch's policy of separatism did in fact lead to an attitude of introversion and to an unfortunate erosion of interest in the well-being and welfare of the wider community. However, Hirsch himself cannot be faulted on that account. Quite to the contrary, Hirsch castigated those whose concern was limited solely to the religiously observant. Most revealing is Hirsch's discussion of the scriptural narrative of Abraham's quest for ten righteous men *within* the city of Sodom. He notes:

> *"The idea of the righteous man in the midst of Sodomite depravity which Abraham visualizes, for whose sake the city might be saved, is not one who keeps to his own four walls, in haughty pride of his superiority gives up the masses and just looks on at their ruinous moral lapses, who thinks he has done quite enough if he saves himself and at most his own household. Yea, such a one Abraham would not class as righteous. He would not consider that he had at all fulfilled the duty which lies on every good man in bad surroundings. The ruin of the masses whom he had long given up would leave such a man cold. He might even possibly feel a certain smug satisfaction in it. That is not Abraham's 'righteous man' out of consideration for whom the salvation of the city should be effected. His righteous man is to be found 'in the midst of the city' and in lively connection with everything and everybody. He never leaves off admonishing, teaching, warning, bettering wherever and however he can. He takes everybody and everything to heart; he never despairs, he is never tired of trying, however distant the hopes of success may be. These are the righteous ones whom he presumes must be 'in the midst of the city' who would feel grief and pain at the death of each individual of these thousands...."*[2]

Moreover, in formulating his position, Hirsch emphasized that his policy demanded not disassociation from individuals, but

---

1. See the discussion in David Henshke, *Ha-Ma'ayin,* vol. XIII, no. 4, pp. 44-47.
2. Commentary on Genesis 18:24, English translation by I. Levi (London 1959), pp. 325-326.

secession from a communal system that he viewed as an institutionalized expression of heresy. In effect, Hirsch argued that the admonition "Do not associate with the wicked, even for purposes of Torah" (*Avot de Rabbi Natan* 9:4) is not applicable to the heretics of the modern era and ruled that heretics and *apikorsim* such as those with whom the Sages forbade all forms of social contact no longer exist in our time. The religious views of the non-observant of modern times have been shaped by parents, educational institutions and a climate of opinion over which they have no control. They are the products of their culture and are not to be held responsible for what they are. From a halakhic perspective they are considered to be in a category identical to those *apikorsim* and Karaites of whom Maimonides declared in *Hilkhot Mamarim* 3:3:

> "However, the children and grandchildren of these errants, whose parents have misled them, those who have been born among the Karaites who have reared them in their views, are like a child who has been taken captive among them, has been reared by them, and is not alacritous in seizing the paths of the commandments, whose status is comparable to that of an individual who is coerced; and even though he later learns that he is a Jew and becomes acquainted with Jews and their religion, he is, nevertheless, to be regarded as a person who is coerced for he was reared in their erroneous ways. Thus it is those of whom we have spoken who adhere to the practices of their Karaite parents who have erred. Therefore it is proper to cause them to return in repentance and to draw then high with words of peace until they return to the strength-giving Torah."[1]

Hirsch wrote explicitly that "secession is not intended as a separation of individuals from one another, a severance of amicable

---

1. Cited by Hirsch, *C.W.*, VI, 207. In an ironic twist, ibid., p. 298, Hirsch notes that a strange outcome might result from prolonged membership of Orthodox and Reform individuals in one religious association. The Orthodox member of such a community grants legitimacy to the Reform position. The Reform members have received a deficient education and are unaware of the nature of their error: "And so I think it could well be that, because I follow an Orthodox way of life in the midst of a community that subscribes to Reform solely from sheer ignorance, I would be the only one in that community that could be accused of bearing the stigma of a *min.*"

personal relationships with brethren who hold religious views different from our own,"[1] and emphasized that, "We must maintain harmonious and friendly contacts with those of our contemporaries who have been raised in the ideas and lifestyle of *minut* and *apikorsut,* of opposition in principle to the truth and the law of Judaism.... We should not, therefore, withdraw from contact with non-Orthodox individuals."[2] However, he cautioned, "all this makes it more imperative for us to keep our distance from the belief system of *minut* and *apikorsut* in which these fellow Jews of ours were raised in order to demonstrate our severance of all connections with that system."[3]

3. It is clear that Bamberger maintained that his advocacy of non-secession was motivated primarily by a desire to raise the standards of religious observance on the part of the general community and to assure that the greatest possible number of individuals be enabled to fulfill their religious obligations (*le-afrushei rabbim me-issura u-le-zakot ha-rabbim*).[4] It was this overriding concern that prompted him to issue a formal ruling conflicting with that of Hirsch. This is underscored by Bamberger's son in *Teshuvot Zekher Simhah* in his statement that, as a result of the accommodations made by the *Gemeinde,* "Many who had hitherto not joined the community of the observant would be withheld from transgression, particularly as a result of the improvements in the *kashrut* of the hospital of the Frankfurt community and similar matters."[5]

In the implementation of a policy such as secession, the sociological realia are often more dispositive than the theoretical or philosophical arguments. Robert Liberles, in his valuable

---

1. Ibid., p. 206.
2. Ibid., p. 207.
3. Loc. cit.
4. *Teshuvot Yad ha-Levi,* I (Jerusalem, 1965), *Yoreh De'ah,* no. 129, p. 199.
5. No. 230. Reprinted in *Teshuvot Yad ha-Levi,* II (Jerusalem, 1972), 242. One of the halakhic questions raised in the correspondence between Hirsch and Bamberger was the propriety of Bamberger's ruling in the jurisdiction in which Hirsch served as *mara de-atra.* The issue is further amplified in *Teshuvot Yad ha-Levi,* I, *Yoreh De'ah,* no. 129 and *Teshuvot Zekher Simhah,* nos. 229 and 230. Bamberger's family maintained that Hirsch had unjustly criticized Bamberger's intervention since the latter's views had been expressly solicited by Hirsch's partisans.

sociological study of the resurgence of Orthodoxy in Frankfurt, is correct in gauging Hirsch's espousal of secession as a manifestation of Hirsch's "modernism." Hirsch did indeed seize upon secession as a "modern" technique for building a vibrant community. Liberles is, however, incorrect in regarding the controversy as one between modernism and traditionalism. Liberles asserts that Hirsch, who had established himself as a proponent of a modern form of Orthodoxy, was giving expression to his modernism in a willingness to break with communal traditions while Bamberger, as a thorough-going traditionalist, was committed to tradition even in its sociological guises and wary of any form of "modernism."[1] It is true that Bamberger and Hirsch did not share an identical frame of reference in terms of their respective education and cultural orientation. In psychological perspective and temperament, Hirsch may have been viewed as "modern." Moreover, in the debate regarding secession in Frankfurt, it is entirely possible that Bamberger, more conservative in outlook, was psychologically disposed not "to rock the boat" and was therefore inclined not to do battle with the establishment more than was absolutely necessary. He may well have been influenced by his close personal contacts with individuals associated with the "establishment" in that city.[2] However, although, in practice, Bamberger did not advocate *Austritt* when there was no compelling reason for doing so, he certainly did not shrink from ideological endorsement of *Austritt*. His ringing endorsement of *Austritt* in other communities, where other conditions prevailed, negates any hesitancy grounded in traditionalism as ascribed to him by Liberles.

4. The halakhic argumentation presented by Hirsch in the second letter regarding secession, the "Open Response,"[3] should give

---

1. See Liberles, pp. 225 and 228.
2. A careful reader of *C.W.*, VI, 244-245, will note that Bamberger had close personal contacts with a number of individuals in Frankfurt, including the learned Rabbi Moshe Mainz and his own son-in-law, Rabbi Seligmann Fromm. The extent to which these individuals may have swayed or influenced his final decision by virtue of the manner in which they presented the facts of the case is an open question, but one that should not be overlooked.
3. See especially *C.W.* VI, 261 and 267-295, including the excellent subtle argumentation on pp. 292-293.

the lie to aspersions cast on his rabbinic scholarship by mischievous detractors.¹ The sources and analysis as presented in that exposition are obviously the comments of no mean *talmid hakham*. They are the product of the mind of a consummate rabbinic scholar. Although Bamberger is regarded as having been the preeminent halakhic authority in Germany at the time, in these written exchanges, Hirsch's analysis of the purely halakhic issues is by no means second best. Of course, whether or not the theoretical conclusions were germane to the fact pattern presented in the Frankfurt controversy is an entirely different question.² The cogency of Hirsch's halakhic argumentation was attested to by Rabbi Ezriel Hildesheimer who did not hesitate to disagree with Hirsch on other matters. Although Hildesheimer was pained and distressed at the rift that had occurred between Bamberger and Hirsch, he expressed the opinion that Hirsch's counter-reply to Bamberger had brought "the question to its final resolution for any person who concedes the truth."³

5. The correspondence between Hirsch and Bamberger is perhaps most noteworthy by virtue of the fact that it highlights a very significant aspect of intramural relations and communal history. Even when the ideological issues are clear-cut, a dispute of this nature reflects a wide array of concerns. As is often the case in the real world, issues become more complex in the process of negotiation and fashioning a compromise. Once the Frankfurt *Gemeinde* offered meaningful concessions to the Orthodox

---

1. See remarks and sources cited in Rosenbloom, pp. 60-63, 75, 89-91 and 419.
2. Hirsch charged, ibid., pp. 306-310, that the concessions granted by the Frankfurt *Gemeinde* created a situation indistinguishable from that already prevailing in Vienna, a community in which Bamberger insisted upon secession. I am unaware of any reply on the part of Bamberger that might resolve that apparent inconsistency.
3. *Yad Sha'ul,* p. 240. Hildesheimer was distressed at the extent to which the Bamberger-Hirsch rift had exacerbated tensions and led to a split in the community. Personally, he continued to be an advocate of the principle of secession but hesitated to intervene in the dispute lest such action make matters worse since he was convinced that passions were too inflamed for rational mediation. Hildesheimer was sorely conflicted and pained at the sight of the "fire of zealotry that consumed both parties in Frankfurt" and broken-hearted that he must maintain silence while secular journalists were heaping criticism and scorn on Hirsch, "who returns the Orthodoxy of our times to its positive glory." Ibid., pp. 238-239.

faction, the issue became less simplistic and a series of conflicting goals and a hierarchical ranking of values came into play. Even halakhically, it became possible to advance conflicting positions. Thus the question of judgment in weighing competing considerations often becomes decisive. And judgment requires knowledge of, and familiarity with, nuances and details of the particular local situation. It is this fundamental point to which Rabbi Chaim Ozer Grodzinsky drew attention in his incisive assessment of the Frankfurt controversy.

R. Chaim Ozer recognized the cogency of both positions as well as the sincere and positive intentions of the protagonists. He wrote:

> *"Regarding the question of association with sinners, in the opinion of the separatists, they see in this a great danger to Judaism that [people] will learn from their actions and by their proximity they may influence the future generation in a negative manner. It is axiomatic that a matter that concerns the foundations of Judaism involves a grave proscription. However, in the opinion of the accommodationists, they see in this matter a great* mitzvah, *not to estrange a large portion of the Jewish people and bring them merit, and they see no loss in this for the faithful who are separated with regard to religious needs. And, thus, this does not involve a question regarding which one says, 'Do you tell an individual, sin in order that you bring merit to your friend?' For, in the opinion of the accommodationists, this does not entail any sin or transgression, rather, to the contrary, it is a* mitzvah *to bring merit to the many. Accordingly, what the separationists see as a great transgression in uniting, in this, the accommodationists see a* mitzvah. *The doubt, according to this, is in the very act itself, whether it is a* mitzvah *or a transgression."*[1]

What was apparent to R. Chaim Ozer, writing in the early part of the twentieth century, has become even more evident with the unfolding of events in recent history. Paradoxically, those events have demonstrated the cogency of the arguments of both proponents and opponents of secession.

The nature of the American Jewish community in its organizational and institutional structure is far different from that of Germany of over

---

1. *Ahi'ezer: Kovetz Iggerot,* I, 243-244.

a century ago. Although there are indeed many points of comparison and similarity, simplistic parallels should not be drawn. Hirsch was not enamored of the academic study of history for its own sake. His own focus was rarely on the past, but rather on the present and the future. He would undoubtedly have had much to say to our community.

Hirsch knew that the vitality of Jewish existence is dependent upon study of Torah. Emphatically, he declared:

> "Our sickness began on the day our communities turned their backs on the study of the Torah. Our recovery will begin on the day when Torah study will regain its rightful place within our communities. . ..
>
> "Reawaken the Torah among people! This is your only hope . . . reawaken the venerable shas groups and batei midrashot to renewed existence and vitality. And the Torah will once again triumphantly demonstrate its healing, saving, life-giving power. The community will no longer be torn by dissension among its leaders and its members. They will again have the one spiritual bond that unites them all.[1]
>
> "The way to help Torah achieve its purpose is not by erecting splendid temples for it and not by collecting its writing in richly endowed libraries. Only if we study Torah, if we irradiate and warm ourselves by its fire and allow this fire to awaken and inspire us, will the Torah become for us what it should be, esh dat, a 'fiery Law.' Only talmud Torah can make us true Jews inspired and permeated by the spirit of God."[2]

With the irrepressible wit and humor that lightened and leavened his often ponderous writings, Hirsch, in a splendid passage, depicts Moses as visiting a contemporary German Jewish community. After having met with self-important dignitaries, committee delegations and trustees, after having being squired around and taken to see elegant synagogal edifices and philanthropic institutions, after having been regaled by choral ensembles, Moses turns away from the trustees in

---

1. C.W., VI, 60.
2. Ibid., p. 37. See also pp. 79-84, 131, and 294 and C.W., I (New York, 1984), 190-193, 249, 292-293, 304-305 and 390-391. These and similar passages should serve to dispel any doubt that Hirsch's philosophy of Torah im derekh eretz was based on a genuine appreciation of the primacy of Torah.

search of children. He stops the first boy he encounters and asks him, "*Passok li passukha* — What *possuk* did you study today?" The lad answers:

> "... I do not understand your question... a possuk? *What is that*? I had classes today in German, French, English, geography, history, physics and natural science. And now I am on my way to my class in religion. I will be Bar Mitzvah *this summer, and that is why I am having two hours of religion each week with my teacher.*"[1]

Hirsch understood that engagement may engender dissension and a full measure of discord. Wistfully, he noted that all too often communal affairs are permitted to stagnate because of the fear that interference on the part of concerned individuals be regarded as indecorous and, hence, in order to preserve cordial relationships, the board of trustees is permitted to settle all matters in accordance with their own discretion. "But then," observed Hirsch, "things are also peaceful in the graveyard and quiet in the mortuary. The dead do not engage in arguments. Once a man has died there is not even a pulse left. Powerlessness itself is a picture of peace and quiet, just like death."[2]

Hirsch was prescient in his optimism. Foreshadowing future developments, Hirsch predicted that if more Jews were proud and undaunted in their religious observance, civic barriers could be overcome. He argued:

> "*If only all Jews who travel or who are active in business life were to insist on observing their duties as Jews, this insistence would bring about the possibility of fulfilling all religious requirements. Wherever he would go, the Jew would then find meals prepared in conformity with his religious standards. Then it would be virtually no sacrifice for him to refrain from doing business on the Sabbath. Why, even in the official institutions of civic and political life, enlightened governments and nations would gladly accommodate a loyalty of conscience which would represent a significant contribution made by a Jewish citizen to the overall society of fellow citizens among whom he*

---

1. *C.W.,* VI, 77.
2. Ibid., p. 28.

>  dwells. ...¹ *The future belongs to the truth* — kushta ka'i."²

Above all, Hirsch was both a realist and a maximalist who always strived to attain the highest possible goals. Presumably, Hirsch would have viewed the accomplishments of Orthodoxy in the latter part of the twentieth century as but a spur to renewed efforts to reclaim the millions who no longer enjoy a meaningful religious identification as Jews. He had advocated communal secession from non-Orthodox institutions, not "a severance of ... relationships with brethren who hold views different from our own."³ Hirsch's charge to individuals within the observant community of his own time, his attempt to arouse their sense of responsibility and to galvanize them into action, are as apt today, in the twentieth century, for our times, as they were then:

> *"...there are many who think they have done enough. ... They are not concerned about public affairs; they think of themselves as yehidim, private citizens who are in no position to influence the community.*
>
> *"They forget that the community of God is composed of yehidim, of individuals united in one group. ... The guilt for any duty left undone falls back upon every single member of the community. ...*⁴
>
> *"The time to act for God, to do our duty, to accomplish our Jewish Mission is always now. ...⁵ We have practically resigned ourselves to apathy with regard to the widespread contemporary non-compliance with God's Laws. We have become phlegmatic with regard to the spirit of irresponsibility — both in matters philosophical and practical — which entangles spirits and hearts. This attitude of laissez-faire governs us...⁶ They [the Sages] knew that we are the era. They knew that the spirit of the era is the spirit of men, to which we all contribute."*⁷

---

1. Ibid., pp. 123-124. This passage occurs in Hirsch's essay, "Religion Allied to Progress," which was earlier translated and published in *Judaism Eternal,* ed. by I. Grunfeld (London, 1959), II, 224-244.
2. Ibid., p. 150.
3. Ibid., p. 206.
4. Ibid., pp. 101-102.
5. *C.W.,* I, 288.
6. Ibid., pp. 291-292.
7. Ibid., pp. 295-296.

*Rabbi Shlomo Jakobovits*

# A Purim in Every Generation

*There Are At Least 109 "Purims" in Communities Around the World!"*

THROUGHOUT THE AGES, MANY A JEWISH COMMUNITY HAS encountered enemies comparable to Haman. Sometimes the Jews succumbed to his persecutions; and in other instances there was a reversal of fortune, and they were saved. At such times, a *Purim Katan,* a local Purim, would be enacted. Its observance on that same date in future years would serve to commemorate their deliverance from impending disaster. Where the sequence of events rendered it appropriate, a *taanit,* a day of fasting, and *selichot* were instituted on the day previous to the new Purim.

The earliest local occasion on record to be accorded the name Purim did not commemorate the saving of a multitude of Jews. In Granada, Spain, the Moslem king appointed Shmuel Hanagid to command his army. In a series of battles in 1038-39, Shmuel led his country to victory. The Jews of Granada rejoiced by celebrating the 1st of Elul as a Purim.[1]

---

1. According to some sources, this was also a family Purim for the descendants of Shmuel Hanagid, to mark his personal deliverance from assassination plots.

## PURIM KATAN IN HALACHAH

The practice of an annual *chag* — the *poskim* refer to it as a *Yom Tov shelo* or *shelohem* — limited to a particular locality or family, is found in *Tanach*,[1] in times of *Bayit Sheni*,[2] and in the Talmudic era.[3] Yet the *halachah* of local Purim is not mentioned as such in the *Mishnah* or *Gemara* nor in the codes of the Rambam and *Shulchan Aruch*.[4] It appear that the custom was widely practiced long before it was formally enshrined as normative *halachah*.

The first affirmation of local Purim in a major *sefer halachah* is in the *T'shuvot* of Rabbi Moshe Alashkar,[5] published in Venice in 1554, ten years before the first edition of the *Shulchan Aruch*. At about the same time, a similar position was expressed in the *Ne'ilat She'arim*, which constitutes the epilogue section of *Sefer Massa Melech*.[6] Both of these authorities are cited by the *Magen Avraham*, *Orach Chaim* 686:4, who thus confirms the full halachic credentials of the "local Purim" by placing it on the pages of the standard *Shulchan Aruch*.

The *Pri Chadash*, in his *Dinei MInhagei Issur*,[7] takes strong issue with these *poskim*. Obviously there can be no denial of the *existence* of local Purims; by that time (seventeenth century), the practice had been well established. What he questions is its degree of legitimacy and the manner of enactment. The above *poskim*[8] hold that a community has

---

1. E.g. *I Shmuel* 20:29.
2. The entire *Third Book of Maccabees* deals with a local one-day Yom Tov observed by the Jews of Egypt during the Hasmonean era.
3. E.g. *Eruvin* 41a.
4. These sources, however, do postulate that a personal miracle-experience calls for a special *brachah* to be recited at that locality for three generations. This ruling imparts some Talmudic authority to the institution of local Purim. See *Brachot* 54a, according to the *girsa* of *Rif*, as cited by *Rambam* and *Shulchan Aruch*.
5. *T'shuva* 49, which deals specifically with the Purim of Lepanto, Italy.
6. Section 7:15.
7. *Orach Chaim* 496:14.
8. Also *Yam Shel Shlomo*, *Bava Kama*, section 37, *Pachad Yitzchak* D:18, and others.

---

The Purim of Cairo (1524), also known as *Purim Mitzraim*, closely parallels the original Purim experience. The Governor of Egypt, Ahmed Pasha, rose to be the powerful ruler of that land within the empire of Suleiman the Magnificent.[1] He was jealous of the wealth and social

---

1. It happens that the empire of Suleiman covered almost the same territory as that of Achashverosh.

the right to establish a local annual Yom Tov called Purim, that such enactment becomes mandatory upon future generations, that this date takes on whatever halachic characteristics are specified in the original *takanah* (e.g., no *Tachanun*, no *hesped*, recite *Hallel* and other *t'filot*, read a special *megillah*, send *shalach manot*, etc.), and that the festive meal is a *seudat mitzvah*. It is even suggested that if such a local Purim is set on a date that in a subsequent year turns out to be a *taanit nidcha* — e.g., the Tenth of Av, which become a *taanit* when it falls on a Sunday — then one *seudah* could be held on the afternoon of that *taanit*.[1]

The *P'ri Chadash* disputes all of these. Basing his position on his interpretation of the *Gemara Rosh Hashanah* 18b,[2] he denies the right to enact such a *takanah,* downgrades the festive meal to no more than a *seudat reshut,* and refers to the observance of such a Purim as *minhag beta'ut,* a custom devoid of legal status.

His view is quoted by the *Aruch Hashulchan, Orah Chaim* 686:7, as a minority opinion. It is also mentioned by the *Mishnah Berurah,*[3] but this authority rules totally in favor of the majority opinion (686:8, 697:2).

The *Chayyei Adam* 155:41, which was written a century before the *Mishnah Berurah,* refutes the *P'ri Chadash* and vehemently upholds the majority view. He allots more space to the subject of local Purim than any other of the well-known *poskim,* and presents a detailed list of appropriate *t'filot,* with the rationale for each. As outlined earlier in this article, he himself had occasion to implement the *halachot* that he enumerates here. Together with these *halachot,* he relates in vivid detail the bitter experience that moved him to establish his own *taanit* and Purim. All this constitutes the final chapter of the *Chayyei Adam,* and the author thus concludes this highly acclaimed work of *halachah* on an intensely personal note.

---

1. See *Taanit* 12, Tur *Orach Chaim* 559.
2. The question being how to understand *Batlah Megillat Taanit.*
3. *Shaar Hatziyun* 697:5.

status of the leading Jews, and announced that unless an exorbitant sum of money was conveyed to him by the 28th of Adar, all Jews in Cairo would be massacred. Clearly his intent was the extermination of the Jews, as the sum specified was beyond anything attainable. But Ahmed was also plotting against the Emperor Suleiman and, on the very day he had set as the Jews' deadline, he was assassinated by soldiers loyal to Suleiman. The 28th of Adar was joyously proclaimed the Purim of Cairo!

The villain of the Frankfurt Purim story (1614), Vincent Fettmilch, actually referred to himself as the "new Haman of the Jews." He was a fiery rabble-rouser who led mob attacks on the Jewish quarter. After two years of anti-Jewish agitation, he ultimately aroused the ire of the Emperor Matthias, who ordered him arrested and hanged. The Jewish community quickly established the 19th day of Adar as a fast day and the following day as the Purim of Frankfurt. A special scroll was prepared, known as *Megillat Vinz* (for Vincent), which was read annually on that day, amid great celebration.

While the Damascus blood libel was at its height in 1840, the Governor of Rhodes accused local Jewry of the same alleged crime and threatened to annihilate the entire community. It was on the 14th of Adar, as the Jews of Rhodes mournfully prepared for what they expected to be their last Purim, that the Sultan deposed the governor and declared the accusation against the Jews to be false. In ecstasy, the Jews of Rhodes added special ceremonies and *piyutim* to the festivities of our universal Purim, effectively celebrating Purim *twice* on the same day!

In some cases, the hated tyrant did not fall but the Jewish community miraculously escaped his sword. Such was the case in Medzibozh, Poland in 1648, when the Chmielnicki hordes bypassed the town. The *Purim Katan* of Medzibozh was set on the 11th of Tevet, to mark their providential survival.

At times, the danger derived from a bloodthirsty mob or an invading army rather than from one powerful individual. Tales abound of such occurrences. One of the most notable took place in Narbonne, France in 1236, when the rash action of one Jew endangered the entire community. A mob rioted, threatening to destroy the Jewish quarter and everyone in it, to avenge the death of a Christian who had been killed by the Jew during an argument. The local commander and his soldiers appeared just in time to avert calamity. The 21st of Adar became the Purim of Narbonne and served as a powerful reminder of the impact one thoughtless Jew could have on the safety of all.

In some cases, the villain was an informer who tried to bring ruin on the community or on an individual through malicious reports to the government. Such was the case in Saragossa, Spain, in 1420. The informer was an apostate Jew. When his plot was foiled, a *Purim Katan* was proclaimed on the 17th of Shevat and a *megillah* was written for the annual celebration. This *megillah* is remarkable for its exceptionally close similarity, in style and terminology, to *Megillat Esther*. It also has the special characteristic of appending to the informer's name the curse *yimach sh'mo* ("May his name be eradicated") every time it appears in the text.[1] This may well be one of the earliest examples of such usage of this expression, which today has become commonplace.

One of the oddest, and perhaps one of the most poignant, reasons for a Purim occurred in 1607 in Verona, Italy. The Jews there had been confined to a ghetto since 1599. It was their request that *they* be the holders of the keys to the gates, and that the ghetto thus be locked each night from the inside, not from the outside. The day this plea was granted, the 18th of Tammuz, was proclaimed a Purim! Its observance continued until Napoleon abolished the ghetto in 1797. The theme of the annual celebration was an expression of satisfaction in segregation; this community felt that ghetto life had more advantages than disadvantages — at least when Jews hold the keys.

Even surviving a natural disaster was cause for the declaration of a Purim. The Jews of Ancona, Italy, during the seventeenth and eighteenth centuries expressed their gratitude to Hashem for their survival on no less than four separate dates, each celebrated by a Purim. They had been saved from revolutionary riots, an earthquake and two fires.

## The Family Purim

Some events were more personal, observed by only one family and its descendants. Rabbi Yomtov Lipman Heller, the *Tosefot Yomtov*, became Chief Rabbi of Bohemia in 1627. The Thirty Years War was escalating, and the government imposed a heavy tax on the Jewish community to help pay war costs. Rabbi Heller headed the Jewish committee charged with the responsibility of levying the share each individual must pay of the collective tax. Naturally, there were those who felt they had been assessed too high, and some of these unscrupulous

---

1. The full expression has come to be *"yimach sh'mo v'zichro,"* which derives from merging these two *pesukim*: *Sh'mot* 17:14 and *Tehillim* 109:13. Usage as an appendage to an accursed name appears to be a comparatively recent practice.

individuals were vicious enough to turn to the government with a list of slanderous accusations against Rabbi Heller. On the 5th of Tammuz (1629), he was summoned to Vienna and sentenced to fine and imprisonment. For fifteen years he experienced repeated sufferings, and the 5th of Tammuz was designated a family *taanit.* This dark era of his life ended when he became the Rabbi of Krakow on the 1st of Adar, 1644. The day was proclaimed a family Purim. He recorded his misfortunes in his *Megillat Eiva,* the *Chronicle of Enmity.*

Rabbi Avraham Danzig, author of *Chayyei Adam,* lived in Vilna. In 1804 a powder magazine exploded and demolished the housing complex in which he resided, killing 31 people. The rabbi and his family survived, but all of them were injured. He proclaimed the 15th of Kislev to be a family *taanit,* and the following day a family Purim.

How many such Purim days are there? The total number will never be known, as there is no central registry of local proclamations. Of those that are known, the most comprehensive list is in the *Encyclopedia Judaica,* where 109 are enumerated. Almost 20 percent of these are in Adar.[1]

Another aspect that cannot be determined precisely is the extent and duration of observances. Celebrations varied very widely. In a few cases, the local tradition was observed only the first several years. But where records exist, the indications are that in most cities observance was maintained for generations, and sometimes for centuries, as in the above case of Verona. The Purim of Shiraz, Persia was instituted in 1400 and observed for over 500 years.

## ঌ Why Purim?

Why was Purim chosen, and not Pesach or Chanukah, each of which likewise celebrates Jewish redemption from the designs of our enemies? The answer lies in the characteristics that render Purim particularly appropriate for this role. Often the community event lends itself to an annual one-day celebration, rather than one of seven or eight days. In some cases, as already cited, the saga was such that a previous fast-day was also appropriate, and this, again, is parallel only to Purim.

---

1. Detailed descriptions of several local Purim sagas can be found in articles in these issues of *Manatschrift fur die Geschichte und Wissenschaft des Judentums*: XXXVIII,XLVI, XLVII, XLVIII.

Beyond this, Purim is the one and only festival on which redemption from enemies is marked by unmitigated celebration. When the enemy is Amalek, we do not apply the restraint of *binfol oyivcha al tismach:* "Do not revel in the fall of your enemy."[1] On Pesach, restraint is very much in evidence; the flag of our joy is flown at half-mast in the form of half-*Hallel,* and there are other indications of concern for the Egyptians. On Chanukah, when so many of our people fell in battle, and so many other Jews sided with the enemy, there is no *mitzvah* of *mishteh v'simchah,* feasting and revelry.[2] For unrestrained joy in deliverance from our enemies, Purim stands alone.

Furthermore, the very nature of Purim, the struggle against Amalek, is such that it returns at various times and in various places. The Torah itself proclaims the Amalek confrontation to be *midor dor* — from generation to generation.[3] In keeping with this maxim, the Alsheikh[4] interprets the Purim narrative as being a direct sequel to the Amalek confrontation of King Sha'ul, five centuries earlier. Accordingly, in every age of persecution we naturally associate the reappearing arch-anti-Semite with Amalek, our enemy of *midor dor.* The failure of his designs in *any* generation becomes Purim, and thus calls for ongoing proclamations of Purim.

Perhaps the strongest support for designating such local observances specifically as Purim comes from the *Megillah* itself. On the basis of events that happened in Shushan, this one city established its own local Purim, on the 15th of Adar,[5] which to this day is still observed in certain localities and is still called Shushan Purim. The precedent is set right there, and it is a precedent unique to Purim.

---

1. *Mishlei* 24:17.
2. *Esther* 9:22.
3. *Sh'mot* 17:16.
4. In his commentary on *Esther* 2:5, 4:14.
5. *Esther* 9:18. See also *Ran,* beginning of *Massechet Megillah.*

Dr. Aryeh Morgenstern
Translated by Yehudah Mirsky

# Resettlement of the Land (Yishuv Ha'Aretz) as Viewed by the Vilna Gaon's Circle

AN HISTORICAL DECISION OF PRACTICAL IMPORT WAS EStablished in the *Beis Hamidrash* of the Gaon of Vilna to the effect that the mitzva of settling in *Eretz Yisrael* is a biblical imperative applicable to our own time. This supports the decision of the author of the *Shulchan Aruch* and is contrary to the view of many *Rishonim* like Maimonides,[1] who did not count it as one of the 613 mitzvot and contrary to the view of Rav Hayyim the *Tosafist*, who held that the mitzva was not in force in his day.

In his annotations to the *Shulchan Aruch,* the Vilna Goan locates the source of *Halacha* that a slave may legitimately force his master to move to the land of Israel in the Tosefta's statement that it is preferable to live in the midst of non-Jews in *Eretz Yisrael* rather than in a Jewish community in the Diaspora. He then adds: "And so in the present day, contrary to Rav Hayyim the Tosafist."[2]

In his own book, *P'as HaShulchan,* the Gaon's disciple, Rav Yisrael of Shklov, cites "Our Master who taught that it is a 'weighted mitzva'

---

1. *Editor's Note:* However, there is a vast literature as to what Maimonides' position on this issue really is.
2. *Yoreh Deah* 267:1, commenting on *Tosefta Avodah Zarah* 5:2.

(which is as significant by itself as all the others put together)." Rav Yisrael goes on to say that the mitzva of *yishuv ha'Aretz* is then, Sinaitic, and not rabbinically ordained, since otherwise it could not be accorded the status of a 'weighted mitzva.'[1]

Oral tradition in Vilna had it that, according to the Gaon, the mitzva of *yishuv ha'Aretz*, like the mitzva of *brit milah*, was first given to Abraham to pass on to his descendants. A textual support for this tradition was adduced from the Midrash in *Bereishit Rabba:*

> " 'And Jacob was very afraid' (Genesis 32:8): he said to himself: Will not all these years that he (i.e. Esau) has lived in Eretz Yisrael strengthen him in his claims against me?"

Jacob's fear, the Gaon reasons, is only explicable if the mitzva of *yishuv ha'Aretz* was in force at the time of the Patriarchs.[2]

An historical document of rare importance, the *Epistle of the Disciples of the Vilna Gaon in Safed*, based on this *halachic* tradition in Vilna, explores the *halachic* meaning and Kabbalistic dimensions of the mitzva of *yishuv ha'Aretz* with unusual depth and sensitivity. There is only one extant copy of this extraordinary work, which was printed in Russia by Rav Yisrael of Shklov in 1810.

To the Gaon's disciples, *yishuv ha'Aretz* is quite simply a mitzva unto itself as a function of the unique sanctity of *Eretz Yisrael*. This sanctity derives not[3] from the mitzvot which can only be performed there, nor from the Torah that may be studied there. Rather, this sanctity directly flows from God's designating this land as destined for inheritance. This Divine choice was given in the Torah's command to Abraham:

> "Go you from your land, your birthplace, your father's house, to the land that I will show you."

The sanctity of the land is, therefore, a Divine ordination, and living there is a value onto itself, and the Abrahamic mitzva is to live there.

---

1. *P'as HaShulchan*, chapter 1 paragraph 14. See also ibid., chapter 2 paragraph 28 where commenting on *Sifra d'vei Rav, Parshat R'eh* paragraph 20's discussion of whether a father may prevent his son from moving to *Eretz Yisrael* Rav Yisrael comments that in that situation a son need not obey his father, since to do so would violate *mitzvat yishuv ha'Aretz*, even if the mitzva were only d'rabanan.
2. R.J.L. Maimon, *Toledot Ha'Gra*, Vol. 1 p.141 (Jerusalem, 1954).
3. *Editor's Note:* See *Yeshuas Malka* of Rav Y.Y. Trunk, Responsa 67.

This sanctity endures forever, irrespective of the transitory episodes of history.

Moreover, in the Kabbalistic conception of the Gaon's disciples, *yishuv ha'Aretz* may hasten the Redemption itself:

> *"Forgetting the land brings about, God forbid, a lengthening of exile and forgetting of the (last) days, for this is Satanic laziness, and causes one to forget the Love of Zion and adoration of Jerusalem; the influence fades and the maidservant rules . . . The house lays in ruins and goes unrestored."*[1]

*Yishuv ha'Aretz* can "resurrect the *Shechina* from dust," free her from the dungeon in which she finds herself.

> *"And none come to raise the Shechina from its prison . . . and how long shall Jerusalem be denied mercy and how long shall the summit of beauty be trampled to the dust . . . and the city and the holy precinct that was the joy of the world be handed over to strangers."*[2]

It is incumbent on the Jewish people, then, to settle the land, to raise the *Shechina* from the dust, in addition to fulfilling the mitzvot bound up with the land and learning the Torah.

The facilitation of settlement, through acts of cultivation and building, themselves bear redemption significance. They uncover the "revealed end" described in the *Gemara Sanhedrin:*[3]

> *"Rav Abba said of the verse, 'And you, mountains of Israel, your branches will give to Israel and your fruits you will bring to My people,' there can be no end more revealed than this."*

※ ※ ※

The Epistle, fashioned by eleven members of the Gaon's immediate circle, is a unique *halachic,* Kabbalistic and literary achievement.[4] It speaks for the land that yearns for its children's return. It glorifies

---

1. Avraham Ya'ari, *Iggrot Eretz Yisrael,* p. 332 (Tel Aviv, 1943).
2. Ibid.
3. 98a.
4. Ya'ari, p.337, missing from his listing is R' Shaul ben Shimshon of Saarje, see my book, *Meshichiyut V'Yishuv Eretz Yisrael,* (Jerusalem, 1987, 3rd Printing) p. 72.

the land's natural beauty while entering a dirge for its desolation. The authors point out the harsh contrast between its hidden Divine potential and wail over the sad and forgetful neglect in which it finds itself.

The authors of the Epistle, who had abandoned their native Lithuania to take up residence in *Eretz Yisrael,* saw their own actions as harbingers of a dramatic shift in the relationship between *Eretz Yisrael* and the Jewish people. This can be seen, for example, in the written requests for financial aid; while they describe their respective courses of study, as did nearly all supplicants from *Eretz Yisrael,* they base their request on the very fact of their residence in *Eretz Yisrael.* Their inability to support themselves was, in contrast to much of the old *yishuv,* not at all deliberate, but a simple function of the tenuous economic and physically unsafe situation in which they found themselves. And their ignorance of Arabic placed them at a severe disadvantage relative to the members of the Sephardic community and the local Arabs as well.

Their financial requests are couched not in terms of Torah study but in terms of the land itself. It is the land and its settlement which are in need:

> "And now we shall explain to you the needs of the land first . . . the land heralds. The land awakens . . . "[1]

Only later, in "our own double request" do they characterize *Eretz Yisrael* as the land of the Torah . . . "In me, the Torah becomes clear, in me fear of God is quickened, in me the soul is set free . . . "[2] They personalize the land, likening it to the maternal *Shechina* to the mother-land asking for the return of her sons and overcome with gratitude at their return:

> "Now thank the Place (i.e. God) who has mercy on the land, remembering me with the return of the sons, who sacrificed for me and dwell in me . . . to cultivate and to keep . . . to join the four amot *of* Halacha *to the four* amot *of the pure and holy land . . . "*[3]

The study of Torah, the four *amot* of *Halacha,* is something added to the land, and not identical to it. It is the son's self-sacrifice on behalf of

---

1. Ya'ari p. 329.
2. Ibid.
3. Ibid., p. 330.

the land that entitles them to the support of the Diaspora. On this, the Epistle leaves no room for doubt. The authors set out two sets of needs requiring attention and support: first "some fitting encouragement of settlement of your desolate land";[1] and second, "for another, building a *beit midrash,* as we do not have one at present."[2] This straightforward dichotomy between settlement and study appears elsewhere. Recounting their efforts to send Rav Yisrael of Shklov on a fund-raising trip to Russia, they record having told him: "You must act on behalf of the holy Torah, to save lives and for the honor of the Holy Land."[3]

In the ordinances of the Kollel Ha-Perushim in *Eretz Yisrael,* written by disciples of the Gaon who founded it, one finds a clear distinction between two sets of priorities to which Diaspora monies ought to be put. The first is the needs of settlement, i.e. acquiring of fields and vacant lots, building buildings, paying taxes and generally maintaining the community. The second is the upkeep of Torah scholars:

"Diaspora donations are set into two categories: to strengthen *yishuv ha'Aretz* and that of maintaining Torah scholars."[4]

※ ※ ※

In a letter of introduction accompanying a fund-raiser to the Diaspora dated 15 Kislev 5991 (1831), signed by the seven heads of the Kollel Ha-Perushim of *Eretz Yisrael,* including Rav Hayyim HaCohen of Pinsk and Rav Yisrael of Shklov, we find a formula (similar to one found in an epistle from Safed dated 5570 (1810) ) according to which funds are to be raised for "a tripartite mitzva," consisting of those three weighted mitzvot which are said to equal all others:

> "How great is this mitzvah of three parts: The Torah study of the community, the saving of precious lives and yishuv ha'Aretz, each of which is as weighty as the entire Torah."[5]

---

1. Ibid., p. 335.
2. Ibid.
3. Ibid., p. 334.
4. Arey Leib Frumkin, *Toledot Hachmei Yerushalayim,* Vol. 3, p.149 (Jerusalem, 1929).
5. *Judaica Exhibition and Auction Catalogue,* p. 774, (Jerusalem, Nissan 5747, 1987).

And in a letter from the heads of the Kollel to Sir Moses Montefiore, dated 7 Heshvan 5600 (1840), we find, as in other documents, a distinction between Torah study in *Eretz Yisrael* and settlement there:

> *"To better His holy people by founding our holy Torah and settling our Holy Land . . . The action below stirs heavenly love to have mercy upon the community . . . "*[1]

Not only do we find this clear distinction, but moreover in one of the Epistles of the Perushim, quoted in the *Epistle of the Officers and Elders of Amsterdam,* we find a fundamental ordering of the two realms, differentiating between *aliyah* and settlement, which are the central dimensions of mitzvat *yishuv ha'Aretz* and the study of Torah there. This ordering, though reminiscent of the ordinance of the Kollel Ha-Perushim, differs in its *halachic* formulation attributed to none other than Rav Hayyim of Volozhin:

"Your Honor's (i.e. the Elders of Amsterdam) desire for their monies to be distributed only to Torah scholars is a wonderment to us. Have they not heard of the difficulties of this year . . . high prices have driven famine through the land . . . even artisans and the like are destitute . . . and moreover, this question was asked long ago at the time of the awesome Gaon, Master of the Diaspora, Our Master, Rabbi Hayyim of Volozhin, the memory of the holy and righteous is a blessing and it was decided that we are obligated to support all those in our Holy Land, not just the scholar. And the reasoning for this is that the mitzva of *tzeddakah* applies to the mitzva of *yishuv ha'Aretz,* which may be fulfilled by any Jew, who is thus deserving of support by the Diaspora. And since then we have abided by this decision in our communities . . ."[2]

An echo of this authentic record of Rav Hayyim of Volozhin's decision, along with a scripture-based reason is found in an oral tradition recorded by Rav Michal HaCohen:

"It has been said by many that Our Master Rav Hayyim of Volozhin, one of the founders of Kupat Rabbi Meir Baal Hanes for those who dwell in the Holy Land, was asked by many faithful Jews: 'Why should charitable monies go to those who have not dedicated their lives to Torah and spent their days in crafts and business? Wouldn't that

---

1. *Montefiore Correspondence,* Jews College (London, file 528).
2. Letters of Community Leaders of Amsterdam, m.s. Collection, *Yad ben-Zvi,* Vol. 13, p. 278.

deprive those whose Torah is their craft who have no other source of support?'

"And to this he gave a brief and winning answer. 'All our efforts are for the settlement of our Holy Land, and who are the settlers, if not the artisans and businessmen? Therefore, we must support them to the best of our ability. Why, do you think, was the date of Gedaliah ben-Ahikan's death made a day of fasting and mourning for all Jews? Because on that day *yishuv ha'Aretz* came to an end. And who lived in the Land then? Wine merchants and vintners.' "[1]

It is only fitting to append to this daring statement of Rav Hayyim, a tradition attributed to his premier disciple, Rav Yossef Zundel of Salant, who made *aliyah* in 5595 (1835).

"The elders of Jerusalem testify that Rav Yossef Zundel of Salant urged the youth of Jerusalem to work for the physical development of the city and the Land. And they continued: 'His love of the Jewish community in *Eretz Yisrael* was so great that he would wander the hills of Jerusalem weeping for their desolation, and used to say that he is even happy to see the building of gentiles, so long as the Land is being built.' "[2]

※ ※ ※

It should, nonetheless, be noted that among the scholarly community of Lithuania, even among those who saw themselves as the spiritual heirs of the Vilna Gaon, there were those who differed with these views of their colleagues as to the meaning and significance of mitzvat *yishuv ha'Aretz*. Space permits discussion of only one, Rav Menachem Mendel Mann, the Rosh Yeshiva of the so-called "Blumkes" Yeshiva in Minsk, one of Lithuania's *gedolim* in the early 19th century. Rav Menachem Mendel was the son-in-law of Rav Avraham ben Rav Anshel of Minsk, author of *The Rightward Pillar* (Minsk, 5571/1811), who made *aliyah* with the Gaon's circle. It is safe to assume that Rav Menachem Mendel was familiar with the above-mentioned ideology of the group regarding *yishuv ha'Aretz*; he nonetheless differed.

In a letter to his brother, Rav Baruch Shimon, the Rabbi of Shklov, he expresses hesitations regarding the latter's desire to move to *Eretz Yisrael*. Rav Menachem Mendel sets forth the Torah as a primary value

---

1. *Ha'Ariel,* Vol. 7, #1 p.4, Tishrei 1875.
2. Eliezer Rivlin, *Ha'Zaddik Rabbi Yosef Zundel Mi'Salant U'RaSatov,* p. 19 (Jerusalem, 1929).

of greater significance than *Eretz Yisrael*. One senses from Rav Menachem Mendel's letter that he saw the process of *aliyah*, with its attendant day-to-day difficulties, as an outright "bittul Torah." To his mind, redemption is dependently solely on the fulfillment of mitzvot and not on the mitzva of *yishuv ha'Aretz*. Moreover, the very sanctity of the Land, to his mind, is not an absolute, but a function of the deeds performed there and the holiness emanating from those deeds in turn. In sum, he says, any spot on the globe may attain the sanctity of the altar of the *Beis Hamikdash*. Rav Mendel writes:

> "With regard to the Holy Land, I will be brief ... Our forefathers did not merit the Holy Land until they had first accepted the Torah. And so in each generation, every man must strive for the Providence of time that will save him from bittul Torah and grow accustomed to occupying all his moments either with Torah and fear of God or with the body's necessary rest ... a great path is yours to travel, and as I have said, the trip to the Holy Land may subject you to bittul Torah. A certainty ought not to be exchanged for an uncertainty. If you labor at Torah you will surely fulfill God's wish 'That you shall be a desirous land to me' and all that is left to God in this world is the four amot of Halacha; and the place where you stand that will be holy land, as holy as the altar of the Beis Hamikdash."[1]

A century later, these same ideas would be expressed by the premier exemplar of the Misnagdic Torah culture of the 20th century, Rav Yisrael Meir HaCohen of Radin, the "Chafetz Chayim." Attempting to dissuade a friend from moving to *Eretz Yisrael*, he says:

> "I have heard ... that his eminence is gathering his strength to travel to the Land of the Holy. In truth, as is known, residing in the Holy Land is a great thing, but Torah study is a greater mitzva, as evidence by the fact that one is permitted to leave Eretz Yisrael *in order to study Torah.*"[2]

These views faithfully represent the world outlook of the majority of Misnagdic Jewry in the last 200 years. *Hassidic* literature of the time

---

1. *Iggeret Shalom*, p. 3 (Jerusalem, 1975).
2. Letter dated, second day of *Tezaveh*, Reb Shmuel Kransnafyorki, reprinted in *Mara D'Ara Yisrael*, Vol. 2, p. 29 (Jerusalem, 1974).

similarly displays an urge to spiritualize *Eretz Yisrael* and devalue *yishuv ha'Aretz* not only in comparison to Torah study but to other mitzvot as well.[1]

This being so, one ought not to regard the Lithuanian *aliyah* of the Gaon's disciples as deriving from the ideological fabric of Lithuanian Jewry, nor as the expression of a merely personal wish to realize the values of Torah study in *Eretz Yisrael* as opposed to someplace else. In fact, the Gaon's circle, and those who made *aliyah* with them, fundamentally differed from their brethren in their avowedly Messianic perspective on *yishuv ha'Aretz* as both a mitzva unto itself and as an action hastening redemption. To this end, they, unlike those who stayed behind in Lithuania, were willing to sacrifice themselves and run the risk of *bittul* Torah for the sake of the religious imperative of the hour.

Study of their writings from *Eretz Yisrael* leaves one, utterly convinced that what we have here is a truly revolutionary spiritual movement which ushered in a new historical era both in terms of the history of *Eretz Yisrael,* as well as the history of Jewry's relationship to that Land. This movement cannot be subsumed under the normal categories of East European Jewry, which when applied to this movement obscure more than they reveal.

---

1. Rav Hayyim Elazar Shapira, the Admor of Munkacz, draws on historical circumstance in responding to a halachic question: from the fact that most of the Hassidic leaders did not move to *Eretz Yisrael,* he infers that *yishuv ha'Aretz* is not a mitzva. See his responsa, *Minhat Elazar,* Point 5 section 12 (Brooklyn, 1974).

[The prevailing Hassidic attitude is strikingly displayed in the comment of R' Moshe Teitelbaum of Ohel to his son-in-law, Aryeh Leibish of Vizhnitz: "How I would miss the mitzva of *Hachnasat Orchim* were I to leave for *Eretz Yisrael.*" *Yismach Moshe,* Vol. I, last page (New York, 1942).]

*Rabbi Bernard Rosensweig*

# The Wrong Response to Modernity

## I.

THE EMANCIPATION, WHICH ACCOMPANIED THE FRENCH REVOlution, shook the very foundations of Jewish life. It is true that the Emancipation broke down the walls of the ghetto and opened the door to legal equality; but there was a price to pay in Jewish terms. This accounts for the hesitation on the part of many Jews in that period to embrace Emancipation fully.[1]

Enlightened society was prepared to recognize the Jew as an individual — *man qua man*. However, the Jew as a Jew, as part of an entity that was known as the Jewish people, with its own distinct religious commitment and communal structure, represented for the Enlightenment a disturbing manifestation — even an act of treason — which it was not readily willing to accept or condone. The Enlightenment offered an exchange: The Jew would be given his legal rights, if in return, he would abandon his national distinctiveness and surrender his judicial autonomy.

The result was that virtually every Jew in Western Europe in modern times was confronted with the painful dilemma of how to maintain the

---

1. While the Sephardic Portuguese Jews living in France, who were highly assimilated, welcomed the Emancipation, their Ashkenazi brethren were much more hesitant and reluctant. They were not that quick to trade their communal autonomy for the rights of citizenship. Cf. L. Poliakov, *The History of Anti-Semitism* (New York, 1975), III, pp. 255-260.

gains of the Emancipation while preserving his Jewish identity and uniqueness.[1] A number of responses to this dilemma — some of them negative — emerged in the 19th century whose impact is still felt to this very day.

One negative response was the rise of Reform Judaism, which believed that it could stem the tide of Jewish disintegration by compromising, adulterating and simply rejecting some of the basic principles of Judaism. Much of this is reflected in a recent book by Professor Michael Meyer, of Hebrew Union College, on the rise, development and growth of the Reform movement and its major figures on a global scale. The book, *Response to Modernity*, is well written, well researched, well documented and is destined to become the major work on the historical evolution of the Reform movement. While the book provides a world-wide view of Reform, it focuses primarily on the two major centers of Liberal Judaism — Germany and America. There is much to be learned from a careful study of this work because "the more things change, the more they remain the same."

## II.

Michael Meyer analyzes the factors which gave birth to the Reform movement. Two factors cited by Meyer as contributory causes for the appearance of Reform Judaism have a familiar ring in our times. He points out that in the eighteenth century higher Jewish education had practically ceased in Germany, ignorance of fundamental aspects of the Jewish faith was rampant and rabbis from Poland, with little understanding of the German reality, had to be imported to minister to German Jews — with all the negative results which accrued.[2] In addition, the bitter struggle between Rabbi Jacob Emden and Rabbi Jonathan Eybeschutz, over the latter's supposed Sabbatean loyalties, split the Jewish community asunder. Meyer quite correctly concludes that "a community so divided was less able to oppose new ideas in its midst or to project the image of a unified authority that might have

---

1. The traditional rabbis could not react negatively to the removal of the physical and legal restrictions — even though they understood some of its painful implications for the patterns of Orthodox Jewish life. Cf. J. Katz, *Out of the Ghetto* (New York, 1978), p. 155.

2. Cf. Michael A. Meyer, *Response to Modernity* (New York, 1988), p. 12.

suppressed emergent centrifugal forces."[1] Ignorance and divisiveness always place the Torah community at peril.

The Reform movement is, however, the end-product of a number of factors which were operative in the seventeenth and eighteenth centuries. It was primarily, as Meyer points out, a response to the emerging new forces, events and circumstances in these centuries and to the changing political and cultural environment which they created. Dramatic changes took place in this period in the economic, political, social and religious spheres; the Industrial Revolution, the Reformation and the Enlightenment brought about revolutionary changes in the areas of thought and action, all of which, obviously, did not leave the Jewish community unaffected. This was particularly true of the wealthier elements of Jewish society who were most exposed to the non-Jewish world and its challenging ideas. It was they who were most affected by the new realities which these developments created, in terms of their thinking, their priorities, their commitment to Judaism and their increasingly tenuous relationship to the Jewish community. It was within this framework that Reform Judaism took its first steps, formed its basic ideas and presented them to the larger Jewish community as an alternative to Traditional Judaism.[2]

Thus, ostensibly, Reform Judaism did not come "to bury" Judaism but "to save" it. Its purpose was to confront the so-called "enlightened youth," which apparently was dissatisfied with traditional Jewish values and appeared to be on the threshold of breaking with Judaism, and to bring it back into the fold.[3] However, the intentions of the Reform movement were totally obliterated by actions and ideals which undermined their stated goals: they attempted to save Jews by truncating Judaism and emasculating its essence.

When we consider who Meyer indicates were some of its spiritual and ideological forerunners, the pernicious nature of the Reform movement becomes much clearer and much more understandable. One of those influences was the semi-apostate Spinoza, who cast doubt on the Mosaic authorship of the Torah. It was Spinoza who projected the idea of the Torah as the constitution of the Jewish people when they

---

1. Ibid., p. 11.
2. Ibid., pp. 9; 11-13.
3. Cf. H. H. Ben-Sasson, editor, *A History of the Jewish People* (Cambridge, 1976), p. 788.

possessed their own state, which lost its binding character with the disappearance of the Jewish commonwealth. The implication was clear: the Torah, as such, was no longer incumbent upon every Jew, and every Jew could, in consequence, evaluate the laws in terms of their subjective value to him. This fit well into the Reform scheme of things.[1] At the same time, Dr. Meyer is able to see some merit in Professor Gershon Scholem's theory linking Sabbatai Zevi and the Sabbatean movement to the origins of the Haskalah and Reform. After all, Sabbatai Zevi did split the Jewish world and "presented an example of religious antinomianism" in which the observance of the Torah was subordinated to the will of the pseudo-messiah. The result was that Jewish Law was no longer unchallenged as the indispensable bond which unites all Jews.[2]

On the other hand, Professor Meyer rejects Moses Mendelssohn as a spiritual progenitor of the Reform movement. Mendelssohn, who remained a practicing Jew all of his life, believed in the revelatory character of the Torah, that its laws were eternal and unchanging and that they were binding on Jews in every historical and political constellation. Meyer indicates that, "Mendelssohn lacked the notion of religious development" which was so essential to Reform and that he insisted that the Torah was not subject to changing times; consequently, a Jew was obligated to keep the entirety of the Law even in a changing world. How could such an approach fit into a movement which championed religious change as a primary principle and exalted the subservience of traditional values to contemporary pressures?[3]

---

1. Cf. Meyer, *Response,* p. 64.

2. Cf. Ibid., pp. 10-11. Some of the pioneers of Reform Judaism had strong leanings towards the Sabbatean heresy. Leopold Loew records that Aaron Chorin, who was the first reformer in Hungary and who provided one of the two reform "responsa" in defense of its tampering with synagogue services, came under Sabbatean influences as a youth. Loew rightly traces to this circumstance the germ of Chorin's liberal ideas. Cf. J. H. Hertz, *Affirmations of Judaism* (London, 1926), pp. 177-178.

3. Ibid., pp. 14 and 64. It is interesting to note that Zvi Kurzweil has indicated that Mendelssohn was a founder of neo-Orthodoxy and that his "place is to be found in traditional Jewish rationalistic philosophy." The controversial Mendelssohn requires a separate article. Cf. Z. Kurzweil, *The Modern Impulse of Traditional Judaism* (New York, 1985), pp. 3-15.

## III.

Reform Judaism, by Professor Meyer's own admission, was not built on the foundations of pre-modern Judaism; in fact, "it was the product of modes of thinking that did not exist earlier and cannot be read back into previous periods of Jewish history." It is true that Reform ultimately attempted to create for itself a "usable past" as a response to the accusation that it was sectarian and schismatic and had severed its ties to the chain of tradition.[1] Nonetheless, Meyer concedes that "the Reform movement was not an internal Jewish development. It came into existence out of a confrontation with a changed political and cultural environment."[2] It was only after the fact that it endeavored to provide itself with Jewish legitimacy by attempting, unsuccessfully I believe, to reconcile its destructive attacks on the essences of Judaism with the religious heritage of our people.

For the Reform movement, the "spirit of the age" reigned supreme and became the dominant yardstick in measuring the validity of timeless Jewish values. Israel Jacobson, who was probably the first practical reformer, felt that he and his group had "the task of bringing a number of customs. . .more into line with changed circumstances and the spirit of the times."[3] Abraham Geiger was the ideological father of the Reform movement. When the role of Hebrew in the liturgy became a matter of serious debate, Geiger defended the position of those who advocated a reduced or minimal role for the Hebrew language. In his defense, he wrote: "History has given here judgment (against the Hebrew language) . . . and all the lamentations against those conditions are useless. No protest is justified against the forces of history."

Rav Samson Raphael Hirsch, in a powerful response, wondered what Jewish life would be like today if our ancestors had adopted this line of reasoning in the period after the destruction of the Temple, or in the age of Constantine when Christianity became the dominant religion in the Roman Empire, or in the centuries of the Crusades, or in the age of Ferdinand and Isabella of Spain in the last decade of the fifteenth century when the whole world seemed to be arrayed against us. With Geiger's reasoning and Jacobson's standard, we would have disappeared long

---

1. Ibid., p. 4.
2. Ibid., p. 9.
3. Ibid., p. 30.

ago from the face of the historical map. The strength of the Jewish people lies precisely in the fact that we have never been in step with the times; rather, because of the unique character of the Torah and its demands, we are ultimately always ahead of the times.[1]

In a very real sense, the Reform movement deified modernity and made it the arbiter and the touchstone of religious values and practices. But why should God and the Torah, which is God's revelation to the Jewish people, be made to fit the egotistical whims of transient man and his changing ideas? Why should Jews bend before every secular wind that blows as if it were the final revelation from Sinai? Why should we adjust the eternal values of the Torah to accommodate the tyranny of some current theory in science, sociology or psychology? Why must we tailor our religious demands to the momentary appeal of contemporary philosophies or political theories which are stylish today and tomorrow will be outmoded and outdated? The strength of Torah Judaism from time immemorial lies in the fact that it has been able to stand above the struggle of contemporary social, political, moral and religious forces and proclaim an absolute "thou shalt" and "thou shalt not" which transcends any given time and guides our lives consistently and effectively.

It is interesting that Rabbi Samson Raphael Hirsch, who propounded the doctrine of *Torah Im Derech Eretz* and who was the father of modern German Orthodoxy, was also extremely sensitive to his surroundings and to the world which it projected. In fact, there were areas in which he and Geiger, whom he knew, did not appear to differ. Like Geiger, he was committed to the Enlightenment and the Emancipation which it fathered; like Geiger, he emphasized the idea of the world mission of the Jews. What differentiated Rav Hirsch from Abraham Geiger qualitatively was Hirsch's unconditional commitment to Divine Revelation and the absolutely binding character of the *mitzvot* in every political or social climate.[2]

In a brilliant insight, R. Hirsch reinterprets a rabbinic statement in Tractate *Shabbos*. The *Gemara* there tells us that when a man comes

---

1. Cf. I. Grunfeld, ed., *Judaism Eternal* (London, 1956), II, pp. 213ff.

2. Cf. Ben-Sasson, *A History of the Jewish People,* p. 839. R. Hirsch distinguished between historical truths and Divine truths which are immutable. He characterized the obligation to observe the mitzvot as being in the category of Divine truths.

into the next world he will be asked a number of questions by the heavenly tribunal. One of the questions which will be asked of him will be: "*Kovato Itim La-Torah?*"[15] which we normally translate: "Did you set aside specific times for the study of the Torah?" In a beautiful twist Hirsch interprets it as follows: "Did you set the times to the Torah, did you accommodate the age to the demands of our eternal Law, or did you trim the Torah to fit the demands of the times?"

## IV.

The Reform movement offered its own solution to the problem of the tension between the demands of Emancipation and the desire for continuing Jewish identity. Henceforth, the early reformers declared, Judaism was to be only a "religion," a denominational cult, limited to a few articles of belief and a handful of unobtrusive observances. Germans of "the Mosaic persuasion" would now be neatly classified alongside Germans of the Christian faith, and enjoy the same status. Gabriel Reisser, who fought for Jewish rights in Germany and who was a lay leader in the Reform movement, proudly proclaimed that German Jews had one father and one mother — the father was our Father in heaven and the mother was Germany. German Jews of this orientation loudly trumpeted their belief that Germany was their Zion and Berlin their Jerusalem. By declaring that Jews were no longer a nation but members of a religious sect, early Reform leaders felt that they were ensuring the right of Jews to full-fledged citizenship.

It was in this context, that Jews were no longer a people, that the Damascus Libel in 1840 (in which the Jewish community of Damascus was falsely accused of the ritual murder of a Capuchin monk) brought forth a peculiar response on the part of Abraham Geiger, the idealogue of the Reform movement. This libel aroused Jewish concern throughout the world and moved Sir Moses Montefiore, Adolphe Cremieux and Salomon Munk to do everything in their power to save these unfortunate, imprisoned fellow Jews. But the incident left Geiger "surprisingly unperturbed." In a letter which he wrote after the Damascus Affair, Geiger indicated that he had been sharply opposed to the mission of Jews which had gone to help their brethren in the east. In his eyes, the Damascus Affair was not a specifically Jewish affair; it was, rather, a

---

15. Cf. *Shabbos* 31a.

universal, humanitarian concern which should have been addressed on that level.¹

In any case, the rejection of the idea of Jewish nationhood and peoplehood became one of the pillars of the Reform movement. In the early nineteenth century, reformers in Hamburg produced their own prayer book in which they omitted passages dealing with the messianic return to Zion, as did Geiger in Breslau in 1854.² To deny to Jews the hope of being able to reconstitute themselves as a nation on its own soil was to deny one of the central principles of the Jewish faith which was reflected in the beliefs and prayers of Jews in all ages. It was to fly in the face of Biblical tradition which confirms the Jewish people as a religious entity with ultimate national aspirations. Nonetheless, it was in this vein that the Pittsburgh Platform of 1885, which was the centerpiece of classical Reform Judaism in America, declared: "We are no longer a nation but a religious community."³

The emergence of political Zionism, with its goal of a Jewish homeland, represented for Reform Judaism "a frightening menace they could not ignore." When a new Zionist newspaper, *Die Welt,* appeared in German, the two leading Reform rabbis of Germany issued a joint statement in which they condemned this publication as a "calamity" which should be resisted. They were horrified to discover that the Zionist movement intended to call its first Congress not in some East European locale but in Munich.⁴ Only the intervention of the local Reform rabbiner, who contended that the Zionist idea was subversive and treasonable, forced Herzl and the Zionist Organization to call its first historic congress in Basel.

In order to mitigate the Reform position, Meyer points out that not only Reform, but German Orthodox rabbis, as well, opposed the Zionist movement on the grounds that "Zionism contradicted the messianic destiny of Judaism." This is a camouflage: the difference between the opposition of certain Orthodox rabbis and Reform spiritual leaders was fundamental: Orthodox rabbis never rejected the principle of Jewish

---

1. Meyer, *Response,* p. 97. Meyer indicates that Geiger modified his position in later years. When the Jews of Romania suffered persecution in late 1860, Geiger sought to gain Prussian intervention on their behalf. Ibid.

2. Ibid., p. 59. Meyer refers to this as the "most audacious innovation" of the Hamburg reformers. For Geiger's liturgical reforms, cf. Ibid., p. 186.

3. Ibid., p. 388.

4. Ibid., p. 209.

peoplehood or the ultimate return of Jews to Zion. They affirmed the Biblical statement: "You shall be unto Me a kingdom of priests and a nation of holy men." They parted company with the Zionist movement as to how the return would take place — through natural means or through messianic intervention. The reformers, as a consequence of their absolute rejection of the national element in Judaism, opposed Zionism in its very core and essence.

Thus, in 1897, the Montreal Conference of Reform Rabbis took note of the First Zionist Congress in Basel with a resolution of "total disapproval" of its desire to establish a Jewish state.[1] In 1917, as the Zionist Movement was moving toward the triumphant moment of the Balfour Declaration, the Central Conference of American Rabbis resolved by a vote of 68 to 20 that "we look with disfavor upon the new doctrine of political Jewish nationalism, which finds the criterion of Jewish loyalty in anything other than loyalty to Israel's God and Israel's religious mission."

After the Balfour Declaration had become a fact, the Central Conference of American Rabbis continued its adamant opposition to Zionism, insisting that "we are opposed to the idea that Palestine should be considered the homeland of Jews. Jews in America are part of the American nation. . . .. The mission of the Jews is to witness to God all over the world."[2] All through the turbulent twenties the impassioned opposition of the Reform rabbinate to Zionism was broken only by the revolutionary stand of a few stalwart souls such as Judah Magnes, Gustav Gottheil, Stephen Wise and Abba Hillel Silver.

Gradually, the inevitable logic of events forced a modification of the anti-nationalist principle which had constituted a major pillar in the Reform edifice for nearly a century. The terrible thirties, reflecting as it did the traumatic changes in political conditions, and their frightening effect on the European Jewish community, forced the issue. The result was a definitive statement in the Columbus Platform of 1937 that obligated Jews to aid in the building up of *Eretz Yisrael* as a Jewish homeland and as a center of Jewish cultural and spiritual life.[3]

However, two important qualifications have to be added. Reform made a complete ideological turnabout not as the result of an internal

---

1. Ibid., p. 293.
2. Cf. *Proceedings of the Central Conference of American Rabbis,* Vol. 28, p. 133.
3. Meyer, *Response,* p. 389.

change in essential principle, but simply in the spirit of a realistic pragmatism — unless we were to claim that pragmatism itself is a principle. The Reform movement simply realized that to maintain its opposition to the national Jewish movement in the light of the historical situation of the thirties would have made it irrelevant even to its own constituency. In addition, vestiges of the classical Reform position are still to be found in the Reform movement. Is it mere coincidence that when it comes to Jews who revel in "Israel-bashing" in the media and making Israel appear in the worst possible light in every controversial situation, that the majority of Jews involved in these exercises come primarily from the Reform lay and spiritual leadership?

## V.

In the attempt to destroy every vestige of nationalistic sentiment, Reform ruthlessly tore out every reference to the return to Zion and the coming of a personal Messiah from our sacred liturgy. Every allusion to Jewish uniqueness was expunged. In their quest to "Christianize" synagogue services, the gap between the officiating clergy and the largely passive worshipers, who said less and less, grew wider.[1] I remember the local Reform spiritual leader in Toronto pleading with his congregants, in a bulletin article, to become more involved in services, to participate more fully and to utter words, rather than acting in the capacity of spectators. What did he expect when his movement had always hailed the Christian church as the model for decorous behavior?

However, the religious deterioration within the Reform temples did not end there. Reform temples, in their rebellion against Jewish law and tradition, began to use the organ, mixed choirs, German prayers, the triennial cycle of Torah reading (even that was abandoned in America for a shorter Torah reading), elimination of the Haftorah on the pretext of allowing more time for the sermon and the substitution of confirmation services for the traditional *Bar Mitzvah*.[2] In the United States, where Reform was more radical, but more consistent, changes in synagogue services were even more far-reaching. In the Temple of Isaac Meyer Wise there were family pews, reflecting the practice of most American churches, and the recitation of German and English hymns,

---

1. Ibid., pp. 338 and 36.
2. Ibid., pp. 33 and 56.

and all *piyutim* were eliminated. In explicitly Reform congregations, *taleisim* were gradually discarded, as were *yarmulkes*. In some congregations, it was forbidden to wear these items during the services, and in others, the *Bar Mitzvah* ceremony was barred. The observance of the second day of the three pilgrim festivals, *Pesach, Shavuos* and *Succos,* was abandoned, as was the second day of *Rosh Hashana,* which is, of course, observed even in Israel.[1] Many Reform congregations replaced what Meyer calls "the raucous sound of the *Shofar*" with the more controlled tones of the trumpet or by mimicking its blasts on an organ.[2] What emerged in Reform were services which were barely distinguishable from their Protestant counterparts.

In this spirit, the Reform movement has, at one time or another, abandoned the multiplicity of rituals and observances which have distinguished Judaism. It has contemptuously brushed aside all those precepts and customs which have preserved the Jew and sanctified his existence as "irksome legalism" and "empty ceremonialism." Not only observances which were associated with the synagogue and festivals, like *Shofar, Lulav* and liturgy, were undermined, but equally the dietary laws, the laws of family purity, the laws of mourning and a whole array of *halachic* demands were either adulterated or rejected. Civil divorce replaced the obligation of a *get.* The right of *chalitzah* (unshoeing), in the case where a man died childless and left a surviving brother, was declared to be null and void and the painful situation of the *Agunah,* the grass widow, was subordinated to the law of the state.

The centrality of the ceremonies and observances in Judaism is too obvious to need a detailed elaboration. No religion, least of all Judaism, can long exist without its historic outer garb. In ancient times, the Greek-Jewish thinker Philo attempted, in good faith, to explain away the forms and institutions of the Jewish people allegorically, as mere symbols of religious truths. The Alexandrian Jewish community which, according to many scholars, was larger than the Jewish community in Jerusalem at the time of the destruction of the Second Temple, ultimately disappeared leaving little in the way of a Jewish legacy for posterity. Authentic Jewish thinkers attest to the fact that when the structure of Jewish law falls away, when the time-tested rites, customs, ceremonies and observances go by the boards, we lose our sense of

---

1. Ibid., pp. 241 and 251-2.
2. Ibid., p. 130.

the Divine and imperil the future of the Jewish people. We may remain an ethical people, but we cease to be a religious people with a specific Jewish commitment.

The Reform movement, however, looked upon the rituals, ceremonies, customs and demands of Judaism, as it was expressed in the Pittsburgh Platform, as objects "to obstruct rather than to further modern spiritual elevation."[1] The builders of Reform were acutely sensitive to the ancient Christian critique of Judaism as being overly "ritualistic" and "legalistic." Geiger himself did not recognize Jewish ritual as "eternally binding Divine commandments." He saw them as "instruments." He saw them as "instruments," and where they did not elevate the soul, he found no reason to continue their practice.[2] The criteria which the early Reformers in Charleston established for the validity of rites and ceremonies was not Divine Law or sanctified tradition, but "their propriety, their general utility, their peculiar applicability to the age and country in which we live to feelings, sentiments and opinions of Americans."[3] Here one must agree with Moses Hess who accused the Reform of having sucked the marrow out of Judaism leaving it a dry skeleton. Reform, he concluded, "has raised baseless negation to the rank of principle."[4]

Reform maligned the traditions, rituals and ceremonies of the Jewish people. Geiger, for example, denounced *milah* (circumcision), as far back as 1845, as a "barbaric, bloody rite."[5] The Central Conference of American Rabbis resolved, in 1893, that converts could be accepted into the covenant of Israel "without any initiatory rite, ceremony or observance whatsoever."[6] The laws of *Kashrut* were abandoned and ridiculed. While Geiger himself personally observed the dietary laws, Meyer concedes that it was simply a concession to his position and not because he felt any inner sense of obligation.[7] David Einhorn, who was one of the leading Reformers in nineteenth-century America, commiserates with his son-in-law, Kaufman Kohler, that in Kohler's Detroit pulpit he was forced to keep the dietary laws, and thus "cannot live as you

---

1. Ibid., p. 388.
2. Ibid., p. 96.
3. Ibid., p. 231.
4. Ibid., p. 208.
5. Ibid., p. 96.
6. Ibid., pp. 257 and 280.
7. Ibid., p. 96.

teach."[1] His other son-in-law, Emil Hirsch, who was one of the most prominent Reform leaders and ministered to a congregations in Chicago, wrote contemptuously of *Kashrut* as "kitchen Judaism" with emphasis on "trivialities."[2]

The impact of these attitudes is far-reaching in its scope. In the Columbus Platform of 1937, the Reform movement did something of an about-face in the area of rituals and observances, and urged its membership to develop the use of concrete symbols both in the home and in the Temple. As a result of that call, and a subsequent *Centenary Perspective* published on the occasion of the one hundredth anniversary of the founding of Hebrew Union College, the Reform movement has made some progress in that direction.

In a survey commissioned by the Reform movement, which was taken in the early '30s before the Columbus Platform was issued, it was revealed that about 20 percent of Reform Jews lit Sabbath candles in their homes on Friday night and recited the *Kiddush.* Only 33 percent conducted a *Pesach Seder*; about one-half fasted on Yom Kippur. They did not even bother to inquire about the dietary laws because so few Reform Jews observed them. A survey which they conducted 25 years later showed somewhat better results. In this survey, 59 percent of Reform families lit candles and 26 percent made *Kiddush*; 74 percent had a *Seder* of some kind in their homes, 93 percent ate matzah during Pesach, but 59 percent also reported that they ate bread. At the same time, only eight percent kept kosher, 24 percent would not mix meat and milk and 24 percent would not eat pork. On Shabbos, 88 percent of Reform Jews indicated that they kept their businesses open, 90 percent worked, 99 percent drove, and 82 percent smoked. While 47 percent claimed to have *mezuzos* in their homes, only two percent admitted to putting on *tefillin,* and only 17 percent indicated that they would employ only a *mohel* for circumcision.[3]

What emerges from this survey is that despite the seeming change in direction by this movement, the response on the part of its constituency

---

1. Ibid., p. 452, note 84.
2. Ibid., p. 280. At the dinner celebrating the ordination of the first four graduates of Hebrew Union College, shellfish was served. Ibid., p. 263.
3. Ibid., pp. 322 and 375. In a footnote, Meyer concedes that "since one must assume that the respondents to surveys are the most committed Reform Jews, the percentage figures for observance are maximal," ibid, p. 473, note 77.

has been quite limited. Gilbert Rosenthal, in an article which appeared in *Judaism* in 1976 on Jewish religion in America, makes the point that Reform "have little loyalty to basic mitzvot endorsed by their denomination. For example, only half of Reform Jews light Sabbath candles, only seven percent attend services weekly; and fully 10 percent have Christmas trees in their homes."[1] The reason is clear — they have no commitment to *Halacha*. When Reform encourages this or that ceremony or practice it is done not because the Torah ordained it or because it is the usage of the *Knesset Yisroel* (Universal Israel), but because it is considered to still be "religiously expressive and useful." In this context, which observance is deemed to be so regarded and for how long a period it is to be retained, obviously depends upon the subjective mood of the congregation or the inclinations of its spiritual leadership. Why should anyone feel obligated to an observance which, according to its sponsors, is not grounded in a transcendent tradition and which can, in different circumstances, be considered irrelevant?

## VI.

The uprooting of sanctified traditions and institutions that are interwoven with the very existence of the Jewish people is the result of a basic approach to, and an underlying evaluation of, the fundamental texts of Judaism — the Torah and the *Talmud*. It is the theological outcome of the rejection by Reform of the binding character of the Torah, both Written and Oral. Over and over again, almost from its earliest beginnings, Reform Judaism repudiated Israel's Law, and with excessive vehemence. Geiger, already as a young man, felt no attachment to the *Talmud*. He rejected the Oral Law as the product of the Divine Will or as part of the Sinaitic Revelation; he claimed that the *Tannaim* and the *Amoraim*, the rabbis of the *Talmud*, were really very much influenced by the times in which they lived, and that they artificially imposed their views into the text of the Bible, while maintaining the fiction of its revelational character.[2] How long would it take for Geiger and his allies to lay their hands on the Holy Torah and challenge its essence and validity?

---

1. G. Rosenthal, "Jewish Religion in America: A Study in Mutuality," *Judaism*, Summer 1976, pp. 292-293.
2. Meyer, *Response*, pp. 90 and 93.

Geiger and the Reformers, who were very much influenced by Spinoza's heretical views on the Bible, began to cast their own doubts on the Mosaic authorship of the Pentateuch. In 1857, Geiger turned his attention to the text of the Bible and "proceeded to historicize and relativize the most sacred text of all." He argued that the Bible, no less than the *Talmud,* had to be understood as the product of its time and was "dependent on the changing historical context that conditioned its final form."[1]

Geiger's position was expanded and amplified by his disciples. Kaufman Kohler and Emil Hirsch, who were the foremost representatives of Reform in America during its classical period, were thoroughgoing Bible critics who looked upon the Torah as a human document. Kohler could write: "The Jew's religion is built not on the Bible nor on supernatural revelation. It rests neither on Moses nor on any other authority. Must we still be cowed by the fears of the thunders of Sinai?" When Kohler became president of Hebrew Union College, one of his first innovations was the introduction of Bible criticism into the curriculum.[2]

His brother-in-law, Emil Hirsch, was convinced that Biblical criticism, which Solomon Schechter characterized as "higher anti-Semitism," had sounded the death knell of Orthodoxy. In an article which he wrote in 1886, he exulted: "Modern scholarship has spoken and its voice cannot be hushed. It has shown that Moses is not the author of the Pentateuch, that Sinai is not the cradle of what is highest and best in Biblical Judaism."[3] Hirsch literally banished the Torah from his Chicago temple when he had both the Torah scroll and the ark removed from his "synagogue."[4] This act was symbolic of the attitude of the whole Reform movement to the Torah. Even those who did not follow Hirsch's lead proclaimed, in effect, that the Torah was no longer their guide and that they had emancipated themselves from what one of them called "bondage to the Bible." A number of years ago the Reform movement published a modern commentary of the Torah. In the introduction, the authors clearly indicated that the commentary "proceeds from the assumption that *Genesis,* as well as the other four books which constitute the Torah, is a human book composed by men."

---

1. Ibid., p. 93. For him, for example, *Deuteronomy* represented a "separate source" from the rest of the Pentateuch. Ibid.
2. Ibid., p. 273.
3. Ibid.
4. Ibid., p. 280.

The implication of this position is clear-cut. The cumulative effect of Geiger's critical work and those of his followers was not only to historicize and relativize every sacred text in Judaism but, even more devastating, it endeavored to rob the Torah of its Divine character. Geiger and his disciples said, in effect, that the text of the Torah was man-made and that it was the product of a given historical milieu. In consequence, what man had made, man could unmake; none of its laws and practices were beyond tampering, modification, or abandonment by any generation. No law was immutable, no text so sacred that it could not be violated by human desire. The position of the Reformers stood in stark contrast to that of the Torah-true community which stands like the rock of Sinai in its proclamation of objective revelation and the binding character of the laws of the Torah, both written and oral, in every generation. Once the Reform movement rejected the revelational character of the Torah, what was the authority for any obligation or norm in Judaism?

This, in fact, is the real point of divergence between Traditional Judaism and that of Reform — the question of authority. The fatal and inherent weakness of those who cut themselves adrift from the historical body of Judaism lies in the lack of valid authority for what they teach and affirm. Apart from private judgment and individual opinion they have no objective criterion for what they tell their people to do or to believe. To talk about sacred Jewish texts as "sources for the spirit of Judaism" as Meyer describes Geiger's approach to the Torah, rather than as timeless imperatives to which we are bound, is to play with words without really providing them with any religious substance. In reality, it is to relativize Judaism and to make it prey to any contemporary fad or subjective whim. In these circumstances, there is no longer an absolute "thou shalt" and "thou shalt not," no longer a religio-moral law that stands eternal and immovable in a fluctuating world of relativity. Man becomes the measure of all things, human and divine. We are back again to the age of the Judges: "There is no king in Israel, every man doeth that which is right in his own eyes."

Yet Geiger, the enemy of traditional Jewish law, had the temerity to demand that he be permitted to act as a rabbi in the Traditional community. His opponents quite correctly responded: "If he likes, let him call himself doctor or scholar, even preacher. Who can object to that? But with what right rabbi?"[1] Geiger endeavored to make the

---

1. Ibid., p. 112.

distinction between his role as a critical scholar and his role as a rabbi of a community who was obligated to observe communal regulations and to treat every custom with respect and veneration. Geiger considered this to be a pragmatic approach to maintain the community and to prevent the Reform movement from becoming just another sectarian movement.[1] However, I believe that David Einhorn characterized it more accurately when he said that "what he appreciated most about America was that unlike in Germany, radical rabbis did not need to be hypocrites. They did not have to play at being Orthodox to avoid offending conservatives within a religious community seeking to serve all.[2]

And for forty years, Geiger strove to take his place on the *Beth Din* of Breslau as a full member. Although he was in favor of the abolition of *chalitzah* and denigrated Jewish divorces, he insisted that he participate in the giving of a *Get* and *Chalitzah*.[3] None of the liberal Jewish historians, including Michael Meyer, seem to realize what an outrage this action constituted in regards to the religious rights and convictions of Torah Jews. Nothing has changed in this respect. The Reform movement, which has trampled underfoot all the religious demands and obligations involved in the *halachic* process of conversion and has made a mockery of its traditional forms, nonetheless demanded, during informal discussions on trying to solve the "Who is a Jew" question, that at least one of their number should be invited to sit on a *Beth Din* which would carry through a proper form of conversion.

## VII.

The ultimate question which has to be answered, in terms of Jewish survival, is, where do these principles and paths lead? Professor Meyer really does not address himself to this major question, although here and there, there are allusions to this crucial problem. Nonetheless, we have the obligation to explore the ramifications of the Reform movement in a spirit of historical realism.

The Reform movement has led itself and its adherents, first and foremost, to a state of religious anarchy. Dr. Maurice Eisendrath, who was the Executive President of the Union of American Hebrew

---

1. Ibid., pp. 112-113.
2. Ibid., pp. 249-250.
3. Ibid., pp. 112-113.

Congregations, the lay body of the Reform movement for many years, once wrote an article in which he said that "bewildered Reform laymen...see before them a plethora of...conflicting practices in Reform synagogues: hats on, hats off; one day Rosh Hashana and two days; kosher kitchens in Reform social halls and ham and bacon in others; *Bar Mitzvah* encouraged and *Bar Mitzvah* barred.... It was the same kind of "57 varieties" of Reform which prompted Isaac Wise to declare in his own day: Every congregation has a leader who reforms as he thinks proper... they call it the free development of the religious idea. I call it anarchy."[1]

In another article which appeared in a major Jewish magazine, Eisendrath called for some kind of minimal code of practice. In his presentation, he conceded that he himself had resisted this idea strenuously as one which would impede and inhibit the free spirit which he felt was the essence of Reform. However, he wrote, that experience "has now convinced me that that which we have today in the Synagogue ... is nothing which resembles true liberty, but it is rather unrestrained license which may soon cause our movement to degenerate into nothing short of self-destructive anarchy."[2] Without a revealed Torah, without a binding corpus of law, without rules and regulations which have their source in respected authority, a deviationist movement like Reform faces the same ultimate fate as that of the Karaites.

More than that, Reform Judaism had produced a Reform Jew for whom the Jewish religion is peripheral to his life, in terms of religious conviction and practice.[3] Whereas a Torah Jew is obligated to ask himself constantly, in so many different contexts, what it is that God and His Law want of him in a given situation, the Reform Jew, unfortunately, barely feels the obligation to take the Jewish dimension into consideration in his confrontation with the major problems of life. Beyond that, a movement which can rationalize its decline, as Michael Meyer does, by reference to the increasing influence of Federations ("Federations, not synagogues, received their more basic and inclusive loyalty") and Israel-oriented organizations, obviously has problems at the very core of its ideology. Can anyone imagine that the commitment of a Torah Jew to maximal Judaism could be watered down by his *K'lal Yisroel* loyalties?

---

1. This article appeared in the *Canadian Jewish News* on May 24, 1961.
2. Cf. M. Eisendrath, "Reform Judaism," in the *National Jewish Monthly,* April 1965, pp. 6ff.
3. Ibid., p. 370.

Quite to the contrary, these larger involvements are an integral part of his overall commitment to Torah Judaism which serve to strengthen his allegiance to his revelationary faith.

Beyond that, the Reform movement, which ostensibly came into being to save the enlightened youth for Judaism, has in fact become, in one felicitous phrase of the late Chief Rabbi of the British Empire, J.H. Hertz, a moving staircase out of Judaism."[1] I remember many years ago, as a student at the Yeshiva, that the late Professor Hyman B. Grinstein, who had written an authoritative history of the Jews of New York, told us that he had examined the membership rolls of the early years of Temple Emanuel. In the course of his scholarly work, he endeavored to trace what happened to their descendants. He found that, with few exceptions, they were no longer affiliated with the Temple or with the Jewish community. It would also be interesting to know the fate of the descendants of Geiger and Rav Hirsch. Rav Hirsch could point to seven generations of Jews practically all of whom are still dedicated to the principles to which he so creatively dedicated his life. One wonders where Abraham Geiger's descendants are today.

The Reform movement, particularly in America, in terms of its principles and structure, has contributed significantly to blurring the lines which separate Judaism from Christianity and, more particularly, its most liberal forms. This was particularly true in regard to the Unitarian Church. It was not unusual for Reform clergy and Unitarian ministers to exchange pulpits or to sponsor joint religious services in which their congregants worshipped together. Some of the leaders of Reform were closely allied to and involved with their Unitarian counterpart in religious and social matters. Eventually, Unitarianism became a threat to the Reform movement because significant numbers in the Reform ranks began to question what, indeed, were the differences between their religion and that of Christian Unitarians, who also considered Jesus to be only a prophet. The result was that the Reform movement was forced to publish tracts delineating the differences between themselves and the Unitarians.[2] I cannot recall a single pamphlet published by any

---

1. Cf. J. H. Hertz, *Affirmations of Judaism* (London, 1927), p. 171.

2. Cf. Meyer, *Response,* p. 289. Another threat to Reform in America was posed by Felix Adler, who contended that Reform Jews were hardly Jews at all. In consequence, he created his Ethical Culture movement, which offered a serious challenge to the Reform Movement. Ibid., pp. 266-267.

Orthodox body covering the same subject or, for that matter, the perceived need to differentiate between Torah Judaism and any Christian sect or group.

It is abundantly clear, against this background, that Reform must bear a significant responsibility for the growth of mixed marriages in the Jewish community; the percentages are frightening. It is true that Reform, in principle, is opposed to mixed marriages. David Einhorn, for example, warned: "To lend a hand to the sanctification of mixed marriages is to furnish a nail to the coffin of the small Jewish race, with its sublime mission." Nonetheless, it has never prevented its members from performing mixed marriages nor disciplined them when they did. In fact, almost half the members of the Central Conference of American Rabbis will perform a wedding ceremony in which one of its participants is a non-Jew; all one has to do is to read the social columns of *The New York Times* on a Sunday or Monday morning and this sickening truth is verified. The fact that in many cases the Reform clergy is simply responding to the pressures of its lay body, which want to give these marriages the stamp of "legitimization," in no way alters the reality or justifies it.[1]

In these circumstances, it is not surprising that the Reform movement has adopted the principle of partrilineal descent in direct opposition to the halachic-historical precedent in which only the Jewish mother determines the genealogy of the child.[2] It is, of course, a reflection of the failure of the Reform movement, a sign of its desperation in terms of the future and a demonstration of its inability to adequately come to grips with a calamity which threatens the foundations of the Jewish people generally, and their movement in particular. They are now reaping the destructive harvest of the noxious seeds of deviation which they planted more than a century and a half ago. There is no room for gloating here, only sadness. With this action they have placed themselves firmly outside the pale of normative Judaism and will force us to create our own *Sefer Yuchsin*, book of genealogy, so that our children will no longer be able to marry theirs without the closest scrutiny.

---

1. Cf. B. Z. Kreitman, "Reform Judaism — a Conservative Point of View," *Judaism*, Winter 1974, p. 28; Meyer, *Response*, p. 371-372.

2. The resolution was adopted at the convention of the Central Conference of American Rabbis in March of 1983.

Thus a movement, which was conceived as a response to modernity and which measured every Jewish obligation and value by the yardstick of contemporaneity, is in danger of ultimate dissolution by the very forces to which it has paid such slavish homage. Professor Meyer's fine scholarship for which he is to be commended, and his sympathetic treatment of his own movement, which is understandable, cannot conceal the historical and theological reality. We have to view this development with great concern, not with exultation; we can ill afford to lose Jews. Now more than ever, in the light of our successes, we should reach out to the deviationist movements with love and urge them to reconsider their ways and to take steps which will lead to more commitment, more observance and more authenticity. Our message to them should be that only those who have cleaved to the God of Israel and have remained loyal to the unadulterated teachings of its laws and traditions in every political and social setting are here to tell the tale to their children and to their grandchildren. That is the real response to modernity.

*Lawrence H. Schiffman*

# From the Caves of Qumran

## *New Light on the History of Rabbinic Judaism From the Dead Sea Scrolls*

THE CENTRAL PROBLEM FACING HISTORIANS OF JUDAISM IN ancient times is understanding how the Judaism we see at the end of the biblical period, circa 400 B.C.E., became the Judaism we see in the *Mishnah,* edited c. 200 C.E., some six centuries later. For the early part of this period, up to the Roman conquest of 63 B.C.E. and the time of Hillel and Shammai afterwards, we have few sources. Some information can be gleaned from the books of the Maccabees, Josephus, a variety of apocryphal texts and from the small amount of material pertaining to this period preserved in Rabbinic texts. Yet these sources afford us little help in our attempt to trace the historical continuity of Judaism from the *Tanach* to the *Mishnah.* For historians, this constitutes a central historical problem.

One of the essential beliefs of the Orthodox Jew is the continuity of the Jewish tradition. This continuity underlies the entire structure of Rabbinic authority which provides the basis in turn for the obligation to observe not only the *Torah Shebichtav* (written law), but the *Torah Sheb'al peh* (oral law) as well. This belief does not imply that nothing has changed. We recognize, in varying degrees, (depending on our different approaches to Orthodoxy) that developments have taken place. These are described in the *Mishnah* and the *Talmud* at length. We believe that these developments are legitimate since they do not break the continuity of the tradition or the oral Torah and since the Torah itself provides the basis for the authority of the sages to sanction such developments as necessary to strengthen Torah practice in times of crisis, to make the transition from the period of prophecy to the cessation of prophecy and later to compensate for the destruction of the Temple and the priestly establishment.

Our tradition has always felt the need to assert its own continuity. The most significant examples of this phenomenon are: the chain of tradition in *Mishnah, Avot* (1:2-2:2), which traces the authority of the oral Torah from Moshe to the son of the *Mishnah's* redactor (collector and editor), Rabbi Yehudah HaNasi (the patriarch);[1] and its partial parallel in the list of the *zugot* (pairs) who occupied the role of *nasi* (patriarch) and *av bet din* (head of the court) in the Hasmonean and early Roman periods in Jewish history, as found in *Mishnah Hagigah* 2:2.

In these two lists, it is fair to say that the greatest emphasis is on that part of the Greco-Roman period most problematical in regard to the claim of continuity. From the end of the Bible through the early Hellenistic period we know from archaeological and literary evidence that little changed in the ancestral way of life of the Jews. That Judaism with which the Jews had been imbued by Ezra, Nehemiah and the last of the prophets served as the basis of their lives, despite Hellenistic influence in their material culture. This changed, of course, with the Hellenistic reform of 175 B.C.E.: the attempt of a group of Hellenizing Jews to assimilate Judaism into the Hellenistic cults and Greek way of life. It is therefore to be expected that even in the aftermath of the Maccabean revolt of 168-164 B.C.E., and the establishment of the Hasmonean dynasty by Jonathan, brother of Judah the Maccabee, in 152 B.C.E., we enter into a period of profound division and sectarianism. This division and sectarianism lasts until the destruction of the Temple. Our sages teach us that this disunity was among the main causes of the failure of the revolt.

However, in the last years before the revolt against Rome, in the time of Hillel and Shammai and their students, in the second half of the first century B.C.E., we again find a trend toward communal unity as the Pharisaic-Rabbinic tradition gained the near universal acceptance of the Jewish people. It was only after the destruction of the Temple that this process was complicated by the sages of the *Mishnah* in the late first century and early second century C.E.

Accordingly, the years from the Maccabean revolt until the period of Hillel and Shammai, those emphasized in the chains of tradition we mentioned above, are precisely the years in which the continuity of our

---

1. Cf. Rambam, *Hakdamah La-Mishnah,* in *Hakdamat Le-Porush Ha-Mishnah,* ed. M.D. Rabinowitz (Jerusalem: Mossad Harav Kook, 1976/7), p. 54.

tradition was most under threat, and for later generations, most difficult to prove historically. Further, even the scant evidence about this period in later Rabbinic sources tell us little about the role of the Perushim (Pharisees), the predecessors of the Talmudic Rabbis, and even from these sources it was possible for many modern historians to minimize this role and to consign it to the pious retrojections of later generations. Josephus helped little in this regard, partly because his information is so brief,[1] and partly because we lacked a sufficient framework in which to evaluate his accounts.

All this was so until the discovery of the manuscripts of the Cairo *genizah* at the end of the last century. Among the many texts and fragments of texts found there was one, called *Fragments of a Zadokite Work* or, alternatively, the *Damascus Covenant,* which would be found later at Qumran among the Dead Sea Scrolls. This text contained two parts; an admonition; and a series of collections of laws on specific topics, such as the Sabbath, courts and testimony, purity and impurity, oaths and vows and relations with non-Jews. These laws responded to the same issues that Mishnaic law discussed, and this fact led some scholars to see the material, falsely we now know, as proto-Pharisaic. A fierce debate ensued about the dating and provenance of this text, and a consensus emerged which dated the text to precisely our period of uncertainty — the mid-second century B.C.E. to the first century C.E. Here, at last, was a non-Rabbinic text which cast some light on the continuity of the Rabbinic tradition. This text already indicated a few significant facts. First, this document straightforwardly argued against the Pharisaic approach, thereby illuminating it. We learned that the Perushim (not named explicitly) were *bonei hachayitz* ("the builders of the wall," cf. *Yechezkel* 13:10), clearly a reference to their making fences around the Torah by adding prohibitions to keep us away from transgression. We also encounter the designation of the Perushim as *dorshei chalakot* (literally, "seekers of smooth things," cf. *Yishayahu* 30:10), clearly aimed at claiming that the laws (*halachot*) of the Perushim are false. In addition, from specific laws in which the sect which authored this document argued against Pharisaic rulings, we can prove that much of the infrastructure of Mishnaic *halachah* was already in place during this period.

---

1. His discussions of the Pharisees are found in *Wars* II, viii. 14 (162-6); *Antiquities* XIII, v. 9 (171-3); XIII, x, 5-6 (288-98); XVIII, i, 2-4 (12-15); *Life* 2 (12); and 38 (191).

Yet the opportunity to gain a much more complete picture of the Judaism of the Hasmonean and early Roman periods came to the fore with the discovery of the Dead Sea Scrolls over the years 1946-56. During this period, a steady stream of texts was unearthed in the Judean desert (mostly by Bedouin and, to a much lesser extent, by archaeologists) which has revolutionized our understanding of this period. While recent controversy has highlighted the unpublished material, the documents already available and those unpublished documents for which extensive information is known, allow us to draw many conclusions regarding the Pharisaic predecessors of the Rabbis.

Indeed, with the collection now before us, we have a library of documents from the Second Temple period. We now know that these documents were collected by the members of a sect which most scholars identify as the Essenes described by the Jewish philosopher Philo of Alexandria (c.20 B.C.E.-50 C.E.), the historian Josephus (c.38-100 C.E.), and some classical authors. We remain uncertain of this identification, however, choosing to postpone judgment until the entire collection has been adequately studied. In any case, this sect occupied a building complex at Qumran, on the western shore of the Dead Sea, in exactly the period we are discussing, from after c.134 B.C.E. through 68 C.E., just after the start of the Great Revolt against Rome of 66-73 B.C.E.[1]

In the collection of this sect were texts which represented not only its own views, but those of a variety of circles which this group regarded as its predecessors, or which it felt were sufficiently close to it to require inclusion of their books.Other manuscripts may have been accumulated for no specific reason at all. Nonetheless, from comparison of these works with the accounts of already known sources, it is safe to conclude that these documents represent a combination of the works of the Qumran sect itself, the biblical heritage of all Israel and the wide variety of books which existed in Second Temple times among various group of Jews.

It is this realization which has radically shifted the focus of Qumran research, in the hands of a new generation of scholars, in the last decade. We not seek to establish, through the study of these texts, the full history of Judaism in this period, not simply the teachings and organizational patterns of a small group of sectarians who repaired to

---

1. See L.H. Schiffman, "The Significance of the Scrolls," *Bible Review* 6, no. 5 (Oct. 1990), pp. 18-27, 52.

the Dead Sea. This means that the value of the scrolls for learning about the Perushim and the Torah is now greatly increased, despite the fact that we can expect to find no primary sources for the Perushim, who eschewed the writing of books of Jewish law or lore. Nonetheless, the anti-Pharisaic polemics and historical allusions in these texts are more than enough to allow us to reconstruct the continuity of Pharisaic-Rabbinic teachings in this period and to demonstrate the dominant role of the Perushim in the affairs of the Temple and the nation for most of the period. Further, we will see that the validity of later Rabbinic traditions can be proven effectively from the Dead Sea manuscripts.

Foremost in establishing these facts is a still unpublished "halachic letter" entitled *Miktzat Maaseh HaTorah* ("Some Legal Rulings pertaining to the Torah").[1] This text is a foundation document of the sect that collected the manuscripts. The text purports to be a letter from the founders of the sect to the Jerusalem establishment, setting forth the reasons for the schism and enumerating some twenty-two *halachot* in which the authors differed with those in control of the Temple. We have determined that the laws of the authors are those of the Tzedukim (Sadducees), the priestly opponents of the Perushim. The text makes explicit reference to the laws we recognize as Pharisaic and Rabbinic. We can demonstrate that the "letter" is to be dated to shortly after the Hasmonean takeover of the high priesthood and the Temple. The authors were Saducean priests unwilling to continue to serve under the Hasmoneans who were following the legal rulings of the Perushim. Hence, we can now prove Pharisaic dominance for the years immediately after the establishment of the dynasty by Jonathan in 152 B.C.E.

Perhaps of more importance are the twenty-two laws. Among them are specific cases in which the opponents of the sect take positions identified in Rabbinic sources as Pharisaic, and others in which their positions appear either anonymously in Mishnaic texts, or attributed to named authorities. Four out of five Pharisee-Sadducee disputes at the end of *Mishnah Yadayim* (4:6-8) appear here. The upshot is that we can show from this text, and I might add from subtle polemics in the *Temple Scroll* as well, that much of the content of Mishnaic *halachah* was in existence at this time, and that *it* — not Sadducee *halachah* — was practiced in the Temple at this time.

---

1. See L.H. Schiffman, "The New Halakhic Letter (4QMMT) and the Origins of the Dead Sea Sect," *Biblical Archaeologist* 53, no. 2 (June 1990), pp. 64-73.

From the material in the *Zadokite Fragments* we mentioned above, of which some ten partial manuscripts were found at Qumran, we can show further evidence for the period of c.134 B.C.E. until the falling out the Hasmoneans had with the Perushim. This dispute is documented in the well-known story of the banquet found in *Bavli, Kiddushin* 66a and in Josephus.[1] Later, there was full-scale conflict between Alexander Yannai and the Perushim. Josephus tells the story of how in 88 B.C.E. the Perushim made common cause with the Seleucid Demetrius III against Yannai. Eventually there was a massacre of Jews by the Seleucids and the Perushim had to change sides, siding with Yannai to rid the country of the foreign armies they had invited in.[2] This story is fully accounted in the Qumran text *Pesher Nachum*, ostensibly a commentary on the *Book of Nachum*, but actually an expression of sectarian ideology. From this document we learn also of the conflict with Yannai and his eventual reconciliation with the Perushim. This reconciliation paved the way for the reentry of the Perushim into a dominant role in last days of Yannai and during the reign of his widow Shlomtzion (Salome Alexandra, 76-67 B.C.E.). Again, the scrolls support the dominant role of the Perushim.

This text goes one step further. Like the *Zadokite Fragments*, it puns the existence of Pharisaic *halachot* and calls the Perushim *dorshei chalakot*. Yet, in addition, it refers to the sect's Pharisaic opponents with the words, *asher betalmud shekaram* ("in whose *talmud* is their falsehood"). Needless to say, they are not referring to the texts we know of as the *Talmudim*, edited much later in the Land of Israel and in Babylonia. Here the use of "*talmud*" is to refer to the way of study which the Pharisaic sages used and which the Rabbis would inherit from them,[3] the dialectic approach to interpreting traditions. This method, the basis

---

1. *Antiquities* XIII, x, 5-6 (288-296). The *Gemara* places the events in the reign of Alexander Yannai (103-76 B.C.E.) whereas Josephus relates them as occurring in the reign of Yochanan Hyrcanus (134-104 B.C.E.). Attempts to harmonize the accounts have often quoted *Bavli, Berachot* 29a, where Abbaye says: *hu Yannai hu Yochanan*. although it is likely that Abbaye only meant to say that both of these Hasmoneans were Sadducees.

2. *Antiquities* XIII, i, 5-XIV, i, 2 (377-383). The parallel in Josephus to the account in *Mishnah, Sukkah* 4:9 of the throwing of *etrogim* shows that this *Mishnah* refers to Alexander Yannai who, because of his conflict with the Perushim, ignored their rulings regarding the water-drawing ceremony.

3. Cf. Rashi to *Sukkah* 28a, *dibbur ha-matchil*: *Gemara*, where the uncensored versions have *talmud* in both *Gemara* and Rashi.

of the tannaitic halachic *midrashim* when practiced on the Bible, and of the *Gemara* when practiced on the *Mishnah,* is proven by the scrolls to have existed in this period.

It is not far from the materials we have been surveying here to the days of the teachers of Hillel and Shammai, as Shemaiah and Avtalyon played roles in the affairs of the nation in the early years of Herod, when he was still only a regional governor (c.45-40 B.C.E.). With the material in the scrolls, of which we have discussed only a small part, we have spanned the years for which we were seeking historical proof outside the Rabbinic corpus for the dominance of Pharisaic tradition in the affairs of the Jewish people and its Temple worship. We have found that much of the content of Rabbinic Judaism can be shown to exist as early as the Hasmonean and early Roman periods. It was this period which we identified as particularly problematic in this regard. We noted that to the Rabbis there was a particular need to claim such continuity but that even they lacked extensive evidence in their corpus of oral traditions, since little survived in the academies from this period. Out of the caves of Qumran have come materials which allow us to prove this continuity in its general outlines. As we learn more and more from the scrolls about the other forms of Judaism which existed in this period — such as Sadduceeism, apocalyptic messianism, Essenism — we will see continuing proof of the view of the Rabbis that this was a period of sectarianism. Yet we will know that throughout this period the Pharisaic tradition continued to develop and played a leading role. We will have uncovered evidence for a stage in the history of our tradition and for that of our people as a whole.

Our century has merited the opportunity of unparalleled research in Jewish history. We have recovered the Cairo *genizah,* which has brought to life the previously dark ages of the geonic period and which has given us outstanding manuscript evidence for Rabbinic and medieval Jewish literature. In the State of Israel archaeologists continue to unearth the secrets of biblical, Second Temple and Talmudic history. We have discovered the Dead Sea Scrolls, as well as the documents from Masada and the Bar Kochba letters. Recently, the great collections of Hebrew manuscripts and Jewish archives of Eastern Europe have opened up to us. Let us take to heart the words of *Devarim* 32:7: "Remember the days of old, study the years of past generations," we will find that the more we learn about our past, the better we are able to meet the challenges of the present and future.

◆§ Holocaust

☐ *Remembering the Living*

*Rabbi Nachum Muschel*

# Remembering the Living

*Over and above remembering the events, heroism and mesirat nefesh of our Kedoshim, we must acquire a fuller appreciation of the nature of the kehillot hakodesh, the sacred communities that made up the tapestry of pre-war Europe. The revival of our rich past is the key to our future.*

I REMEMBER THE SUMMERS I USED TO TRAVEL AS A YOUNG BOY TO my grandfather's farm, there to spend six to eight weeks surrounded by nature, with scores of my cousins. This was our own self-made summer camp, presided over by uncles, aunts and a *Zaide* who generated respect and sweetness, who embraced us with his Torah. After the war they were no more because the tyrants put an untimely end to most of their spiritually rich life . . .

❦ ❦ ❦

I remember . . . as I was returning on the train at the end of the summer, a train ride so exciting to a young boy, my face glued to the windows of the speeding car, I looking out at the fields, the trees, and the rivers . . . Then, about 15 kilometers, two stations away from my home, down there on the horizon would rise a beautiful, shining dome towering over all other structures. It was the dome of the beautiful new *shul* — the synagogue that was built in my town. The dome that was visible from such a distance reminded me that it was not only attractive and distinct, but that our new *shul* was built by the townspeople, most of whom were poor. But, these townspeople had given of themselves with love and devotion to build this synagogue, to underscore with their very lives and acts that one cannot permit a city that houses a proud Jewish community to allow its private roofs to be taller than those of their synagogue. It is this sight of my town that remains forever associated with the skyline of memories of the people that made up my community. Actually, in my city there was no one, not the richest person in town, not the least religious of them, whose home would exceed in beauty or appeal that dignity of the central new *shul,* the *Beit Hashem.*

※ ※ ※

I remember . . . One Friday night, as I returned home with my father from *shul* and we sat down to the Shabbos table with my two older brothers. I was about five or six years old, and I was greatly surprised by the absence of our beuatiful silver candelabras which always adorned the Shabbos table and gave me a special feeling. I could see myself in the shining bases of the beautiful glistening candelabras, but this time my mother had lit candles in very simple brass candlesticks. I was disturbed, and I dared asking my father, "*Tateh,* where are the candelabras? Our beautiful candelabras are not on our table this time." My father motioned to me to wait until after *Kiddush.* When he finished, he sat me down with my brothers and said, "*Kinderlach,* true it is a big *mitzvah* to light Shabbos candles, and it is very special when we adorn the *mitzvah* and add beauty to it. We were taught to do just that in the Torah *posuk* (verse) "*zeh kay-li ve'anvayhu,*" but yesterday I found out that there was a Jew that came from Germany to our town who was arrested by the police for crossing the Polish border without a passport and without a visa. The police were willing to let him out, but they demanded bail of 1,000 *zlotys.* I heard about the case. I also heard that he didn't have the money to provide the bail, and that no one came forward to help. So, I decided," my father continued, "to pawn our candelabras to get 1,000 *zlotys* and to bring the man out of jail. You see," he continued, "Shabbos candles are important, but *pidyon shevuim,* redeeming people from captivity, is by far more important. And the *chachamim* also teach us, '*Bemakom sh'ayn anashim hishtadel l'hiyot ish.*' When no one else steps forward, try to fill the void."

My mind started to wonder, is this what one has to give? Is this how to give? Is this to whom one gives?

❦ ❦ ❦

I remember . . . There were many *shuls* and *"shteiblach"* in my town and significantly they were all crowded — almost the entire city population *davened* there. Every morning, every evening, the streets would empty out of people, and the *shuls* and the *minyanim* would be filled with adults and children, with the strong and the weak. And many among those who *davened* would be the students of the *batei medrash,* the young men who were distinguished in their black garments, adorned with locks of *payot* and the beginning signs of beards framing their faces. I would watch them during their *davening* or learning. I would envy their zeal and enthusiasm and the genuineness which I saw in them as they approached Torah and *tefillah.*

There was one specific young man, a neighbor that I knew from the community. Chaim Shmelke was his name. He was so pleasant, always a smile on his face. He would always find a moment to chat with me, to test me with a riddle, and show me a smiling face while he challenged me to learn something new. One day as I was returning from my school, seeking a shortcut I went through an abandoned little alley. I came by an empty large lot. Suddenly, sounds of young men marching and exercising like a military group reached my ears. I turned in the direction of the sound, and I saw a group of young men dressed in uniforms adorned with Stars of David. They were singing *"Sh'tei Gedot L'Yarden,"* marching, running, jumping and exercising in response to the leader's direction. I came close and, much to my surprise, I recognized that the young men were the same young men I usually saw in the *shul,* but here their dress was different. In *shul* I knew them wearing different garments, different hats. I kept looking, and there was Chaim Shmelke.

I couldn't believe it. I called towards him, "Chaim Shmelke, is that you?" He turned his glance towards me, came to the end of the lot, put his hands around my shoulder, and with his usual pleasant expression, said "Yes, it's me, but don't think that I changed. I am the same young man with the same faith and the same love for Torah and *tefillah* that you know. But, we cannot depend on the thoughtfulness and graciousness of nations. Difficult days are coming for the Jewish people. We must be prepared. We must practice and bring closer the day of our going to *Tzion,* to settle it and to secure the freedom of our people." But he used the word *"cherut"* instead of "freedom" and emphasized it especially, and then he said, "The name of the organization is *Cherut,"* and he pointed to the sleeve where the words *"Cherut Snif Jabotinsky"* were inscribed. "But, my friend," he said, "please don't tell anyone you saw me here. Not everybody would understand." I walked away confused. The word *"cherut"* rang in my ears. People dream about *Tzion* that is under Jewish rule. It embedded itself in the core of my conscience 'til this day, even though Chaim Shmelke's body is no more. It went up in smoke during the Holocaust.

☙ ☙ ☙

I remember . . . this *shul* in which I davened. It was known as the *"Sanzer Kloiz."* About 500 people davened there, pouring out their hearts and deep emotions using beautiful *nusach* chants. They were people of Torah stature. I remember some of them. There was the Royter Alter, an elderly gentleman with grayish reddish hair, glistening eyes, and sweet disposition. I sat in *shul* between him and my father as he pondered all the time on every comment of the *Or HaChaim* of each *parshah*. He would share with me his enthusiasm, his discovery, and demanded of me either to know it or to listen to his explanations.

There was Wolftsche Wechsler, the aristocrat of our town, a respected personality and an outstanding *baal tefillah*. His beautiful *nusach* stirred and moved everybody to piety. To this day I still remember hearing his powerful voice on Rosh Hashanah and Yom Kippur, thundering in the quiet *shul* as he was saying *"hineni he'ani"* and cried out with a scream that filled me with jitters, *"ve'sigar besatan l'val yastineini"* calling up God to "be angry with the Satan who speaks evil of Jews" and then we, the youngsters, would stand around him and observe how literally streams of tears would flow down from under his *talis*.

And then there was Reb Mayer Malter who stood on the *bimah* all the time. During *davening* he would clap his hands above his head, he would jump and bend, *daven* and clap and we, the youngsters, would look and hear the people around him whispering, "He is one of the 'Lamed Vavniks.' "

And, above all, I remember there was the Rav, a picture of distinction, beauty and pleasantness, a *hadras ponim* in every sense of the word. Everybody, everybody paid him great respect. He enjoyed a king's place in our *shul*. He was the grandson of the Sanzer Rebbe, the Divrei Chaim, *zt"l*.

And it happened, one Shabbos as I was leaving the *shul* with my father and reached the gate to go out, I stretched my hand and made an effort to kiss the *mezuzah* that was barely within my reach. I stopped for a minute, and a gentle hand touched me from the back. I turned my face. I stared directly into the face of the *Rav*, Reb Nachum Ephraim, the rabbi of the *kehillah*. He was standing behind me, smiling down at me, looking straight into my face. My blood rushed to my face, and I felt warm all over as he turned to me and said, "I hear that you are attending Hebrew Gymnasium, that Zionist school. I am surprised. You know this is a dangerous road to go." I was dumbfounded for a moment. I was caught off guard, but I gathered strength. I turned back to the Rav and I said, "Rebbe, I learned in the Gemara '*Rav Meir rimon motza, tocho achal klipaso zarak,*' that Rabbi Meir found a pomegranate. He ate its content and discarded the shell." (This statement is quoted in the Gemara as an explanation of why the great scholar, Rabbi Meir, allowed himself to study Torah with Elisha Ben Avuya, who became a heretic.) Reb Nachum Ephraim, without removing his eyes from mine, continued to smile and he said, "*Nochumke, du bist nisht Rabbi Meir.* (You are not Rabbi Meir.)" I was surprised that the rabbi of this big *shul* knew my name. His words pierced my ears. They taunted my conscience. I was confused. To this day, perhaps somewhere in my subconscious, these words still reverberate.

Indeed such was the nature of those saintly communities. The education was all around you. The Torah training embraced you from all ends. Jewish life was the main concern. Everything else was secondary. The mothers did not send their children to go to sleep. Instead they would say, "*Gai lain Krias Shema.*" (Go say *Shema.*) Members of the family were not invited to come to eat, but were reminded to "*Gai vash dich.*" (Go wash for *hamotzi.*) And when the youngsters seemed to have nothing to do, they weren't sent to watch television. Their father or mother would say, "Why are you wasting your time? Take a *sefer* and look into it." And your uncle who met you on the street didn't ask you for the results of the ball game. He inquired what you learned. He wanted to hear a *posuk* quoted. He gave you a brief test, and by the time you came home, your father already had the results.

And, in the tight, small kitchen of your home your mother didn't just cook the food and the aroma didn't just spread all over. But she taught *halachos* in how to take challah, how to salt meat, how to keep a house kosher, how to give *tzedakah*. And if, when she koshered the meat, she found some question in the chicken that she just opened, then you, young man, had a job. You had to take the chicken and go to the *Rav* of the city, to the *Dayan,* and ask a *shailah,* a question, a request for clarification of the law. It was in your home, not in your school where you were taught how to enter the home of the *Dayan,* how to greet, how to ask, how to answer, how to respect, and how to leave. And when you came to the *Rav,* you came into the *beis din shtiebel.* It was full of *sefarim.* The *Rav* would look at your face, ask your name, how old are you? Where do you learn? In this brief exchange, you would discover that the rabbi knows all details about your family. He would open the package and examine the chicken. You would repeat what your mother had said. He would look again. Sometimes he would say, "Good, it's kosher." On other occasions he would say, "Too bad, it's *treif.*" And then he would send you on your way, and he would add, "Remember, give my regards to your father and to your *Zaide.* Tell them it's from Rabbi Mayer Arak."

Reb Mayer Arak, I later learned, was the famous Torah scholar who was well known in the Torah community throughout Poland. These seemingly insignificant details made up the colorful beauty of Jewish life in those *kehillot hakodesh.* For full Jewish life is not one simple component of a general existence that embraces sociological, economic and intellectual facets. Rather, the opposite is true. The sociological, economic and intellectual factors, they are but small details in the total glory of a full Jewish life.

And, today, it's our duty to perpetuate this principle, to emulate this life mode. It is our duty to replicate the beauty of that lost world, to reconstruct it in our homes, in our communities; not merely as a good show with us being the fine actors; not as a mere stimulation which produces but a superficial appearance; but, as a genuine revival of a lifestyle that has depth, that guides, that nurtures, that endures. It is time to transplant into our homes and into our communities the proven sources of strength which withstood the test of time, rather than expend our energies on reviving but the weaknesses, the inconsistencies of the years that the *galut* appended to our demeanor, and that history charged them to be in a category of "*mayshiv chachamim achor.*" As the Gemara explains, sometimes in a period of tragedy, even the wise ones lose their insight, and make errors of judgment.

What must concern us today is the importance of remembering and of cultivating that memory as living experience in the next generation.

Hopefully, we will recognize the powerful call for true *Ahavat Yisrael,* for reaching out to another Jew, to another community, to feel someone else's need and pain, to feel and to act. Recognizing the strength of faith, of genuine faith under all circumstances, the need to allow *emunah* to saturate every aspect of our being is unquestionably another urgent call emanating from the experience of the Holocaust. But, above all and everything else, we have the duty to recognize the mission that is ours, the mission that we must fulfill toward those who perished, towards *Am Yisrael* and towards Hashem Himself.

In this context, it is vital that we acknowledge the feeling that nests deep within our hearts, the feeling that resounds with a question that is barely heard, but a question that persists, the question of "why?" *But not why did it happen, but rather why was I saved?* Why did God spare me? Why did I emerge from the hellish fire? To address this question, it would be helpful to bring to our consciousness the comment made by Harav Kook *zt"l* on the passage that concludes the *tefillot* on Yom Kippur as we say *"Elokai, ad shelo notzarti, ayni k'dai, ve'achshav shenozarti, ke'elu lo notzarti."* Rav Kook explains, "Oh God, I know that I was not destined to be created at another time, at another generation. I could have been, but clearly my essence was not intended for a different time. It was obviously intended for the here and for the now. Your plan, oh God, was to create me and to bring me now into this period, into this time, into this place. Mine, therefore, is the duty to make my being worthwhile here and now. Mine is the duty to negate an existence that would be *'k'eelu lo notzarti,'* as if I were not created at all.

We, too, were placed here and now to fulfill a mission, to replicate, to substitute, to build.

## ~§ Humor

☐ *Is There a Cure for
  Shalach Manot Syndrome*
☐ *A Pre-Schooler Confronts Divinity*

*Charlotte Friedland*

# Is There a Cure for Shalach Manot Syndrome?

IT IS NO REGRET TO BE ON MY *SHALACH MANOT* LIST. IN TWENTY Purims I have not had the heart or nerve to drop anyone from my roster, and new households are added every year. My husband calls it creeping socialism. Presented with the updated inventory year after year, he reminds me, in rising decibels, that our vast food distribution program qualifies for a federal grant. "Make it official," he dares. "File the papers and become a non-profit agency!"

He firmly believes that our bulging register is symptomatic of a compulsion on my part. Nicknamed SMS (*Shalach Manot Syndrome*), the disorder is characterized by the curious inability to cross out a name. Its victims irrationally add more and more recipients to their compendiums, gradually increasing the number and magnificence of the holiday treats.

A quick example. Back about fifteen years ago, we had one daughter, a saucy child with golden curls, registered in the Pre-1A of a local yeshiva. She had two teachers, one for Hebrew subjects and one for English. Who could turn down this little cherub when she innocently asked if we could bring *shalach manot* to her two beloved teachers? The charming notion was carried out and the following year she sweetly asked us to repeat it. Why not?

The precedent had been set. Another daughter and four sons later, we found ourselves setting out each Purim morning to a dozen of the children's teachers and rebbes. When our eldest hit junior high, we cheerfully absorbed the entire departmentalized faculty. No longer was it a matter of one *morah* and the teacher around the block. Now we would load the 24 "teacher *manot*" into the car and deliver them wherever the instructors resided. Who can forget shlepping five miles through the snow to find the obscure address of Madame Antoinette, the high school French teacher? Was she surprised! Was she puzzled! Was she Jewish?

The teachers are just the tip of the Purimberg. Our relatives, neighbors and friends, the children's friends, the friends' children, the neighbors' relatives, all found places in our directory. Each *erev* Purim, our kitchen took on greater and greater resemblance to the national FedEx Center.

Distribution was another matter. With over a hundred destinations, the packages were sorted by neighborhoods into boxes, then piled into the car to be dropped off in the brief period between the morning *Megillah* reading and the *seudah*. While I placidly plucked the ducks for our meal, my husband would go tearing around the neighborhood, racing against the sun to be home in time. Unable to cram the kids and all the cartons into the car at once, he began making two, then three trips.

We bought a van. Not for this purpose alone, of course, but I did have it in mind. Falling prey to SMS, I gleefully calculated how many more baskets we could fit into the expanded cargo space and began to scribble additinal addresses at the bottom of my list. With trembling hands, my husband held a *Mishnah Brurah* under my nose and pointedly read the "bottom line" *Halacha* of *shalach manot* aloud:

"One is required to send to his neighbor . . . two types of cooked food . . . i.e., two gifts to one person."

I thought it was pretty low of him to bring religion into this.

But in my heart of hearts I suspected he was right. SMS is a serious affliction. I sensed that, unchecked, the obsession could wither our bank account, sap our energies and destroy family harmony. I was starting to dream hamantashen. But what could I do?

He warned me that if I could not overcome my weakness myself, he would have to take control. With a ruthless gleam in his eye, he grabbed a pen and X'd out over half the list as I cringed in horror. The first to fall was Madame Antoinette. I cajoled the restoration of one or two rabbis, but he stood firm on the rest.

It was decided then. We could cut the list and risk the displeasure of the world. When Purim came, a mere 50 baskets went out. I was convinced that my friends would never speak to me again, let alone the rest of our ex-recipients. But no. In a merry line, the *shalach manot* appeared at our door, gaily intimating a reciprocal gift. The few "extras" with which we had armed ourselves disappeared in a flash. I wound up frantically shuffling packages as messengers waited at our door. In all, the number of *shalach manot* we gave out that year broke our record. And I'm sure I handed some families back their own goods.

Next year, we resolved, we would have to come up with a better solution. A clever fund-raiser came to our rescue. Recognizing that SMS is a growing epidemic, some worthy institution came up with the idea that we should send them money. In return, they would send out little cards to all of the people on our list (except one) announcing that we have decided to give charity this year, rather than waste our dough on them. At least that was the gist of it.

It sounded like a noble arrangement. We joyously sent in our checks, prepared our single *halachadik* package and sat back. Those nifty cards would stem the usual flow of *shalach manot,* right?

Wrong. We got back a hundred little cards with the same message *and* the customary line-up of gifts at our door! Once again, I found myself in the kitchen, frantically pouring hamantashen from one receptacle to another.

We gave up, resigning ourselves to the idea that our annual *shalach manot* assembly line would wind from the kitchen to the dining room, march into the living room and eventually tumble downstairs into the basement. Snatches of "The Sorcerer's Apprentice" wafted through my house.

Like anyone living with an SMS victim, my husband took pains to keep temptation from my sight. For years he hid those advertisements offering to send *shalach manot* anywhere in the world. I never knew of such a service, until I came across an old magazine that had escaped his secret crypt. Just contemplating the possibilities made me dizzy. The entire planet opened up for the Purim gift-giving! Imagine the surprise on the face of Tanta Ruthie in Israel! What about Oscar in Australia, and Cousin Dina, Shamir, Gorbachev . . .

Then again, anything sent by an agent would not have our personal style to it. Style is very important in SMS. It's not enough just to send something. That something must convey tasteful self-expression.

A few years ago, you will observe, the humble paper plate was replaced by the disposable aluminum pan. Then came reed baskets;

then baskets in a prismatic spectrum of colors. Next came those chic miniature shopping bags and finally tins with vivid Florentine motifs. This is where I get off. A patent leather shopping bag is just not *me*. And I am definitely a basket, not a tin.

When my children informed me that our *shalach manot* had become boring, we looked for frills to dress them up. What we found in the stores shocked even me. From the dark depths of crass commercialism had emerged new concepts in *hidur mitzvah*. Foils and cellophanes and mother-of-pearl; doilies in silver, gold and copper; ribbons and bows of tinsel and velvet. We bought it all.

But I drew the line at plastic grass. The kids thought it was cute, but I knew better. I had grown up Out There and I recognized the "new" adornment to be nothing more than recycled stuff. I piously rejected the grass. In fact, I would refuse to buy a *shalach manot* chocolate bunny, even if they stick a yarmulke in it.

The contents of our baskets (sans grass) seem comparatively mundane, despite our efforts to keep up with the trends. When I was a child, we used to lovingly place a couple of bakery hamantashen, a fruit and a little bottle of grape juice onto a plate and deliver it with pride.

Now that I am an adult, all of that has changed. When I sent out my six ounces of grape juice, I was presented with wine. The following year, I upgraded to champagne and got back a big Sabra. I shipped off the Sabra and in came Baron Herzog Cabernet Sauvignon '72.

In exchange for our humble hamantashen we received a mouthwatering array of cakes, pies, and trendy tarts, all home-baked. The rustic jam arrived next and then the imported caviar. When I opened the quiche and homemade spaghetti, I knew I was dealing with a deadly case of GSMS (Gourmet SMS) and promptly called it quits.

Just between us, I picked up the latest tip this year. Go oat. I predict a healthful supply of oat bran hamantashen and other high fiber pastries masquerading as traditional Purim treats. Tucked alongside them look for the inevitable molded chocolates shaped like a gragger, a Megillah, or a portrait of the Queen herself.

One last word about remuneration. Yes, tipping. Once again hearkening back to the old days, I remember delivering *shalach manot* for my parents and being rewarded at each stop with a smile and a thank you. Maybe even a compliment on my costume. It was nice.

Today I open the door, accept the package, and the kids stand there with their palms up, like bellhops. The first time it happened, I started vacantly at their upturned, expectant faces and asked if something was wrong. Their expressions fell and they trudged back to their car.

I discovered my faux pas when my own children came home from our *shalach manot* rounds, their pockets bulging.

"How did it go?" I asked.

"Oh, we did pretty well," they grinned. Is this the sound of a mitzvah? The pockets were turned inside out and quarters, silver dollars, even bills scattered on the table. Astounded, we began to count up their loot.

"Does everyone give tips like these?" I inquired.

"Some more, some less," came the savvy answer. "It helps if you look real cute."

We gathered up the tips and put them in an envelope marked "Tuition." With just one or two more Purims a year, we might have it.

Is there no solution? Is there no cure for SMS? I have given this matter considerable thought and have concluded that it is too late to save myself. For you, however, there is a way out: Send me some money. In return, I will fax a copy of this article to everyone on your list! For a small extra fee, I will inscribe your name across the top and print in red letters, "Do Not Send *shalach manot* to This Person."

If we can get this idea going as a national movement, SMS could become a thing of the past. But send only money. No *shalach manot,* please.

*Elisheva Schlam*

# A Pre-Schooler Confronts Divinity

W ITH AN UPTURNED BOTTOM LIP AND A FLIP OF HER DARK black curls, my toddler proclaimed, "I'm not saying *Shema* to Hashem," as I tucked her in one recent evening.

This from the mouth of a child whose parents boast a combined 32 years of religious education? Am I raising a heretic? Has she rejected God at the ripe old age of three?

Frantic, but trying to evoke the voice of reason, I put the videotape in my mind on rewind and stopped it at Sinai Hospital the day my progeny was born. Is this the fate of mothers who don't opt for "rooming in?" All I wanted was a little shut-eye those first few nights. Was I wrong to presume the bonding or education process or whatever could commence three days later?

I fast-forward to my daughter's *Kiddush* celebration. Maybe I had been too preoccupied with greeting guests and preparing food and had not fully concentrated on the spirituality of the moment.

On and on, through milestones in her young life, my internal video raced, from leaving her as a nine-month-old for my full-time job, to the time she got lost in Macy's Herald Square.

And then, I ejected my mental videocassette and thought back to a conversation of earlier this week. Atara and I had settled comfortably on the living room couch to read *Torah Shapes*. We reached age 5 and there, in vivid color, were the holy Tablets encased in a bold red square. Next to the square was a drawing of a bearded man with sandals and what appeared to be a white kimono. I assumed this was a rendering of *Moshe Rabbeinu* and got ready to turn the page. But that was not to be.

Atara pointed to the figure, opened her baby browns and asked, "Is this Hashem?"

It wasn't just an idle query. She learned forward to look into my face and her eyes were saying, "Aha! I finally nabbed him — right in this pink and yellow cardboard book." At the time, I gently told her that it was not Hashem, but *Moshe Rabbeinu*, and moved on.

But now her unsatisfied look was coming back to haunt me. The abstract concept or explanation of Hashem that had been offered until now didn't seem to be working for her. She was hoping to find something her stubby little fingers could touch and hold and call Hashem.

How do you discuss the ideals of a Higher Power and the precepts of faith with someone whose major life works have been graduation from diapers to pull-ups and overcoming the bottle urge (if only during the day)?

I wasn't too sure of the answer to the above question, but I considered that she had already managed to absorb to some extent the concepts of love, death and, well, money. Those were abstracts. There had to be some component of *Hashem* that could be apparent to her as well.

I stroked her back, running my fingers around the outline of one of the 101 Dalmations adorning her nightgown. Defiantly, she turned, stood up and gazed out the window. It was that hazy, twilight evening time when you can actually see the switchover from day to night, if you watch carefully. Still in an upright position, Atara wanted to know why it was turning dark.

Well, there's an opening, I thought. I bent her to a sitting position and explained that little children need to go to sleep each night after a long, hard day of playing. *Hashem* makes it dark especially at bedtime so they can close their eyes and sleep.

At that moment, something seemed to click and my answer elicited a reluctant smile. Maybe it was recognition of the story of the six days of creation that her playgroup *Morah* had so painstakingly reviewed no less than 800 times. Or possibly, she was struck by the natural order of the world and appreciated Hashem's sensitivity to her need for ten hours of darkness each night.

I'll never know exactly what triggered her smile of acceptance, but that simple statement seemed to clarify some of the conflicts that plagued her busy little mind. I assume we'll encounter a few more hitches along the rough and tumble path that lies ahead, but for now, at least, Atara's gone back to saying *Shema*.

# ❧ Jewish Thought

☐ *Illuminating Faith*
☐ *Kabbalah as Experience: Moshe Idel's*
    *Critique of Gershom Scholem*
☐ *Fundamentalism Reconsidered*
☐ *To Radically Alter Our Lives*

*Dr. Yehuda Gellman*

# Illuminating Faith

*An analysis of
Rabbi Avrohom Yitzchak
Hakohen Kook's Orot Ha-emunah*

OURS IS AN AGE OF EXTERNALS — GLITTER AND TINSEL. How do you look? How do you talk? How do you dress? What do you profess to believe? What do you eat? If that's o.k., then you're o.k. The world is much too complicated for us to look deeper, to see beneath the surface; not enough time, and not enough patience.

Also, there are too many dangers. We must stay strong to keep the outside out. We must be able to easily identify the enemy, and our friends. We need constant encouragement that we are in the right place. We want to be able to check often and quickly, to make sure we are not being insidiously infiltrated by the outside. How do you look? How do you talk? What do you eat? That's enough for me. I am secure.

... And in my security, I succumb to a terrible danger, the danger of superficiality, of inaction, and of weakness of the will.

... And the world grows cold for me, and loses its excitement and its freshness, as I move along the surface of life in increasingly intricate

---

*Editor's Note*: Dr. Gellman's review is a succinct summary of many key points in *Orot Ha-emunah.* However, in some instances, in order to grasp Rav Kook's full meaning, it is necessary to read the full text of the pertinent passages as well as to compare them to other related passages in the corpus of his works.

patterns, but always moving, alas, only on the surface. No adventure for me, no discoveries, no surprises.

Ours is an age of lack of self-esteem. We don't trust ourselves. We want to be protected, for we feel small, afraid, far from the center of spirituality. In being humble, we think we are modest, but really we are weak. In being excessively cautious, we think we are being exceptionally *frum,* but really we just don't trust ourselves. We see ourselves as vulnerable enclosures whose boundaries must be clearly demarcated, whose territory must be secured, whose way in the world must be defensive.

"Excessive fear of sin destroys the goodness in a person, and makes of him a lowly creature, who does nothing but lie there, shaking." So writes Rabbi Abraham Isaac Kook, in the opening paragraph of *Orot Ha-emunah.*[1] "A person must believe in his life, in both his physical and moral powers." The lack of *emunah* in oneself is the greatest of all the curses in the Torah, "Your life will be in the balance . . . and you will not believe in your life."[2] You will be plagued by self-doubt (Your life will be "in the balance") and lack inner confidence. Because of this inner anxiety, "In the morning you will say, 'Who will give evening?' and in the evening, 'Who will give morning?'"[3] "*Katnut ha-emunah,*" "insufficient *emunah,*" is a lack of confidence in oneself, and "comes from the inability to raise one's own self-worth to the point of understanding how he is deserving of the Divine Greatness."[4]

When we believe in ourselves we are not afraid — cautious, yes, but not afraid.[5] And when we are not afraid we can look at the world again, and see in it the kaleidoscopic possibilities of existence. We can look outside, and see beneath the surface. And beneath that surface, we may even find something of ourselves.

※ ※ ※

---

1. *Orot Ha-emunah,* edited and arranged during the lifetime of Rav Kook by Rabbi Moshe Gorwitz, from Rav Kook's writings and by his request (Jerusalem, 5745). Quotations are cited here by page and paragraph number. The above quote is at 1.1, that is, page one, first paragraph of the page.
2. *Devarim* 28:66.
3. *Devarim* 28:67.
4. *Orot Ha-emunah* 106.2. See *Menachot* 103 b; and see Rav Zadok Ha-cohen, *Sefer Zichronot,* Section I, for a similar interpretation.
5. See Rav Kook's *Midot Hara'ayah,* p. 144 for the distinction between caution (*zehirut*) and fear (*pachad*).

*Orot Ha-emunah* was written by Rav Kook more than 50 years ago, but only now has been published for the first time. Who can guess why it has been withheld from the public all these years? Not a book in the usual sense, but a loose collection of separately written paragraphs constituting a kind of spiritual diary, *Orot Ha-emunah* is one great call not to be afraid, to look below the surface, and to ascend thereby to great spiritual heights. "When a person believes in himself he discovers great contentment in his spiritual endeavors, and ascends upward."[1] In this work Rav Kook explores *emunah* by comparing and contrasting it with *kefirah* (atheism, denial), *avodah zarah* (idol worship), and "minut," which is the term favored by him to refer to Christianity, and by examining its relationship to the doing of mitzvot, and to general culture.

From these writings there emerges a profound teaching that belief in oneself is conceptually and existentially inseparable from *emunah* in God. For first and foremost, for Rav Kook, *emunah* is a state of being. As he writes elsewhere, "*Emunah* is the most basic self-revealing of the essence of the soul."[2] And this self-revealing is really the Divine within us made manifest: "Too much fear spoils *emunah*, because one doesn't trust himself and his understanding, thereby diminishing his awareness of the Divine spark in his soul."[3] The essence of *emunah* is an awareness of the perfection of the Infinite and that "whatever [experience of the infinite] enters the heart is but a minute spark of what can be imagined."[4] *Emunah*, then, is a self-affirmation in which one experiences one's own self-revealment as the revealing of the Divine within. *Emunah* is a state of being.

It follows that *emunah* is not constituted by an act of "belief" or by a linguistic, cognitive affirmation. The latter are important both as external expressions of *emunah*, and as a means of bringing to *emunah*.[5]

But even in their absence, *emunah* can be alive. And more, *emunah* can live even where there is no conscious awareness of one's self-divinity and even when one denies the Divine: "Sometimes you will find a *kofer* with an inner, shining strong *emunah*, flowing from the source of transcendent holiness, stronger than a thousand believers, who are

---

1. *Orot Ha-emunah*, 100.4.
2. See *Ma'amarei Hara'ayah* of Rav Kook, p. 70.
3. *Orot Ha-emunah*, 100.4.
4. Ibid., 41.4.
5. Ibid., 20.1 and 31.3.

"small of *emunah.*"[1] How is this possible? Because "the inner spiritual basis of the holiness of *emunah* transcends all language." A *kofer* can manifest the Divine power of his being even while denying faith with his mouth, and a believer can be lying, shaking with fright, all the while proclaiming his faith through chattering teeth.

*Kefirah* can itself even emanate from holiness. This can happen for example, when linguistic affirmations are rejected precisely because they are sensed to be inadequate, as but a weak shadow of the power of being. Thus, "there is denial (*kefirah*) that is like consent, and consent that is like denial."[2] Inadequate articulations of Judaism may force their own rejection, out of the depths of holiness. If we are to return the *kofer* to the practice of Torah, our elucidations of Torah contents must be adequate to the power of his being.[3]

Rav Kook's concept of *emunah* provides hope for our seemingly faithless world. For, "There are many *apikorsim* who are deniers, in accordance with the standards of *Halacha.* However, when we examine their soul we will discover in them a connection to the Divine content, in a hidden form. And that is why in our[4] generation there is a tendency toward merit and kindness even toward absolute deniers."[5]

That does not at all mean that it does not matter for Rav Kook if you are atheist or believer, as long as the inner *emunah* manifests its power in you. Far from it. Linguistic affirmations of faith lead in the direction of transcendent truth, whereas protestations of atheism lead in the direction of falsehood and inauthenticity. He who is faithful to

---

1. Ibid., 21.2.

2. Ibid., 25.2.

3. Ibid., 25.3, where Rav Kook calls for new "explanations" of Torah. The same passage occurs with modifications in *Orot Hakodesh,* volume I, p. 152. I believe the passage in *Orot Ha-emunah* to be the more accurate of the two.

4. Note: See *Iggrot,* Volume II page 188, where Rav Kook compares the deniers of prior generations who were in fact by and large lost souls, with those of *Ikvoso D'meshicha* (messianic period), who are "Good from within and bad from without," in the words of the *Tikkune Zohar.*

In a private conversation, Dr. Gellman pointed out that Rav Kook's hopeful attitude to the contemporary irreligious Jew has ample precedent. See *Baal HaTanya: Likkutei Amorim,* chapter 42; *Likkutei Torah* beginning of *Parshas R'ey. Sfas Emes* to *Succos* page 91B and 104A. *Shem Mishmuel Rosh Hashana* page 31 in volume on *Moadim.*

5. Ibid., 18.3.

conceptual assertions of *emunah* has a covenant with God that he will merit that *emunah* which is beyond conceptualization and language. From that high vantage point he will apprehend the correspondence between the elements of the conceptualized *emunah* and its transcendent counterpart.[1]

Yet sometimes, when we look outside, and beneath the surface, we do see something of ourselves.

Idol worship, too, in its deepest essence knows the power of being of *emunah,* but covers it over with corruption and evil: "In the filth of *avodah zarah* great is the spirit of *emunah,* in its wildness and coarseness, its frenzy and horselike power."[2] *Avodah zarah* knows the visceral, immediate engagement with the Divine in the world, and total, passionate, self-actualization and self-affirmation.

This "core of holiness'[3] in *avodah zarah* is passed into the Jewish people via Abraham, who began as a worshiper of idols. It is written "From the womb of the morning, yours is the dew of your youth."[4] *Bereishit Rabba* interprets this as being addressed to Abraham. He too was afraid and self-doubting, because of those years he had spent in the worship of idols.[5] He is told, "Just as dew is the blessing for the world, so too are you a blessing for the world." We might think the *Midrash* means to encourage Abraham *in spite* of his worshiping of idols. But Rav Kook quotes the *Midrash* differently: "Just as dew is a "good omen" for the world, just so, those years you worshiped idols are a good omen for the world."[6] The source of dew is in the heavens. Then the dew transcends to the ground, to a lowly place, to be raised heavenward by the rays of the morning sun. Just so, the core of *avodah zarah* is in the

---

1. Ibid., 31.1-31.3. In kabbalistic terms, conceptualized *emunah* corresponds to the *sefirah* of *Malchut,* and the *emunah* above articulation to *Binah,* the "higher freedom."

2. Ibid., 3.3. I have corrected errors in the text, although the same errors appear in the manuscript, a copy of which I have been privileged to view.

3. See Rav Kook's *Arpalei Tohar,* p. 32, and *Iggrot,* volume II, p. 43.

4. *Psalms* 110:3.

5. *Breishit Rabba* 39.8. See also, *Midrash Tanchuma Lech Lecha.* The Midrash apparently follows the view that Abraham recognized God only when a fully mature man, and not at age three.

6. *Orot Ha-emunah* 77.3. These lines occur in the manuscript, but are inadvertently omitted in the printed edition.

holiness of *emunah,* but *avodah zarah* plummets to the lowest forms of human existence from there to be raised back to its source, heavenward. The passion and engagement that *avodah zarah* encompasses in self-affirmation is taken up by Abraham into the true religion. *Avodah zarah* is returned to its source.

※ ※ ※

Our history "begins in disgrace, and issues in praise." For in the beginning "Worshipers of idols were our forefathers." The process of history brings the praise *out of* the disgrace. Thereby, and "God had brought us close to His service."[1]

Abraham first came to knowledge of God via contemplation of the world. Had it not been for the passion and engagement in the world which he inherited from *avodah zarah,* his religion might have been nothing more than an arid exercise in abstract philosophical reasoning.[2] The power of *Halacha* with its life engagement traces its ancestry back to Abraham, the father of *emunah.*

Christianity, on the other hand, knows nothing of the power of life of ancient *avodah zarah.* Since it arose after the desire for *avodah zarah* was nullified, it is empty of life at its core.[3] At its center, instead, stands an abstract, philosophical system of cold reasoning. As a result, "the general religion of the nations receives a form of shaking and weakness, which does not mix well with the breadth of life, but instead assumes the form of dark monasticism, which is less able to go with life than any sort of *avodah zarah.*"[4]

Kohelet says, "And I find more bitter than death the woman, whose heart is snares and nets, and her hands as bands; whoever pleases God shall escape from her, but the sinner is trapped by her."[5] Our Rabbis identify this woman with "minut," that is, Christianity.[6] Thus, Rav Kook writes: "The Epicurean *kefirah* is death, whereas the distortion of *emunah* is worse than death."[7] What is the "Epicurean *kefirah?*"

---

1. See Rav Kook's *Olat Re'iya,* volume II, pp. 260-261. In practical terms, Rav Kook warns us of the "nothingness' of *avodah zarah.* See *Orot Ha-emunah* 5.2.
2. See first source cited above in note 21.
3. See Rav Kook's *Eder Hayakar,* p. 30.
4. Ibid., p. 31.
5. *Kohelet,* 7:26.
6. *Sifrei, Shelach,* section 70.
7. *Orot Ha-emunah,* 6.2.

Epicurus taught an austere physicalist ontology, including only physical entities and physical interactions between them. He was an arch anti-metaphysical philosopher. On the other hand, Christianity, the "distortion of *emunah,*" knows the intricate structures of the "science of God," systematic theology. Yet Epicureanism is death, while Christianity is worse than death! To be anti-life is worse, far worse, than being anti-metaphysical! The power of life can exist hidden, deep within the dead body of the anti-metaphysician, to be aroused and awakened in a resurrection of the dead. But there is no life at all in the forces of anti-life.[1] For this reason, Divine Providence has allowed the spread of materialist philosophies of *kefirah,* as a defense against something far worse.[2]

Because so divorced from life, Christianity makes impossible demands that have no chance of being implemented. She has no concern for the realities of life. "Therefore, she says to offer the other cheek in return for a slap. Obviously, people can only believe that this is a sublime trait, but cannot attain it."[3] The result is inevitable failure and perpetual guilt. In a subtle inversion, *chesed* metamorphising into *din*! The aim of Christianity then becomes the alleviating of guilt, by the granting of forgiveness. But the forgiveness is not a prelude to a holier life. "Forgiveness becomes the whole goal."[4] The believer/sinner (for they are one) needs the Church to receive forgiveness. "By the sinner is trapped by her."

To believe that which can be practiced is the special genius of Jewish spirituality. This is the "balance of the Torah" which knows how to weigh the ideals against possibility of implementation.[5]

*Emunah* is an ineffable state of being. How does it relate to the details of Torah practice? "*Emunah* is the highest poetry (*shira*) of the world, with its source in the Divine nature in the depths of the

---

1. Rav Kook's critique of Christianity in *Orot Ha-emunah* bears an uncanny resemblance to Friedrich Nietzsche's critique of Christianity (and also of Judaism!) in *Genealogy of Morals,* and elsewhere.
2. *Orot Ha-emunah,* 6.2 and 6.3.
3. Ibid., 94.3.
4. Ibid., 16.2. It should be kept in mind that Rav Kook's experience with Christianity was largely confined to the Catholic Church in Poland.
5. Ibid., 94.3. The reader might wish to ponder the question whether excessive religious demands within our community are always intended to raise our spiritual level, or sometime are really devices for creating guilt.

soul."[1] High poetry is unstructured, without meter and rhyme. It has total freedom of imagination without restrictions. It is a spontaneous outpouring of individual creativity.[2] The Torah is the translation of the higher poetry into measure and beat, into conventions and rules. Torah is the poetry of *emunah* in its practical rhythm. "There are those filled with the glory of the poetry, who are pained by the restrictions of the practical life, but they accept the yoke of the kingdom of heaven.[3]

But there are also impatient souls "who cannot bear the measure, and they are full of rebellion. But even in this rebellion the Divine pleasantness lives, albeit in an unclear way."[4,5]

Rab Kook once wrote "Just as there are laws in poetry, there is poetry in laws."[6] When one loves a poem, he does not experience the restrictions of its form. The possibility exists to live a life of mitzvot as a form of poetry.

The poetry of *emunah* is not to be found exclusively in Torah. It informs every aspect of human endeavor that is "Divine creativity":[7] "The pure understanding sees the appearance of the Divine in every improvement of life ... It is all included in Divine creativity."[8] The realization of our humanity is included in the power of *emunah* — "Everything is included in her, and everything exists in her."[9]

---

1. Ibid., 88.2. The word *"shira"* is sometimes used by Rav Kook to mean "song" as in *Arpalei Torah,* p. 38, and sometimes to mean "poetry." I translate it here as "poetry" since in *Orot Ha-emunah* 40.2, the *"shira"* of *emunah* is contrasted with prose. It may be that Rav Kook intends the term to denote that which is common to both song and poetry.
2. On occasion Rav Kook referred to himself as a "free poet," meaning he was free from the constraints of the usual conventions of poetry. See my Hebrew article, 'Aesthetics in the Thought of Rav Kook," in S. Rosenberg and B. Ish-Shalom, eds., *Yovel Orot* (Jerusalem, 1987).
3. *Orot Ha-emunah,* 88.2.
4. They experience the ineffable level of the higher poetry, but fail to perceive that in their world the highest poetry must be transferred into the world of action. The higher light must pass through the prism of the world in which we exist.
5. Ibid., 88.3.
6. Quoted in *"Pirurim and Pitgamim,"* p. 23.
7. Strictly speaking, this is not Rav Kook's view, in light of his assertion in *Orot HaTorah* that the inner essence of all "human improvements and *chochma"* is the light of Torah (chapter 12,4). See also *Orot Ha-emunah* 69.1, line 9, where it is also indicative that the essence of *chochma* is in Torah.
8. *Orot Ha-emunah* 44.1.
9. ibid., 95.2.

❀ ❀ ❀

The bifurcation of reality into that which is the Lord's, and that which is Caesar's, originates in the anti-life of Christianity which severs the material world from its foundation of holiness.[1] This poison has also infected the body of the Jewish people. For there are those amongst us who in their zealousness to fight evil believe we must suppress science, arts, and political activity because they are not part of the Divine aspect of the world. Hence, "They hate culture, the sciences, and statecraft, in Israel and in the world."[2] This is a lack of *emunah*.

The Jewish people excels at integrating opposing forces into a balanced whole, the power of Torah, the power of *Tiferet*. Therefore we must not stifle any talent, any human propensity, from developing to its fullest. It must first be allowed to exhaust the individuality buried within it. Once its full nature has been revealed and drawn out, then, and only then may the Jewish genius for integration and synthesis, including the rolling back of excessive development, be brought into play.[3] If we impede the power of human creativity in the name of "faith" we sin against *emunah*.

"The enslavement of human reason and its silencing destroys the world. The holier the source of enslavement, the greater the damage."[4]

What are we to do? It is not enough for intellect and *emunah* to dwell side by side within our soul. For we must not allow *emunah* to settle in a corner of ourselves where our intellectual powers have not reached. Our *emunah* would then be weak, and not worthy of us. We must unite intellect with *emunah,* so that in proportion to our intellectual achievement, *emunah* will be raised up.[5]

"This is true not only of the individual, but also of the nation in general, and of the whole world, in the generality of humankind."[6]

These are the teachings of Rav Kook in *Orot Ha-emunah*.

... and the world grows warm for me, as the increasingly intricate patterns of reality reveal themselves in the rays of the morning sun, in an ongoing adventure of discovery. *Orot Ha-emunah* — the lights of *emunah*.

---

1. Ibid., 69.1.
2. Ibid., 43.4.
3. Ibid., 24.3. See *Orot Hakodesh,* volume I, p. 189, for more on the dialogue between individual development and the process of integration and balancing.
4. *Orot Ha-emunah,* 67.2.
5. Ibid., 57.2.
6. Ibid., 57.3.

*Micha Odenheimer*

# Kabbalah as Experience: Moshe Idel's Critique of Gershom Scholem

FOR SIXTY YEARS, THE STUDY OF KABBALAH IN SECULAR universities around the world has been dominated by the theories and approach of one man: Gershom Scholem. Scholem, a brilliant, charismatic German Jew, emigrated to Jerusalem from Berlin in 1923, and lived there until his death eight years ago. Scholem virtually founded the academic discipline of the study of Jewish mysticism. His historical studies span the entire gamut of post-Biblical Jewish history, from the Rabbinic age until *Hassidism* and beyond.

For many intellectuals, Jews and gentiles alike, Scholem's studies and determinations have been their sole source of knowledge about Kabbalah. In most modern works on Jewish history, Scholem's theories — such as the idea that the Kabbalah of the ARI was a response to the traumatic exile of the Jews from Spain, and that the Shabbatean movement was made possible by the mass dissemination of the ARI's Kabbalah — are treated as if they were established facts.

Recently, however, Moshe Idel, a young professor at the Hebrew University, where Scholem taught, has shaken the academic world by challenging many of Scholem's basic notions. The controversy surrounding the work of Moshe Idel has spilled out of the classroom and the learned journals of history into popular newspapers and magazines in both Israel and the United States. Idel's revisions (his major work, published by Yale University Press in 1989, is called *Kabbalah: New Perspectives*) have led to his portrayal in the press and in portions of the academic world as a new wave academic, a rebel against the authority of established wisdom, a heretic in the temple of the academy. Ironically, Idel's "heretical" ideas have brought academic research closer to the Jewish tradition's own conception of Kabbalah than anyone would have previously guessed possible.

Orthodox Jews have traditionally looked at the study of Judaism in the secular university with some degree of suspicion — and rightfully so. The founding fathers of the academic discipline of Jewish studies were German Jewish products of the Enlightenment, who had internalized the ideas and values of 19th-century German culture in which they lived. They were certain that their era and civilization represented the highest point of moral and spiritual development in human history, and they judged all previous cultures and eras through the lens of pure reason — the radiant emblem of the Enlightenment. They wrote with condescending approval of those parts of Judaism which conformed to their notion of rational thought; what did not fit easily into their preconceived categories was suppressed or ridiculed. Their social ideal was the integration of Jews and Judaism into German culture as a whole; for most 19th-century German-Jewish scholars, Judaism itself was not a living option. Moritz Steinshneider, one of the founders of "The scientific study of Judaism" ("der Wissenschaft des Judentums"), is once reported to have said: "Jewish scholarship has one task left: to give the remains of Judaism a decent burial."

Gershom Scholem was himself a rebel against Wissenschaft's smug and stifling conception of Judaism. The Wissenschaft scholars held Kabbalah in particular contempt; they saw mysticism in general, and Kabbalah in particular, as expressions of the superstitious and antirational forces from which the Enlightenment had come to redeem mankind. Scholem, in turn, derided both Wissenschaft and German Jewish culture in general. He believed that German Jewry's embrace of German culture and identity was a betrayal of their Jewishness, and that their "rational" analysis of Jewish history and thought denuded Judaism of its richness, depth, and vitality. In choosing the study of Kabbalah as his life's work, Scholem in effect proclaimed that in just that stream of the Jewish tradition that the Wissenschaft scholars had condemned as worthless, the inner core of Judaism's life and the hidden mainspring of Jewish history could be found.

A young German Jew in post-World War I Germany could rebel against the bourgeois, assimilationist tendencies of his parents' generation in one of three ways. He could become a communist or socialist — although this choice meant an implicit acceptance of assimilation. (Scholem's older brother chose this path.) He could become an observant Jew, or he could become a Zionist.

Scholem considered the possibility of becoming an Orthodox Jew for some time. In Berlin, he studied *Talmud* with a teacher associated with Agudat Yisrael, but eventually he decided against Orthodoxy. "For some reason, I just couldn't see it," Scholem once said about the possibility of becoming *halachically* observant. Perhaps for the same unarticulated reason, Scholem, having arrived in Jerusalem, refused an opportunity to study Kabbalah with a living Kabbalistic master — a member of the famous Beit El school in the old city of Jerusalem. "When I met him I was 26 and he was about 70 years old. I told him I wanted to study Kabbalah,.." Scholem had said, in an interview published in his book of essays *Explications and Implications*. "He looked at me for a long time, checking me out. He looked at the lines of my forehead, and only afterwards did he speak to me. He said: 'I am willing to teach you, on one condition — that you don't ask questions.' This made a great impression on me. I said to him, 'I have to think about it.' Afterwards, I told him that I couldn't do it. He was an amazing Jew. He had a radiant face. He made a great impression on me." But despite this great impression, Scholem decided to study Kabbalah on his own.

Scholem's choice of Zionism was not only a political position, but a spiritual stance — and it could therefore not be combined with Orthodox observances or beliefs. Zionist, for Scholem, was not just a response to anti-Semitism or an expression of Jewish nationalism. Zionism was the fruit of the inner, hidden dynamic of Jewish history, and contained within it the seeds of Jewish religious renewal. Scholem did not see *Halacha* or traditional Orthodoxy as playing any role of importance in this renewal. In Scholem's paradoxical formulation, it was *secular* Zionism that was the key to the spiritual and religious renaissance that he desired and predicted for the Jewish future.

Scholem's theories about Kabbalah cannot be separated from his Zionism. Scholem himself thought that Zionism would transform Jewish studies by freeing scholars from the necessity of apologetics, and from gentile and even anti-Semitic views of Judaism whose influence in the Diaspora was almost unavoidable. Scholem, presumably, did not take into account the possibility that the ideological weight of secular Zionism might itself have a distorting affect on the study of Jewish history and religion. Yet Scholem's Zionism may be the hidden key to understanding many — though not all — of the points over which Idel and Scholem contend.

Four of the major points on which Idel has challenged Scholem can be described as follows:

## 1. The origin of Kabbalah:

> One of Scholem's central assertions is that Kabbalah itself was the result of the exposure of Rabbinic Judaism to Gnosticism, a dualistic philosophy and path to salvation of Greek and Persian origin. Gnosticism is a system of intricate mythological speculations concerning the nature of God and the supernal realm, speculations that Scholem saw repeated or elaborated on in the writings of the Kabbalists. Thus, Kabbalah itself, according to Scholem, originated through the penetration of an alien heresy into Rabbinic Judaism.
>
> Idel understands Kabbalah as in internal development whose wellsprings are to be found within Judaism itself. He points out that the similarities that exist between certain Gnostic texts and some Kabbalisitc symbols and ideas can be just as easily explained by positing a Jewish influence on Gnosticism rather than the reverse. The recent discovery of the Nag Hamadi Library — a source which was unavailable when Scholem made his assessments — has shed new light on the history of Gnosticism, and has indeed, according to Idel, demonstrated that Gnostics were influenced by Judaic symbols and concepts. Scholem, on the other hand, according to Idel, "never satisfactory explained why great Jewish sages in the second century would adopt a doctrine they knew to be heretical."

## 2. The relationship between Rabbinic Judaism and Kabbalah:

> Scholem believed that a basic tension existed between Rabbinic (*halachic*) Judaism and Kabbalah. Scholem depicted Rabbinic Judaism as "strangely dry and sober." "The ritual of Rabbinic Judaism," Scholem has written, "makes nothing happen and transforms nothing." Rabbinic Judaism's concerns, according to Scholem, are strictly legalistic, and thus one step removed from

the living source of spiritual inspiration. Kabbalah, on the other hand, is like an underground stream moving through the heart of Judaism, carrying with it the vital power of mythic and mystical ideas. At critical junctures, especially during crisis periods, this stem bursts forward, infusing Judaism with new life at points in Jewish history when Rabbinic Judaism could not provide the Jewish people with sufficient spiritual sustenance.

Idel does not believe that a basic tension exists between Rabbinic Judaism, or *Halacha* and Kabbalah. Instead he perceives a myriad of connections between Rabbinic ideas found in the *Talmud* and Midrash, and Kabbalistic concepts and symbols. These connections reinforce his belief that Kabbalah grew organically from within Rabbinic Judaism, and even that Kabbalah contains within it the elements of an authentic oral tradition which extends back to the prophets and the priests of the Holy Temple. "What greater testimony can we have," Idel has said, "than that of the greatest experts on Jewish texts of their time — men like Avraham Ibn Daud (Raavad), the Ramban, Rabbi Yosef Karo and the Vilna Gaon? If Kabbalah went against the grain of Rabbinic tradition, they would have clearly seen it. Yet all of them were convinced that Kabbalah was a true interpretation of Judaism, and a tradition that was totally consonant with *Talmud* and Midrash. As scientific researchers, we are not required to believe their testimony. On the other hand, we may not ignore it either."

3. **The relationship between a) the exile of the Jews from Spain, and the ARI's Kabbalah, and b) the ARI's Kabbalah and the Shabbatean movement.**

Scholem believes that the trauma of the exile from Spain and the messianic longings which this event aroused are reflected in the ARI's Kabbalistic cosmology, with its emphasis on catastrophe (the breaking of the vessels) and *tikkun* which will bring the Messiah. The popularization of the ARI's Kabbalah then prepared the way, according to Scholem, for Shabbetai Zevi by awakening and giving form to messianic longings among the Jewish masses.

Idel argues against both these claims. He points out that the ARI never mentions the exile from Spain in any of the records we have of his teachings. Idel also contends that the catastrophic and messianic concepts which the ARI emphasizes are to be found in earlier Kabbalistic works that predate the Spanish exile by decades or centuries. Idel says that the ARI's works could not have influenced the masses, preparing the ground for Shabbetai Zevi because, while the ARI was widely recognized as a saint and a great master, his doctrines were known only to a select elite.

## 4. The last, and in many ways most important distinction between Scholem and Idel which I will discuss, is the question of the nature of Kabbalah.

Is Kabbalah mainly a system of thought, or is it a path to mystical experience and even union with God? Scholem, for the most part, understood Kabbalah as a set of mystical and mythical ideas. Although he was certainly aware that there was an important experiential dimension to Kabbalah, mystical experience was only rarely the subject of his scholarly work. His main focus, and that of his disciples, is on the close analysis of texts. From reading Scholem, it is possible to gain the impression that the texts themselves, and the ideas they articulated, were the end product of the Kabbalistic endeavor.

Idel takes the opposite approach. He understands even the most theoretical texts as having mystical experience as their origin and goal. "It's important for academic scholars of the Kabbalah to understand what it means to live Kabbalah," he says. "These texts were written by and for people who attempted to be aware, with every movement they made, in every thought they had, of the effect they were causing on high, according to the map that had been drawn for them by Kabbalah. Try practicing that kind of awareness for a couple of hours, much less a couple of years, and you will see how quickly your state of consciousness changes and you begin to perceive things in a totally different way. The ideas found in Kabbalistic works are only the beginning, only the starting point of what Kabbalah is about."

What does all this have to do with Scholem's Zionism? An essential part of secular Zionist ideology was the idea that Rabbinic Judaism — which Scholem identified with *Halacha* — was not the only legitimate expression of Jewishness. Scholem saw in Kabbalah — perhaps because he wished to — an alternative to Rabbinic Judaism. The messianic longing and drive towards redemption contained in Kabbalah provided secular Zionism — whose power lay in its ambition to create a new history for the Jewish people — with an ancient pedigree. Kabbalah for Scholem — as David Biale in his book *Kabbalah and Counter-History* has shown — is a counter-tradition, a secret alternative to the exclusive claims of *Halacha* on the Jewish people and Jewish history.

Thus, Scholem's secular Zionism can shed light on his desire to portray the relationship between Rabbinic Judaism and Kabbalah as one of tension, and to de-emphasize the continuities that exist between Rabbinic texts and Kabbalah. Scholem's readiness to attribute a Gnostic, non-Rabbinic origin to Kabbalah can also be explained in this fashion. Moreover, Scholem's Zionism helps us understand his attempt to link historical crisis, such as the expulsion from Spain, and Kabbalistic theory, and his emphasis on the connection between Kabbalah and the messianic movement of Shabbetai Zevi. Kabbalah, in Scholem's interpretive scheme, is both a response to Jewish suffering and a catalyst of Jewish activism — much like Zionism is.

Idel points out that Scholem's tendency to emphasize the tensions between *Halacha* and Kabbalah may have led him to depict Kabbalah as a system of thought and not as a guide to religious performance and mystical experience. One precedent for this kind of reading of Kabbalah can be found in the Christian Kabbalists of the Renaissance, who saw in Kabbalah an ancient tradition of wisdom, which they could only adopt as their own by lifting it out of its natural context: the entire corpus of Rabbinic literature, the performance of the commandments and the mystical experience of communion with the God of Israel towards which this form of religious life leads. Scholem once half jokingly said that if he believed in the transmigration of souls, he would suspect that he was a reincarnation of Johannes Reuchlin — a 16th-century Christian Kabbalist. Idel, half seriously, recently remarked that he considered this a revealing speculation: "It's significant that Scholem saw himself as the reincarnation of a *Christian* Kabbalist." Idel did not mean to suggest in this remark that Scholem had a secret admiration for Christianity, but to raise the possibility that Scholem's Zionist negation of Rabbinic Judaism and *Halacha* in some way echoes or parallels Christianity's negation of Kabbalah's natural context.

If Scholem is a Zionist scholar of Kabbalah, the next question is naturally: Who is Moshe Idel? Idel was born in Romania in 1948, the same year the State of Israel was founded, and came to Israel with his family when he was 15. Idel is a scholar rooted in the reality of post-Zionist Israel, an Israel where the ideologies that created the State have broken apart — either because they were found wanting or because what they set out to accomplish has been fulfilled. Ben Gurion's motto "from the *Tanach* to the Palmach" — i.e., that everything created between these two eras is redolent with the scent of the Diaspora and is thus irrelevant to modern Israel — is no longer an operative guideline even for the secular Israeli. The radical break with the Diaspora which was marked by the founding of the State is a fact of life. What occupies Israelis now, more and more, is the sense of continuity and identification with Diaspora history that they feel despite this break.

Israel, 40 odd years after its founding, is a heterogenous society where the tightly defined borders between different groups have begun to open and crack under the strain of living together in one jolting, crowded reality. A State where an Orthodox Sefardi is the Minister of the Interior, where the whole country is held in suspense waiting for the television address of a 96-year-old Lithuanian *Rosh Yeshiva,* where Agudat Yisrael and the Communist left may sit together in one coalition, is a State with a reality too complex for any ideology to interpret or control.

This is the reality in which Moshe Idel does his best work. Idel shuttles back and forth, at times, between the university and Meah Shearim, where he has extensive contacts with Kabbalists in such communities as Toldot Aharon. Idel is interested in practicing Kabbalists and mystical experience as much as he is in the study of texts. He is the first academic scholar of Kabbalah for whom the oral tradition of Kabbalah is as significant as the written one. Idel does not negate the possibility that Kabbalists can develop supernatural powers of clairvoyance or telepathy. Idel's idea of scientific objectivity includes the probability that there is a great deal yet which science does not know. In the field of Kabbalah research as well, Idel's real quarrel with Scholem and his disciples lies in his belief that academicians just don't know enough yet about Judaism's secret tradition to write authoritative histories or to spin definitive metatheories.

Idel, besides being his scholarly antagonist, may someday be perceived as one of the first fulfillments of Scholem's dream: that the State of Israel would produce scholars freed from the crushing burdens which bent the Jewish self-image in the Diaspora. One of the last of these burdens may well have been Zionism itself.

*Rabbi Dr. Jonathan Sacks*

# Fundamentalism Reconsidered

'WHEN I USE A WORD,' HUMPTY DUMPTY SAID IN A rather scornful tone, 'it means just what I chose it to mean — neither more nor less.'[1]

Lewis Carroll's remark is uncannily appropriate to the rhetoric of current religious argument. The key Humpty Dumpty word in contemporary discourse is the term 'fundamentalism.' It is used with passion. But no one quite knows what it means.

Is it, as James Barr suggests,[2] a term relating to Conservative Evangelical Christianity, or does it apply to Catholicism as well? It has been applied, in the last decade, to Muslims, Sikhs, Hindus and Jews. But if Fundamentalism refers to the holding of certain doctrinal positions, then certainly there is no doctrinal common ground between these faiths.

Sometimes it is used to refer to a certain attitude to sacred texts, but again without any strict consistency. It may mean one who regards those texts as Divinely revealed, or literally true, or inerrant, or authoritative, or immutable or invested with unimpeachable sanctity. Clearly these views are very different from one another.

Others use it to refer to a range of religious and cognitive attitudes. According to Barr these include personal pietism, a reluctance to create denominations and religious establishments, a distaste for the

---

1. Lewis Carroll, *Through the Looking-Glass,* Chapter 6.
2. James Barr, *Fundamentalism,* London: SCM Press, 1977. See also his *Escaping From Fundamentalism,* London: SC, Press, 1984; and his *Holy Scripture: Canon. Authority, Criticism,* Oxford: Clarendon Press, 1983.

professional ministry, a preference for informality and a refusal to give a hearing to other points of view. Only some of these — perhaps only the last — will strike a chord with those who use the word in a Jewish or an Islamic context.

Yet others again use it in the context of political activism. Fundamentalism here refers to the very different politics engaged in by the so-called Moral Majority in the United States and by radical conservatives like the late Ayatollah Khomeini in Iran. The word has been used to describe the reaction of the Islamic community to Salman Rushdie's book, *The Satanic Verses.* When used in the context of Israel, it is most often ascribed to the territorially maximalist group Gush Emunim.

For some, Fundamentalism is an attitude to society, culture and modernity. In this sense it is certainly a reaction *against* modernity and an attempt to reinstate classic or traditional religious values. But the object of criticism certainly differs between faiths. In Christianity it seems to be secularization; in Islam, westernization; and in Judaism, assimilation.

One result is that when the word is used in a Jewish context it is sometimes taken to refer to all Orthodox Jews, on the ground that Orthodoxy involves a belief that the Torah is the word of God and not — even partially — the work of man. Such a belief, Conservative and liberal theologians argue, is incompatible with modern historical scholarship and therefore fundamentalist.

At other times it is used to refer to those who understand the Torah literally; or to those who argue that all *halachic* change is impermissible; or to those who invest the words of great Torah sages with absolute authority; or to those who see no value in secular culture — four very different sub-groups within Orthodoxy. As one writer has noted, '*Any* position . . . that is more traditionalist, or closer to the *Halacha,* than that of a person using the term is potentially "fundamentalist." Hence 'the label "fundamentalist" finds itself pinned on to a range of groups and individuals who may in practice have little or nothing in common with one another.'[1]

Finally, as we noted, it is predicated of the disciples of the late R. Zvi Yehudah Kook — the religious members of Gush Emunim — who lay great stress on the sanctity and settlement of *Eretz Yisrael shelemah,* the

---

1. Jonathan Webber, 'Rethinking Fundamentalism: the Readjustment of Jewish Society in the Modern World,' in *Studies in Religious Fundamentalism,* edited by Lionel Caplan, London: Macmillian, 1987, 108.

land of Israel in its broadest boundaries. Here it has nothing to do with religious belief as such, but to a particular relationship between belief and political action.

※ ※ ※

Nor is this all. The emotive or evaluative charge of the word has shifted significantly over time. Barr attributes the origin of the term to the series of booklets published in America between 1910 and 1915 called *The Fundamentals.* They set out with uncompromising rigor the fundamentals of Christian faith. Shortly thereafter, those who held firmly to Christian dogma in the face of the then current strands in Biblical study came to be known as fundamentalists. The *Shorter Oxford English Dictionary* dates the word's first appearance at 1923. Originally, then, it was a term of praise.

More recently, though, it has become a term of abuse, 'suggesting narrowness, bigotry, obscurantism and sectarianism.' More recently still there has been a counter-attack by traditionalists. Thus one Orthodox rabbi could write, some weeks ago, 'The Rambam, the Vilna Gaon, the Chassam Sofer and all other *gedolim* were fundamentalists who respected and understood the scientific knowledge of the time.' There is an attempt here to reclaim the positive association of the word.

A word used with such constantly changing connotations is in danger of losing all sense and reference. It means just what the speaker chooses it to mean, no more and no less. There is a need for some ground-clearing to be done if invective is to be elevated to the level of argument.

The subject is large, and in what follows I have addressed only a part of a part of it: Fundamentalism as a way of reading the Biblical text. In what sense can Orthodoxy as such be said to be fundamentalist? In what sense does that term apply only to particular schools of thought within Orthodoxy? And in what sense does it not apply to Judaism at all?

Throughout, I would ask the reader to divest the word of negative associations. If Judaism commands us to be fundamentalists, let us be so, proudly and undefensively. But let us be so, also, precisely and accurately. *Kiddush* and *havdalah* are linked commands: for there is no sanctification without the making of clear distinctions.

※ ※ ※

Orthodoxy involves belief in a proposition denied by most non-Orthodox Jews, namely, that the Five Books of Moses are the unmediated word of God. They are, that is to say, *revelation*. It is in this sense that Conservative Jews often speak of Orthodoxy as a whole as fundamentalist.

Here, for example, is one recent Conservative account of the distinction between 'fundamentalist' and 'historical' approaches to the Bible. The 'fundamentalist view . . . held by many Orthodox Jews, some Protestant Christians and almost all Moslems . . . contends that the whole Pentateuch was given by God to Moses at Sinai.' The 'historical view . . . held by the great majority of the Conservative and Reform movements in contemporary America, much of Christendom and most Biblical scholars . . . is that the Bible consists of a number of texts, composed by a variety of people in a number of places and times and later compiled in written form by a redactor.'[1]

The belief in Torah as revelation is not simply *a* fundamental of Jewish faith. It is *the* fundamental. For were it not for our faith in Torah, how could we arrive at religious certainty about the creation of the world, the meaningfulness of human existence, the justice of history and the promise of messianic redemption? Our knowledge of these things, fragmentary though it is, is derived neither from logic nor science but from our faith in Torah and its Divine authorship. In this sense, therefore, Orthodoxy *is* fundamentalist.

It is strange, though, that the word should be used in this sense, as if to suggest that belief in revelation were obscurantist or 'unscholarly.' The phrase 'And God spoke' is full of mystery. But no more so than the phrase 'And God did.' The mystery in both cases lies at the point of contact between the Infinite and the finite, the metaphysical and the empirical.

The beliefs in creation, miracle, Divine providence, reward and punishment and redemption all share this same feature with revelation, that they involve attributing an event to the authorship of God. They do not rule out the possibility that an empiricist — one who refused to admit the idea of a metaphysical cause — might interpret those events differently. There are no religious events that are self-authenticating; none that can be interpreted *in only one way* (with the exception of *Matan Torah* itself: See Rambam, *Hilchot Yisodei HaTorah*, 8:1 and 8:2). As the Torah's description of Pharaoh's reaction to the plagues makes

---

1. Elliot Dorff and Arthur Rosett, *A Living Tree,* New York: State University of New York Press, 1988, 20.

clear: a miracle can always be interpreted as magic. Religious belief, that is to say, always requires faith. But faith is not a denial of the evidence of the senses. It is a trust in something beyond the senses. There was something beyond the mighty east wind that parted the waters at the Red Sea. There was something beyond the human hand that first inscribed the words of the Mosaic books. That something in both cases was God.

※ ※ ※

To believe in revelation, therefore, requires faith. What is perplexing, though, is the Conservative argument that there can be Jewish faith *without* belief in revelation. For, broadly speaking, there are two kinds of 'non-fundamentalist' approaches to the Torah. There is the empiricist-historicist view that the Torah is to be seen as an altogether human work, to be understood within the categories of secular history. And there is the Conservative position that the Torah is not revelation but *inspiration*, the word of God *as interpreted by man*. The first view is consistent. It dispenses with religious faith altogether in reading sacred texts. The second view, though, is not yet a view at all until we have some criterion for distinguishing between the *Divine* and human elements in the text.

Some Conservatives, for example, have argued that the law of *mamzerut* (illegitimacy), which they see as morally offensive, must therefore be the works of man. Some liberals have said the same about the Biblical prohibition of homosexuality. But this is an extraordinary view of man. On what conceivable ground can we assume, *a proiri*, that man can have only offensive ideas? Why not inspiring ones also? If so, then all items of Jewish faith — the covenant, the promise, the hope — are possibly human constructs also; and we have no way of knowing which are not. If so, Jewish faith as a totality has no more objective reality than the religious imagination of a small group of dreamers long ago and far away.

The Conservative position is given spurious credibility by two separate confusions. First is the assumption that it is supported by secular Biblical scholarship of the last two hundred years. It is not. That scholarship assumes at the outset that texts are to be understood independently of Divine revelation or inspiration. It therefore supplies no support to, or refutation of, any particular metaphysical view of the way God speaks to man. Second is the assumption that since Judaism contains a view of inspiration (to the other prophets) and revelation (to Moses), the former idea is coherent without the latter. Again, it is not. As Maimonides makes clear, our belief in prophecy is dependent on the laws laid down in the Torah itself.¹ Without revelation, in other words, we would not believe in inspiration.

A further factor in making Conservatism seem coherent is its apparent similarity to 'conservative' positions within Christianity, ones that admit historical criticism of sacred scriptures. Again the comparison is misleading. For this kind of Christian theology takes *another* kind of revelation to be central: the revelation of God in human form. Once theology is built on that foundation, it can take a critical view of scripture. For scripture is not then revelation itself, but the record of that revelation by witnesses to it. For Judaism, revelation does not refer to the person or presence of God but to the word of God. By this fundamental criterion, all other manifestations of the Divine are to be judged (Rambam, *Hilchot Yisodei HaTorah,* 8:3). A view, therefore, that can be made intelligible within Christianity cannot be transferred to Judaism and assumed to be intelligible there also.

※ ※ ※

The second sense in which the term fundamentalist is used is to describe a particular approach to Biblical *authority*. As Barr puts it: 'For fundamentalists the Bible is more than the source of verity for their religion, more than the essential source of textbook. It is . . . practically the center of the religion,' he suggests, 'because it is the more accessible and articulate reality, available empirically for checking and verification, that provides the lines that run through the religion and determine its shape and character.'²

Now in such a sense, fundamentalism is well known to Jewish history as the heresy known as Karaism. It is what Yeshayahu Leibowitz picturesquely describes as 'bibliolatry.' The Pharasiac and rabbinic tradition are precisely built on the rejection of the idea that we can derive instruction directly from the Biblical text. In additional to the written law, there is an oral law, the latter being the authoritative explication of the former. Maimonides includes rejection of the oral law as 'denial of the Torah.'³ In this sense, Fundamentalism is a negation of Orthodoxy.

It is this, above all, that makes Fundamentalism a phenomenon of Protestant Christianity with no equivalent in Judaism. For Judaism

---

1. M.T. *Yesodei haTorah* 7:7, 8:3.
2. Barr, *Fundamentalism,* 36.
3. M.T. *Teshuvah* 3:8.

insists, first, that the Biblical text requires *interpretation*; second, that the interpretation is provided by *tradition*, which has the same authority as revelation itself; third, that to be applied to the present, that tradition must itself be interpreted by *authoritative exponents* of Torah, whether in the form of a Sanhedrin, or a recognized court of Jewish law, or an acknowledged *posek* — *halachic* authority.

Interestingly, in one way, it is precisely the liberal forms of Judaism that come closest, in contemporary Jewish life, to the Protestant fundamentalist model. For it is they that argue that the traditional understanding of Torah, concertized in *halachic* precedent, can be overturned in the name of personal autonomy, or 'fresh ethical insights.' They, like Protestant Fundamentalism, represent a reaction against the authority of community, traditional, precedent and established practice. They argue that such things have, over the course of time, distorted the essential teachings of religion, and that piety demands a fresh encounter with the texts, untrammeled by the history of the way those texts have been understood by the community of faith. That is not to say that liberal forms of Judaism are fundamentalist. It *is* to say that they are 'protestantisations' of Judaism.

※ ※ ※

The third aspect of what is called a fundamentalist approach to the Bible is the belief in its *inerrancy*. The Torah is true and free of error. In this sense, certainly we believe that the Torah is 'a law of truth.' But of what kind of truth do we speak?

Do we speak of *literal* truth? On this point, within Judaism itself there were forceful arguments as to the empirical content of Biblical propositions. The dominant strand of early rabbinical thought ruled out any naive liberalism in reading the Biblical text: and this as a matter of principle. For the Torah uses a whole series of physical and emotional attributes in speaking of God. These anthropomorphisms offended against rabbinic ideas of the incorporeality of God. Writing these implications out of the text was a major element of some of the *targumim* or early rabbinic translations, and constitutes a large part of Maimonides' philosophical program in the *Guide of the Perplexed*.

Indeed Maimonides ruled that to attribute physical characteristics to God was a form of heresy,[1] and added: 'You will perhaps say that the

---

1. M.T. *Teshuvah* 3:7.

literal interpretation of the Bible causes men to fall into that doubt, but you must know that idolaters were likewise brought to their belief by false imaginations and ideas.'[1] The fact, in other words, that one might believe that God had physical attributes because one read the Torah literally was no excuse.

There remained such questions as whether, for example, Jacob's wrestling match with the angel, or Balaam's talking donkey, or Jonah's sojourn in the belly of a whale, were to be understood literally as taking place in physical space, or as dreams of prophetic visions, to be understood as metaphors or allegories or mystic intimations. On such questions, for example, Maimonides and Nachmanides in the Middle Ages took different approaches.[2] Nonetheless, three medieval philosophers of such different intellectual orientations as Saadia Gaon, Judah Halevi and Maimonides could agree that if a scriptural verse conflicted with the dictates of reason, it was to be interpreted other than literally. Maimonides explains *why* the Torah uses figurative language; so that each will understand the Torah's truths at a level appropriate to his or her understanding, some literally, some metaphorically.[3]

※ ※ ※

This much, though, is generally conceded by critics of Orthodoxy. What makes one a fundamentalist, they argue, is not an insistence on the *literal* truth of the Torah but on its truth *per se.* But it is here that liberal Jewish theologians, impressed by Barr's strictures against Protestant Fundamentalism, fall into an error which Barr himself is careful to avoid. For clearly, anyone who turns to the Bible for guidance in belief and conduct takes it as true *in some sense.* This applies to fundamentalists and non-fundamentalists alike. Critics of Fundamentalism must therefore maintain that it ascribes the *wrong sort* of truth to the Bible. Which sense is that?

Barr is clear. The 'sort of truth that is important for the fundamentalist' is, he says, 'correspondence to external reality.' A fundamentalist is one who reads the Bible for *factual information.* That, for him, is its purpose as a book. 'Veracity as correspondence with empirical actuality

---

1. *Guide of the Perplexed,* I, 36.
2. See *Guide of the Perplexed,* II, 42-46; Nachmanides, *Commentary to Genesis* 18:1.
3. *Guide of the Perplexed,* Introduction.

has precedence over veracity as significance.'[1] Or again: 'correspondence with external reality must be affirmed as an inalienable and essential property of the Biblical texts.'[2] Or again: 'the fundamentalist conception of truth is dominated by a materialistic view, derived from a scientific age.'[3]

Now there are certainly those who read the Torah this way. But equally, there are those who do not. When the sages ask, 'Why was this book written?' or 'Why was this passage placed next to that?' rarely indeed do they answer: because that is how things happened. Their normal mode of answer begins with the words, 'To teach you that . . .' The sages were concerned, that is to say, with Torah as *instruction,* legal and ethical. Indeed that is what the word Torah means. That is its genre, and how it is to be read.

There is no more striking example of this than the famous rabbinic comment with which Rashi begins his commentary to the Torah. 'Rabbi Yitzchak said: The Torah should have begun with the verse (*Exodus* 12:1), "This month shall be to you the first of months," which is the first of the commandments given to Israel.' Behind R. Yitzchak's remark is the assumption that the Torah is essentially a *book of commandments:* the constitution of the covenant between God and Israel. It should therefore have begun with the first command to the children of Israel. Evidently R. Yitzchak was prepared to contemplate a Torah which omitted entirely the narratives of creation, the flood, the patriarchs, the exile and the first stages of exodus. Thus far did one sage express his indifference to the factual information — historical and cosmological — contained in the Torah's first sixty-one chapters.

Nor, though R. Yitzchak's view is extreme, is it uncharacteristic. As many scholarly studies of Midrash have disclosed, the sages were remarkably indifferent to the historicity of Biblical narrative. They employed techniques of deliberate anachronism and what Yitzchak Heinemann calls 'creative historiography.' Their interest lay in deciphering every possible *halachic* and ethical nuance of the text; not in laborious researches into its facticity. To have done otherwise would have been to have missed the point of the narrative and misconstrued its genre. Torah, as the Torah itself so often insists, is not an assemblage of

---

1. Barr, *Fundamentalism,* 49.
2. Ibid., 50.
3. Ibid., 93.

facts: It is a set of rules and models of how Israel should live and be blessed. It does not set out primarily to answer the question, 'What happened?' but the question, 'How then shall I live?'

※ ※ ※

To be sure, belief in Torah as revelation rules out the kind of critical approach advocated by Barr. It is important to see why. Consider one of Barr's examples: the Biblical account of creation. Barr's own view of the matter is this: 'About the actual processes of the origin of the world as we know them he [the putative human author of *Genesis* 1] knew, of course, nothing, and set against our knowledge of these processes his account is certainly "wrong." Since, on the other hand, the processes and sequences which are known to us through modern science were certainly totally unknown to him, this "wrongness" is quite irrelevant in our understanding the story.'[1]

Now this is a very disingenuous comment. It makes *all* the difference as to whether we believe that *Genesis* 1 is a statement about creation by the Creator, or a naive pre-scientific account by a religiously inspired but cognitively primitive member of the species of *homo sapiens*. It may be irrelevant to our understanding of the chapter, but it is critically relevant to our understanding of the world.

The believer in Torah as revelation is not naive. He may accept R. Ishmael's dictum that 'the Torah speaks in the language of man.'[2] The Torah — as Maimonides emphasizes — was revealed to a particular people at a particular time in specific historical, social and intellectual circumstances. It uses language and metaphor intelligible to one age: It may have to be decoded and re-encoded at another age. That is a major element of the process known as Midrash. But there is a vast difference between the idea that 'the Torah speaks in the language of man' and the idea that the Torah speaks with the voice of man. We believe it does not. It speaks with the voice of God.

It is here that the believer can and should turn the tables on the Bible critic. For the Torah does contain statements about its own purpose as a book. 'Moses commanded us the Torah as the heritage of the congregation of Jacob.'[3] The Torah is firstly, *commanded*; it is a

---

1. Barr, *Fundamentalism,* 42.
2. B.T. *Berakhot* 31b et al.
3. *Deuteronomy* 32:4.

book in the imperative rather than the descriptive mode. Secondly, it is commanded to *us*, an enduring heritage; it is a book whose commanding force is not diminished over time. To read the Torah thus is to read it as it asks to be read. To read it otherwise may be an exercise in scholarship, but it is not to read it *as* Torah.

Biblical scholarship since the nineteenth century has been dominated by historicism. This emphasizes 'the uniqueness of all historical phenomena' and maintains 'that each age should be interpreted in terms of its own ideas and principles.'[1] It reads texts in the context of the past. It seeks their original meaning, not their present interpretation. It asks what a passage meant *then*, not what it might mean *now*.

That is how we read texts *academically*. Michael Fishbane has rightly noted that when read academically 'old texts are appreciated as alien to, or at least distanced from modern sensibilities and understandings — approachable only by crossing the philological-historical divide that separates their contents from our modern minds and intellectual habits.'[2]

But that is not how we read Torah *convenantally*. To read Torah publicly in the synagogue, to learn it in fulfillment of the command of *talmud Torah*, is to re-create Sinai. It is to hear Torah as spoken and promulgated *now*. It is to open oneself to the word of an Author whose intentionality is not governed by the normal laws of time and foreseeability. The 'Bible,' read as the product of human minds long ago and somewhere else, ceases to be *Torah*, the world of God addressed to me, here and now. And what one must ask of the Bible scholar is: Is his reading of the text any closer than that of the fundamentalist to the Torah as perceived by the community of faith? Does it read the book as it asks to be read and as it has been read since it was first accepted?

※ ※ ※

There is a great deal more to be said about the narrow subject of 'fundamentalism' as a way of reading sacred texts, without yet touching on the social and political dimensions of the phenomenon. But I hope enough has been said to show that the use of a term drawn from

---

1. *The Fontana Dictionary of Modern Thought,* edited by Alan Bullock and Oliver Stallybrass, London: Fontana/Collins, 1983, 285,6.

2. Michael Fishbane, 'The Academy and the Community,' *Judaism* (Spring 1986), 153.

the inner dynamic of Protestantism has only an obfuscating effect when transferred to Judaism. James Barr himself has scrupulously argued just this point; but it has generally been ignored by his Jewish borrowers.

The late Professor Leo Strauss, in his *Philosophy and Law,* made the very telling point that the Enlightenment, in its assault on religious traditions generally and Biblical faith specifically, never truly engaged with the concept of revelation. It merely took its non-existence as given, and proceeded to interpret the Bible accordingly, as if it had proved what in fact it had merely assumed. The traditional belief in revelation, meanwhile, was neither refuted nor refutable. 'For that reason, Orthodoxy, unchanged in its essence, was able to outlast the attack of the Enlightenment and all later attacks and retreats.'[1]

The attention of Biblical scholarship has shifted dramatically in the last two decades, away from historicist methods toward the literary approaches of Robert Alter, Frank Kermode, Meir Weiss and Meir Sternberg, structuralist readings inspired by Roland Barthes, and the 'canonical' approach of Professor Brevard Childs. Each of these stresses the unity of the text as opposed to its fragmentation, through the methods of historical criticism. Childs' approach in particular attaches great weight to the text as understood by the faith community in which it is read.

In each of these new developments one senses a restlessness with the results of historical scholarship. Indeed Meir Sternberg, in his recent *Poetics of Biblical Narrative*, writes of the last two hundred years of Biblical research: 'Rarely has there been such a futile expense of spirit in a noble cause; rarely have such grandiose theories of origination been built and revised and pitted against one another on the evidential equivalent of the head of a pin; rarely have so many worked so long and so hard with so little to show for their trouble.'[2]

Fascinating though these developments may be to the believer, they are incidental to what I have called the convenantal reading of the text. The sages made a subtle and important distinction when they said: 'If you are told, There is wisdom [*chochma*] among the nations, believe it.

---

1. Leo Strauss, *Philosophy and Law,* Philadelphia: Jewish Publication Society, 1987, 11.

2. Meir Sternberg, *The Poetics of Biblical Narrative,* Bloomington: Indiana University Press, 1985, 13.

If you are told there is Torah among the nations, do not believe it.' All post-Enlightenment scholarship proceeds on the axiom that its findings must be universally accessible and testable. That is its particular glory and what qualifies it for the title of *chochma*. Torah, however, proceeds on the assumption that its words and the living commentaries thereto are addressed to a specific community: the community to which Torah was given and by which it was accepted. That is what differentiates Torah from *chochma*, and *perush* — commentary and application — from research. Biblical scholarship may be *chochma* but it is not Torah. For only the community of the commanded can experience the Torah *as command.*

❧ ❧ ❧

The concept of *Torah min ha-shamayim,* Torah as revealed command, is a relational one. It presupposes One Who commands, and those who are commanded. It embodies two ideas: the *giving* of the Torah and the *receiving* of the Torah. The giving of the Torah is — like creation, miracle and Divine intervention in history — a difficult idea. It speaks of the meeting of the Infinite and finite, the breakthrough of the transcendent into the world of the senses. Maimonides describes the revelation at Sinai as 'one of the mysteries of the Torah.' He adds: 'It is very difficult to have a true conception of the events, for there has never been before, nor will there will ever be again, anything, like it.'[1]

This is not defensiveness on Maimonides' part. It flows from his, and our, concept of scientific knowledge. We can only generalize from the known to the unknown on the basis of observable regularities. Necessarily, therefore, unless we were witnesses, we cannot have empirical knowledge of unique events. The giving of the Torah was a unique event. Therefore we cannot know it empirically. Instead we can know it only through tradition and, ultimately, faith.

But if the *giving* of the Torah is a 'mystery,' the *receiving* of the Torah is not. And here it is worth spelling out the hermeneutic implications of *Torah min ha-shamayim.*

To read Torah convenantally is to hear the voice of God Who is above time and space addressing me in my full existential singularity. It is to enter into its words, not as they were addressed to the wilderness generation, but to me, here, now. It is to read the awesome curses of

---

1. *Guide of the Perplexed,* II, 33.

*Leviticus* 26 and *Deuteronomy* 28 in full knowledge of the blood libels, the Crusades, the pogroms, the Inquisition, the expulsions, the *Shoah*. It is to read the promise of the ingathering of full knowledge of the state of Israel. It is to hear the infinite intentionality behind those words.

To read Torah convenantally is to be lifted on the wings of the Divine presence beyond the relativities of the human situation. It is to know that if there is a command in the Torah which we do not understand, that is a failure in our understanding which we must labor to overcome, not the mark of a human intrusion into the text which we must labor to emend. It is to recognize the sanctity of the Torah scroll, with which we dance on Simchat Torah, over which we mourn if it is defiled, which we bury if it is destroyed: the only object in Judaism which we recognize as animate, possessed of a soul.

To read Torah convenantally is to do so as part of the historic community of Israel, the 'congregation of Jacob' whose heritage it is. It is to hear its words filtered through the tradition of interpretation accepted as authoritative by the community of faith.

That is how Jews read Torah and how faith demands that Torah be read. *As* Torah. Which is to say: as authoritative instruction on how to live and how to interpret the meanings that underlie our experience of nature and history. Revelation defines the set of hermeneutic presuppositions that constitute recognition of the genre Torah. There is no reading of Torah which is not accompanied by faith.

If this is Fundamentalism, so be it. On it, I stake my faith as a Jew.

Rabbi Mayer Schiller

# To Radically Alter Our Lives

*An analysis of Rabbi Hillel Goldberg's "The Fire Within: The Living Heritage of the Musar Movement"*

I RECEIVED *THE FIRE WITHIN* SHORTLY BEFORE SHABBAT BEGAN some days ago and finished it before *minchah* the following afternoon. A man's response to any spiritual work is always heavily colored by where he happens to be "holding" in his own *avodah* at that time. Hence, there is always an element of subjectivity involved in a review of a work geared to eliciting a passionate response. Perhaps, on that particular Shabbat, I was ripe to be touched. Yet, I was far more than just touched by Rabbi Hillel Goldberg's work. I was profoundly, deeply moved and, thereby, conclude that it was not just my receptivity that was involved but the intrinsic power of this passionate work.

Yes, for the reader looking for the basic details of the *Musar* movement, of Rabbi Yisrael Salanter, of his first-generation disciples Rabbi Simcha Zisel the "Alter" of Kelm, Rabbi Yitzhak Blazer and Rabbi Naftali Amsterdam, as well as detailed descriptions of the schools of Slobodka and Navarodok, this work will provide him with a wealth of information. But, for every reader who yearns to whatever degree to better his relationship to God, it will perform a much more significant task. It will challenge him, page after page, to subject his own existence to the same careful scrutiny that the *Baalei Musar* subjected theirs and which (as becomes obvious to all after reading a few pages) the author clearly subjects his own. Of course, this is precisely what Rabbi Yisrael wanted, to challenge our spiritual complacency incessantly, to cause us to burn with an ardor for self-betterment despite the deadening hands of *Hergel* (rote observance) which seems an inevitable result of the passage of time in an insular environment (a situation which almost all of the Torah camp finds itself in).

*Hasidut* as opposed to *Musar* provided many possible means for the individual to sidestep a direct confrontation with his own spiritual state. Although, in truth, just as demanding as *Musar* (and probably at its deepest levels even more so), *Hasidut* could easily be misperceived or watered down by its adherents. It was, in fact, the case that many "Hasidim" took within the confines of their movement either the high road or low road around a clear assessment of their station in God's service. By high road, we refer to the tendency of some to harp on the mystical teachings of *Hasidut,* the study of which can often focus on other worldly data to the exclusion of this worldly performance. The low road is well known to all and is taken by the masses who use the camaraderie and provinciality of *Hasidut* as a means to guarantee the Orthodoxy of themselves and their children. This stance, however commendable and certainly successful in maintaining faith and observance, draws little if nothing from the *avodat HaHasidut* and is certainly not conducive to self-scrutiny and spiritual productivity. *Musar* allows for no escape. Involvement in its study and practice means that one is constantly looking at his own existence and challenging every aspect of it. There is little talk of Heavenly realms and no communal activities which do not raise the question of one's spiritual state. Perhaps, this is the very reason why *Hasidut* achieved widespread popularity and *Musar* did not. Perhaps, that is as it should be and for most men a self-confident, boisterous and somewhat smug condescension is the best means to preserve Orthodoxy. That is an intriguing question. What is clearer, though, is that *Musar,* by puncturing man's smugness at the core of his being, must result in a constant spiritual renaissance in the hearts of its practitioners.

❁ ❁ ❁

*The Fire Within* brings home the teachings of *Musar* in a deeply personal manner. Rabbi Goldberg is not the typical absentee author of contemporary Orthodox literature. He is involved as a real human being every step of the way. We are not just introduced to the demands of Kelm or Slobodka or Navarodok, but we are shown how their teachings are eternally relevant, how they deeply moved the soul of the author and how he struggled to come to grips with their demands. We are further allowed to see the author often hesitating, unwilling to probe some *Musar* teaching or practice. In sum, we have in *The Fire Within* not merely a history, not merely a spiritual autobiography (no mean feat itself) but a skilled interweaving of *Musar* teaching and *Musar* living all set upon a contemporary stage with real life doubts and difficulties as background.

In keeping with the mood established throughout the book, Rabbi Goldberg was not satisfied with merely studying *Musar* teachings or researching the *Baalei Musar's* lives. He journeyed (pilgrimaged might be a better word) to assorted contemporary *Musar* figures in order to study under them, but more importantly, to carefully observe (and record for our benefit) their daily lives.

Once again, here the author is not a detached observer. He goes to the *Baalei Musar* not as an author or a researcher, but as a Jew seeking to receive instruction, criticism and inspiration in order to better serve God. Each one of these encounters is a gem in its own right. Before long the reader finds the likes of Rabbi Binyamin Zilber, Rabbi Eliezer Ben Zion Bruk, Rabbi Yehudah Leib Nekritz and a host of others to be, not distant storybook saints, but real life people whose lives challenge his own on every page. Their demands on themselves, by implication, became demands on us as we encounter them.

The resurgence of Torah Judaism in recent decades leaves us all with much to be proud of. Yet, there is no doubt all of our varied communities have significant weaknesses, sore spots at vital parts of their organism. All too often, in order to defend the superiority of one's particular orientation against the claims of other communities, we ignore our own warts while glorifying in our strengths. It is an easily understood temptation, yet one capable of wreaking immense spiritual havoc in the long run.

Communal self-satisfaction is only the sum total of individual smugness. A lack of honesty about one's person leads inevitably to a lack of honesty about one's community. The result of all this is that both as communities and individuals we plod on, as yesterday so today and inevitably tomorrow. One is tempted when surveying this scene reminiscent of Jack Horner's assessment of his post-plum-removal state

*To Radically Alter Our Lives* / 263

to refer to a prediction of Rabbi Yitzhak Meir of Ger. The *Hidushei Ha-Rim* once wrote that before the Messiah's appearance there will be large communities of observant Jews. The Satan will be quite content to allow them to function because in an unsuspecting moment he will sneak up to them and steal away their *nekudat hapenimeyut*, their innermost soul. Thus, they will go on but with the heart missing.

Rabbi Goldberg is unique on the contemporary scene because he is willing to inject himself into his work. Almost all writing emanating from the Torah camp today deals with ideal types who are depicted as saintly and generally, beyond emulation by us less-than-perfect humans. There is certainly a place for such literature. Now, though, one senses that the time has come for a Torah literature of realism, depicting how regular people struggle to live up to God's demands. How does *Musar* or *Hasidut* affect the ninety-nine percent who will not be remembered for centuries? How do we (as teachers, businessmen, parents, etc.) and how should we seek to realize Torah in our lives in the rough and tumble world of doubt, despair, boredom, elation, etc.? Where is the Orthodox Proust to depict life as it is lived? Rabbi Goldberg has begun this process. *Musar* has touched him deeply in moments of darkness and light. It is this sense of confronting *Musar* in the world we all perceive which renders his work so compelling.

*Musar* is the ultimate guarantee against spiritual complacency. One cannot read *The Fire Within* without thinking long and hard about oneself, one's community and the world in general. The reader emerges from it spiritually refreshed and rededicated. It is a most important work, the purchase and reading of, which should be placed on our immediate agenda. It is after its reading, though, that its true relevance comes home. *The Fire Within* is only significant if, when all is said, it is lived.

# ◆§ Outreach

☐ *From a Mother With Love*
☐ *At the Forefront of the Baal Teshuvah
      Movement: The Beginnings of NCSY*

Judy Berg

# From a Mother With Love

DEAR SANDY,

I know your name is Zahava now, but you have to indulge me; I'm your mother. Besides, I still remember looking at you in the delivery room and thinking, "If we name her Sandra and call her Sandy, she'll be Sandy for life. After all, how could you get another name from Sandy?" Never assume. As a child, you were cute, funny, busy, a pest, endlessly curious, sometimes exasperating, mostly wonderful. The years flew by and one day you were in college.

The next thing I knew, you were working in Arizona, meeting this terrific man, and when I looked again, I found myself dancing at your wedding. When Benjie was born, the circle was complete and life was wonderful. Nothing but smooth sailing from then on. Never assume.

One day you told me you'd decided to keep a kosher kitchen. I replied, "That's nice," and, practical person that I am, I immediately thought of a set of Grandma's dishes I had stored that I could give you. Well, I don't think that was quite the reaction you were hoping for, but then I didn't realize at the time that you were contemplating considerably more than just separating dairy from meat. Life got very interesting after that and events moved quickly.

By the time I realized what a cataclysmic life change you were making, I was completely confused. Where had all this come from? Why was it necessary? What was it all about? And most importantly, what had become of my daughter? We had some rocky times back then but not, I think, because of the obvious reasons. I think we both misperceived each other's motives. As with many mother-daughter relationships, problems arise when territorial lines are crossed and unspoken criticisms are felt. Defenses go up, feelings are hurt and suddenly, there we are, sitting across from each other like two strangers with nothing to say to each other.

How, I wondered, did we get to that point and how were we going to fix it? You had become someone I didn't know anymore and I was scared to death that I'd never find you again. Looking back, I can understand what happened. It seemed to both of us that we were no longer on the same side. You thought that I was disinterested in what you were doing because my reactions were not more enthusiastic. I thought that you disapproved of me because I hadn't given you a more traditional Jewish background. As it turned out, we were both wrong, and as time went on, we carefully began to find our way back.

Fortunately, we had the children to use as sort of a buffer zone. We talked about them a lot, as I remember. Then, as more time passed, we found other things to say. We grew more comfortable in our new situation. We talked about recipes and decorating. We began to talk about wordly things and spiritual things. And eventually, we began to understand that we weren't so far apart after all. As a matter of fact, it became more and more apparent that we were getting closer all the time. We were both learning a lot.

You were taking classes and doing a lot of reading. You were getting advice and support from all of the wonderful new friends you had made. I was learning too. Here are a few of things I learned: Always carry a package of kosher lollipops in the glove compartment of the car for grandchildren. You can buy it if it says "OK" or "OU," but if it says "OU-D," they sometimes won't eat it. It's always wise to eat something on the way to the *Seder*, and never, under any circumstances, upon meeting a rabbi, shake his hand while saying how happy you are to meet him. I've also learned to keep my mouth shut...mostly.

I've witnessed how wonderful it is to live in a community where people genuinely care about each other to the extent that they treat each other like family. I saw this first-hand when I came to stay with you for a week after Ariela was born. Every day at 5:00, the doorbell rang and someone was standing on the porch with containers of wonderful-smelling, lovingly prepared food for the new mother and family. This went on all week. Busy women with families of their own and many other things to do taking time to "do" for someone else. What an amazing thing. Everyone concerned about each other, caring about each other, and living the Golden Rule.

More than anything, though, I've learned that our differences do not have to result in divisions.

When you and I were much younger, I read a poem about parents and children that said something to the effect that your children are only yours for a little while and that when they grow up and leave home, your job is done. That made sense to me at the time, but now that you are grown and gone, I know that the opposite is true. There is no bond in this world as strong as the one between parent and child and now that you are an adult and we can relate to each other as women, that bond seems to be even stronger.

In spite of the different paths our lives have taken, our common experiences and shared history bring us always closer. You have not yet had the pleasure of knowing your children as adults. There is no greater joy for a parent than to see one's child become the person you'd always hoped she'd be, and although a parent's job is never really finished, your father and I can look at the person you are today, and feel very proud.

I have just a few more things to say, words that aren't said nearly often enough. Maybe some that have never been said. First and most important, I love you. You are good and dear and all that a daughter should be. Second, I want you to know that I support your decision to become an observant Jew. How can I not? I see how happy you are, how much more content and how much better you feel about yourself. It seems that you have finally found the place you have been looking for all your life. How lucky you are.

Lastly, I admire you. I know that it is not always easy for you. There is great discipline involved in your day-to-day life and I am aware of how hard you work and how much of yourself you give to making your home a loving and spiritual place. Yet with all you do, you still manage to be a wonderful mother to your precious children, a loving wife and daughter and a truly good person. If this had been your goal, then consider yourself a success because you are achieving it every day.

Well, I think I have said all I wanted to. You told me to say what was in my heart. You said I couldn't go wrong. You were right. Maybe we should all just say what's in our heart to those we love more often. Never assume.

I am grateful for being given this opportunity to tell you how I feel and I pray that we will continue to be blessed with understanding, with happiness and with love. *Baruch Hashem.*

Love, Mom

*Rabbi Pinchas Stolper*

# At the Forefront of the Baal Teshuvah Movement
## The Beginnings of NCSY

*Rabbi Pinchas Stolper recounts the beginnings of NCSY in the 1960s, a time when all the "experts" predicted the project was doomed to fail.*

IN SEPTEMBER 1959, THE LEADERSHIP OF THE ORTHODOX UNION charged me with the responsibility of developing a young movement in American Orthodox synagogues, knowing full well that such a venture had not previously succeeded. The resources available were minuscule: myself, a part-time secretary — little more.

Few believed that it was at all realistic to expect youngsters in the "hinterlands," dotted with Orthodox congregations on an assortment of levels — most communities then lacking a day school; where Torah observance was minimal; the Talmud Torah a failure; and where social dancing was the dominant youth activity — to attend a program where *halachah* was stringently observed and attend Torah study groups. Certainly no one expected them to return a second, third, and fourth time.

None of the institutions, programs, support systems, special schools for *baalei teshuvah* or exciting personalities of today's rapidly expanding *teshuvah* movement then existed. But the work went forward. Progress was marked with notable speed. We were meeting a felt, crucial need. Soon additions were made to the staff.

By January 1963, I was able to report in *Jewish Life* magazine:

> *In the past two years, more synagogues and more of their young people were participating in youth programs than ever before. The key factor in this development was the Orthodox Union's National Conference of Synagogue youth. "NCSY" has grown with unusual speed into a movement truly national in scope. Its chapters and regions function through the length and breadth of this country. The most notable aspect of the sudden response of congregations to this area of activity, however, is not simply numerical growth. Rather, it is the demanding character of the program — and the fact that the drive for its adoption rises from the teenagers themselves.*
>
> *The success of the program bears out the contention that teenagers can be true to a positive definition of the meaning and potential of adolescence. Young people will accept and are accepting a program of maximum commitment to Jewish belief and observance, to the demands of the laws of Sabbath,* kashrut, *prayer, and study, and the whole* Mitzvah *concept, when presented within the context of their teenage sub-society.*
>
> *They are our core and leadership group. A substantial portion of the membership of NCSY comes from homes which are not religiously observant. It is among this element that the NCSY concept has met its decisive test.*
>
> *Thousands of boys and girls proved through their enthusiastic response that what they really want is a program for Jewish living, an environment of Torah, a path of return to the living traditions their parents in so many cases had forgotten or perhaps had never known. NCSY has grown beyond all dreams and expectations. The plans of yesterday have been attained and exceeded. Hundreds of congregations have established youth programs where none existed before.*
>
> *Most significantly, NCSY has become a rallying point for idealists willing to serve youth without compensation. Growth in numbers has been more than matched by NCSY's growth in quality and intensity.*

By 1969, NCSY could justifiably be called a "movement" of *baalei teshuvah* with a contagious, electric quality. Young people, we had found, are prepared to respond when the call is uncompromisingly clear. In its unique ability to sink grass roots in America's great backyard, NCSY had demonstrated that American youth is in search of Torah.

By 1980, the stream had grown into a flowing river. By then the *teshuvah* phenomenon merited broader analysis. The following represents a digest of my article in the Winter 1980-81 issue of *Jewish Life:*

> *The* teshuvah *movement, still in its earliest stages, demonstrates that this generation has been entrusted with a unique opportunity which generations preceding ours did not enjoy. If our community is unable to adequately respond to the potential of this phenomenon, we are in danger of squandering a moment in history which offers Orthodox Jewry the opportunity to regain its dominant and pre-eminent position within the Jewish People. Once, my mentor, the late Ga'on Rav Yitzchok Hutner, told me that the* teshuvah *phenomenon "represents an opportunity which arrives only once in many generations, offering the privilege to accomplish unusual and mighty tasks."*

## ৺ A Trend Reversed

The *teshuvah* phenomenon represents a reversal of the trend of disaffection and abandonment of tradition which characterized the past generations since "The Enlightenment." That trend is not replaced by a new current which has turned the Orthodox Jewish community into a magnet which attracts rather than repels the disaffected and searching to the exclusion of all other ideologies, philosophies, and trends.

In America, many tradition-minded Jews submitted to the emasculation of halachic practice by the Conservative movement, in the mistaken belief that an Americanized, "de-Europeanized," Judaism which made fewer demands might be a factor in retaining the loyalties of Jewish youth. They would discover, to their dismay, that the next generation of American Jewish youth would have little appreciation for a watered-down, compromised religion which lacks passion and authenticity and is soft on commitment and consistency.

Seen in this light, the *teshuvah* phenomenon is much more than an isolated development which has affected the Torah community during the past thirty years. It is a new, unanticipated major force which has the potential to transform the direction and fortunes of the entire Jewish People.

By now, the *teshuvah* phenomenon has become the property of all of *Klal Yisrael*. Few believed me when I returned from NCSY events in the early '60s and told stories of young people from Upstate New York, Virginia, Texas, Chicago, the South, and Midwest and Western cities like Peoria, Kansas City, and Denver who had begun to observe Shabbat, keep kosher, were forming local Torah learning groups and wished to study in *yeshivot*. For years afterwards, despite the fact that the ten events of 1959 had become sixty events in 1962 and eighty in 1964, touching the lives of thousands of young people, there were still some who did not believe the stories, and perhaps to this day do not believe them. In time, there emerged entire communities of *baalei teshuvah* — as in Atlanta, Los Angeles, Providence, Memphis, and elsewhere. Suddenly, *yeshivot* began filling with *baalei teshuvah* and new *yeshivot* were created for them: in the United States, Yeshiva University's James Striar School and Yeshiva She'or Yoshuv; and in Israel, Ohr Somayach, Aish HaTorah, D'var Yerushalayim, Darchei Noam, Diaspora Yeshiva, N'vei Yerushalayim and others. Today, a large proportion of the students at Yeshiva University and as many as sixty percent at Touro College are *baalei teshuvah*. At Einstein Medical College there is a Talmud *shiur* attended mostly by *baalei teshuvah*. Educators often say, "I wish I could work exclusively with *baalei teshuvah* — they are so responsive, so quick, so receptive and so eager."

Entire communities have begun to feel the impact of the enthusiasm and devotion of the *baalei teshuvah* to learning and *mitzvot*. In becoming part of mainstream Orthodoxy, *baalei teshuvah* have injected a new vitality into the very community which encouraged and absorbed them. A fresh ferment of spiritual searching spearheaded by *baalei teshuvah* in our midst has shaken complacency and hopefully portends a process of renewal.

## ✥ Starting the Process: Principles of Redirecting Our Youth

What were the educational principles, methods and goals which allowed for the success of the NCSY concept? The aim is to build within youth a resolve to reject that which is false in society and to identify with the Torah community through a commitment to the *mitzvah* life in practice and ideal. In this sense, the approach promotes and is associated with the natural rebelliousness of youth. Since their surrounding society is not religious, a healthy manifestation of the maturing process is channeled in favor of religious ideals and goals. Educationally, it functions as an all-encompassing youth society that seeks to capture the total person intellectually and emotionally, and to evoke the crucial decision to identify with Jewish life.

Emphasis on experience, identification, peers, and environment has worked not only with young people from secular or indifferent home and school backgrounds, but also with *yeshivah* students, many of whom have admitted that they first became "religious" in NCSY.

Intellectual probing is one of the few weapons that are of value to a youth society that disdains arbitrary and unreasoned dogmatism. It is for this reason that many "yeshivah dropouts" have "found themselves" Jewishly in NCSY, where thinking and questioning are encouraged instead of avoided. The *Rebbe-Talmid,* mentor-disciple principle, views the *rebbe in locoparentis,* charged not simply with imparting information to his pupil, but with educating him in the full sense — molding his character and his mind. He is not restricted to texts; all the world is his text. He is a living example; he teaches through deed, conduct, and attitude. He sets a tone; his actions are determiners of values. He represents the "do as I do, live as I live" philosophy. He is a text person, not a textbook.

A second educational principle is that of experience and environment. Lacking a Jewish environment at home or in the street, parents send their children to a Jewish school. All too often, this is a weekday experience, in contrast to the historical pattern of Jewish life and Jewish schooling, where both environment and school related to the student during every day of the year. If education fails to reflect life, its joys and sorrows, ups and downs, of what value is it? *Chumash* and *siddur* have minimal force in the life of the young person who never shed a tear on Tisha B'Av or never was *freilich* on Purim.

A third, and possibly, overriding principle is the fellowship of one's peers. Many of life's strongest impressions are formulated in the presence of young friends. One dynamic, articulate, and popular adolescent can influence more young people than a roomful of rabbis.

Why does one weekend in such a setting often evoke so powerful a response from young people?

Adolescents — especially Jewish adolescents — tend to be passionate and uncompromising. Possessed of a penetrating intuition, they are quick to sense what is sham or hypocrisy. They recognize the genuine article. Our young Jews are searchers after truth, and with their newly discovered sense of Jewish purpose are capable of pursing truth. Teenagers are often intensely mystical. They are willing to emulate a good adult model, but primarily look to outstanding peers for leadership. Above all, their growing maturity and independence make them respecters and pursuers of competence, of ability, or work, and of responsibility. The teenager is not yet set in his ways. He can be molded, influenced, inspired, taught and directed.

Our premise here is that the Jewish teenager is hungry for Torah, unaware of this though he — and his elders — may be. But will young people actually accept a program of maximum commitment to Jewish belief and observance?

The answer is yes — if the program is presented within the context of their own teenage world. Yes — if programming is keyed to the highest, not the lowest, denominator, refusing to treat youth like children, respecting their maturity, their questioning and inquiring minds. Thousands of boys and girls have proved through their intense response that this was precisely what they were looking for. The year-round *mitzvah* and Torah study programs which are so central a part of the NCSY concept, together with the much-remarked appeal of the movement's many local, regional and national get-togethers, have won a response which warrants much reflection. The setting is warm, friendly, invigorating. The faculty eats, sings, prays, and dances with the young people. They let their hair down, open their collars and relate as real people. Shabbat is lived, not only taught. Hundreds of teenagers have responded to this moving experience with, "I never knew Shabbat could be like this."

The entire experience promotes a sense of belonging and identification. The participant is involved on every level — rarely is he a spectator. *Shiurim* and discussions, "What It's All About" and "What To Do — And How" sessions, soul-stirring and exhilarating dancing, thoughtful tales and contemplation and introspection to bring a sense of self discovery, awakening — and the "Jewish decision.' *Seudah Shlishit* and *Havdalah* are emotional high points that leave indelible impressions. Here they find the dynamic, fast-moving joy of youthfulness. Here exciting themes, bursting with Jewish values, interpenetrate the pattern of daily life. Here, in this coming together in a world of their own, is found that inexpressible *ruach* which bespeaks an inner universe discovered.

The emphasis is on informal discussion groups, on searching, probing questions and answers. No questions are ever barred. Very often the answer is in itself less important than the realization that answers do exist. At our "Ask the Rabbi" sessions, participants are encouraged to ask any question in writing without signing their names. Generally we shun sermonizing and preaching; the emphasis is on environment and free, open discussion, discussion that brings understanding and knowledge, not guilt.

The younger advisers, older than the participants by but a few years, concern themselves with asking questions, creating friendships, showing that they care. They listen to problems whether in the group or individual setting. Faculty and advisers are always accessible and available.

Lest it be supposed that by the late 1960s the undertaking had been of no more than test-tube size, it should be noted that in one year, over seventy events of two-to-fourteen days duration were conducted for a total of 10,000 young people. Each boy donned *tefillin* at weekday morning services, and each participant, boy or girl, joined in *Shacharit*, *Minchah,* and *Maariv* services; fervently recited the Grace after Meals; attended study sessions; laved hands before meals; scrupulously observed the Sabbath; and participated in exuberant, soul-piercing, *ruachdik* social events — all marked by the absence of social dancing, beach parties, or the type of public social intimacy that American teenagers often take for granted. The aim is for the whole person; the appeal is to mind and soul, to intellect and emotion alike.

If the average person were asked in September of '59, "What one factor would make an American Orthodox youth program most likely to fail?" he would point to one word: *tzniut*. Over the earlier years, strenuous objections were repeatedly expressed in some quarters to NCSY's emphasis on *tzniut* — a strictly enforced ban on social dancing or mixed swimming at regional or national events. In the early years, there were cases of stormy meetings of adult leaders who were sure that an American Orthodox youth program would fail if it adhered to high standards of *tzniut*. In a few instances, the adults, unable to decide whether or not to continue affiliation with NCSY, left the question to the kids, who invariably — and to the utter amazement of some — voted in favor of the policies of NCSY. This may reflect youth's instinctive feeling that social dancing, with its sensuous overtones, is out of place in a Jewish religious setting, for few of them would have had much insight into the halachic rationales for this position. This policy, like others, is now accepted and observed as a matter of course in every one of NCSY's hundreds of regional events.

Someday it may be possible to fully document this dramatic story. It would be replete with examples of lives revolutionized, of communities brought to new life; of non-*mechitzah* synagogues whose NCSY chapters sponsor regular *minyanim* in the *beit midrash* annex with a *mechitzah*, and young people struggle against all odds to become Jews, while in the main sanctuary sit a few elderly persons, trying their best to be real Americans. Well may one ponder the future of these synagogues where we can envisage the picture of *"Vena'ar katan noheg bo"* — "A lad will lead the elders."

The classic example is that of a sixteen-year-old Philadelphia girl whom I overheard tell a fellow NCSYer: "I went to Talmud Torah and learned many things, but they never taught me any religion. I never *bentsched* once, before I came to NCSY."

During the past four decades, NCSY has continued to refine its methods. There is greater emphasis on formal education, and an elaborate complex of specialized educational programs and modules has been developed — all based on the initial insight that when properly challenged, youth will respond.

## ✎ Poetry

☐ *Kolk*
☐ *Reaching In*
☐ *Conversations*

*Eleanor Freemer*

# Kolk

They came from a town called Kolk
These old men, embraced by their
yellowed prayer shawls,
lying deep and silent
in this holy plot of ground.

The tiny *Kolker Shul* where my father
and these companions worshipped
is gone. Gone are the pungent smells
from tobacco-stained fingers
that wrapped the tefillin around
once strong arms, that cradled the holy Torah,
with which they joyously, wildly danced.
Each morning those fingers wound the leather straps
across their foreheads where memories were stored,
of family martyrs in a place without graves,
without markers for those who stayed
behind in that distant shtetl of
*Kolk*

Your siddur's edges were curled up
from years of turning those pages with
dampened fingers; letters were washed out by tears
from eyes that had no need to see the words.
You all now share this resting place,
this haven in a New World cemetery
huddled behind a broken gate
whose sign reads in faded Yiddish
*Kolk*

---

*Editor's Note*: This poem was prompted by the author's daughters' return to Orthodoxy and their many questions about their family's past.

My father peacefully sleeps among his comrades.
In death they are all that is left of a town
where once they lived. Its name
was spoken only among themselves.
No oral or written testimony
bears witness to what they saw or felt,
of their pleasures, or of their fears.
Alone in their shul they beat their breasts,
crying out in prayer to Hashem,
A Kaddish for those they left
who sleep an uneasy sleep somewhere in
*Kolk*

Pappa, I stand here and say Kaddish for you
and for those who never made the journey.
What can I tell your young,
those who are our future, about our past?
I cannot talk of the lost years, you never spoke of.
Your thumbprint is on me.
Your eyes gaze out from your grandchild's eyes
Your voice echoes from my grandchild's lips,
but this is all I have of you.

Now, these children, grandchildren,
great-grandchildren, seek markers,
resting places in a shtetl no longer there.
They search among the broken headstones
covered by weeds for our beginnings.

They ask,
"Where are the maps to show us the way?
Where are the sages to tell us our history?
Where are the candles to bless the night?"
There are no answers.
The earth is silent.
It keeps its secrets.
We are left with just a name
written in faded Yiddish
swinging on a cemetery gate
*Kolk*

*Chevy Schwartz*

# Reaching In

*Making Contact
With an Autistic Child
for the First Time*

A flash
of whimsical silence
thundering
back to the
frail reality
that sits
uncomprehending
before sparkling eyes,
Take my
gift of
love
and need me
please
Colorless memories
blanket
these blameless
green mirrors
The eyes
that scream,
that hurt,
and with terrified totality

escape
this blur of color and sound
we call our world
I reach out
and hum a melody
pure and sweet
suffer no sacrifice
just listen
and let the fluid
song seep
through and ripple
a sleeping emotion
just once
look into my eyes
I search
and sing
this aimless tune —
slowly,
the lashes lift
two puzzled pupils
stare —

trying — oh
so hard
and then the lids droop
and the rythmical rocking
prevails
I sing of nothing
and of everything
hoping
and not hoping
All is still
save a melody
that wanders

somehow
to the heart of this child
in an instant
green swords
aim directly into
my disbelieving eyes
confused,
yet wanting more
What else can I give
my precious one?
My heart and my time
are not enough

*Devora K. Wohlgelernter*

# Conversations

Come and I'll tell you a secret
just between you and me
I know you won't like to hear it
But it just wasn't meant to be

I think the Good Master missed her
that He wanted her by his side
I think that He longed for her beauty
I think that's why she died

Wait little daughter, I'm coming
I just have to finish things here
Temima has a party tomorrow
I promised her I'd be there

You'll see her again little Mother
When you go to her heavenly home
She'll come to greet you smiling
You'll hold her hand in your own

She'll tell you she's not been unhappy
that she's been protected and warm
How silly of you to have worried
When your heart was all broken and torn

Don't cry so much little Mother
Eternity will come soon enough
Try to enjoy what you have here
'Til you leave this troublesome earth.

# ✥ Science and Judaism

- ☐ *Holy Alliance: Reflections on Contemporary Science From the Tents of Torah*
- ☐ *The Revolution in Evolutionary Thinking: Role of Divine Providence*
- ☐ *The Age of Our Universe*

Rabbi Yitzchok Adlerstein

# Holy Alliance

*Reflections on
Contemporary Science
From the Tents of Torah*

## I. Rav Aryeh Kaplan:
## A Modern Chronicle of B'reishit

GOOD TEACHERS, OUR RABBIS OBSERVE, ARE LIKE GOOD chefs. Each can take what is difficult to digest and transform it into a tasty dish on an attractively set table. Rav Aryeh Kaplan succeeded as few others did in faithfully serving up the profundity of past Torah giants. He sublimated his enormous originality, using his gifts to make the arcane accessible to the many. His topical works are meticulously annotated, tracing back each and every idea to proof-texts of earlier times and more authoritative authors. *The Living Torah,* his masterful translation of *Chumash,* could have offered a single, lucid approach to each phrase. Instead, it gathers the thoughts of a host of the *Rishonim* (medieval commentators). Each thought is too precious to dismiss or overlook. Taking it all in, he recognized the greatness of previous generations, and our need to defer to their *mesorah.*

In one area — explicating the first chapters of *B'reishit* — Rav Kaplan pushes beyond his role as articulate spokesman for the past. Early in his career, he organized years of research into *The Handbook of Jewish Theology.* He later published parts of it as *The Handbook of Jewish Thought (Maznaim,* 1979). What follows is a condensation of material that Rav Kaplan did not include in his published volume. We can only speculate that he felt that his approach was both tentative and controversial. We do know, however, that Rav Kaplan was greatly pained about the supposed conflict between Torah and science. Exaggerating this conflict presented a barrier to many people who might otherwise embrace authentic Judaism. He delighted in finding areas where they worked synergistically, especially because he believed that the Torah (particularly *Kabbalah*) predicted that a time would come in which the mind would successfully begin to unravel some of the wisdom with which God endowed this world.

Rav Kaplan begins a chapter entitled "Biblical Interpretation" with some fundamental tools: recognizing multiple strata of meaning in a Divine work; proper and improper assumption of allegory; understanding words in the context of their usage in other passages. The key to proper understanding of God's intent in the Torah is our tradition of interpretation. Precisely because of the depth of *Hashem's* Torah, though, even traditions of interpretation sometimes become difficult to understand. Therefore, we sometimes offer original interpretations, even where those of the *Rishonim* are available.[1]

He turns to another tool: the recognition that God speaks the language of man. Torah must be "accessible to all people for all times." Rav Kaplan says, "If God had written the Torah using current scientific terms, it would have been completely unintelligible to the shepherd thousands of years in the past, while primitive to the scientist thousands of years in the future." The Torah, which is not primarily a scientific work, alludes to extremely complex processes in simple, allegorical language. So, when the Torah speaks of calling "X" by the name of "Y," it uses familiar terms to describe abstruse concepts, ones that could not readily be understood in ancient times.[2]

He switches to the creation story itself. Although the Torah, *per se,* does not fix the moment of creation,[3] there is evidence from a host of

---

1. Ohr HaChaim, *B'reishit* 1:1. s.v. V'Hagam.
2. We are familiar with anthropomorphisms in Torah. We realize that God has no form, and that "His outstretched Hand" is a substitution for "His Power." But the word "Power" itself is not properly ascribable to God, and is therefore just an approximation. See *Moreh Nevuchim,* 1:53 end.
3. This statement should not be confused with the creation of Adam, which the Torah localizes precisely according to our traditional chronology as a bit shy of 6,000 years ago.

disciples, including Torah literature,[1] that the initial act of creation took place billions of years ago.

On the first day, God created the electromagnetic force. It is this force that mediates all chemical activity, and therefore is responsible for the shaping of all biological events. God **called** this "light" "day," approximate terms which had to be used before this force was understood. God also created the interaction of electromagnetic energy with matter. The absorption of energy is the "darkness" that God labeled "night."

On the second day, the matter that God had previously created took form within a geometric space-time matrix defined by matter itself. With matter taking form in this way, the spiritual world of God was separated from the physical. This separation is the "firmament" that God termed "heaven," since no words yet existed to convey the idea of the abstraction of space-time.

The next stage (i.e., the third day) saw the completion of the distribution of matter through the creation of the gravitational force. (For this reason, the phrase "and it was good" is absent on the second day: the interaction of matter and space was not yet finished.) Matter had previously existed in a fluid, "chaotic and void" state. The "gathering of waters" that God **called** "seas" involved more than water itself. All matter condensed because of the non-Euclidean warping of space-time that we call gravity. Also completed were necessary physio-chemical properties of future flora. These properties would leave plant life waiting at the threshold of existence, ready to develop much later.[2]

On the fourth day, God initiated the cosmogenic processes through which matter would cool and coalesce into galaxies, stars and planets.

God next created a process that would eventually produce animal life. The Torah uses the verb "created," instead of the more familiar "made," since the latter implies completion of something that was already created and formed.[3] The process initiated on the fifth day, however,

---

1. See the next selection.
2. Rav Kaplan points to the similar notion in *Chullin* 608, resolving the tension between *B'reishit* 1:12, where the earth is depicted as "bringing forth" all forms of plants, and *B'reishit* 2:5, where the Torah tells us that nothing grew before Man's cultivation. The earlier passage, says the *Gemara*, actually means that the earth brought forth a potential for life that lay dormant until later.
3. Radak, *Y'shaya* 43:7, and others.

was a new creation because it does not inhere in the nature of inorganic material. The *Midrash* tells us that God did this by forming an image in the sea, and enabling it to spawn life, unlike man-made images which cannot reproduce themselves.[1]

On the sixth day, God refined the evolutionary potential to insure the development of higher mammals. This potential was completely fulfilled regarding the animals. The Torah writes that "God **made** the beasts of the earth." Not implicit in God's work so far was the evolution of a being of such complexity that it could serve as a host to the soul, a spiritual gift from God. This indeed was something new, and we therefore learn that "God **created** Man."

## II. Rav Aryeh Kaplan: Kabbalah and the Age of the Universe

Why does the world appear to be so old? Rav Kaplan tackles the thorny issue of the apparent antiquity of the Earth in an address to the Association of Orthodox Jewish Scientists in 1979. He notes that people have dealt with the problem for over a century, with mixed results. He cautions that solutions should emerge from Torah sources themselves, rather than from apologetic excursions. We should not embrace tentative solutions so absolutely that they intellectually paint us into corners in which we do not belong, as did the impassioned arguments of some Torah thinkers centuries ago for belief in a geocentric universe.

He considers several schema. Some ignore the problem, conveniently bifurcating their personalities into "religious" and "scientific" modes, each with its own understanding of the universe. No well-integrated personality could be satisfied with such a Rabbi Jekyll and Mr. Hyde approach. Some insist that no credence be given to scientific inquiry, which is inherently fraudulent and suspect. Those who sit in the lap of legitimate science cannot accept this. Some reason that the six days of creation each lasted billions of years, but with no support from Torah literature. Still others maintain that the world was created with a history, one that made it look old at the time it came into existence. Rav Kaplan rejects this notion with a venegeance; there is simply no Torah support for it. In fact, this approach was first put forth by a non-Jewish scientist

---

1. *Midrash Tehillim* 86:3, *Yalkut Shimoni,* loc. cit.

several years before Darwin made his proposal. Contemporary scientists scoffed at it then; it is certainly unsatisfactory today. It also goes against the grain of authentic Torah teaching: would God clutter His universe with misleading clues, pointing the honest observer to an Earth older than it is?

For lack of a Torah-based approach, we unconsciously gravitate to the position of Christian fundamentalist and Creationists, whose "science" has been rejected by some of the finest scientific minds. It is not an association of which we should be proud.

There is an alternative. *Sefer HaT'munah* is a kabbalistic work ascribed to the first-century *Tanna*, Rabbi Nechunya ben HaKanah. It sets forth an idea that would win the acceptance of many later thinkers:[1] Sabbatical cycles, or *shmitot*. According to this view, when the *Talmud* speaks of a world which lasts 6,000 years, to be destroyed in the seventh millennium, it only refers to one *shmitah* cycle in a series. Altogether, there are seven such cycles, each of seven thousand years, adding up to one *yovel* (Jubilee). Thinkers differ about which of the seven cycles our known world occupies. Rav Kaplan continues:

> "*The* Sefer HaT'munah *thus establishes the age of the world, at least according to some classical interpretation, at 42,000 years . . . This teaching itself was subject to a highly significant interpretation by Rabbi Yitzchok of Acco* [born at the end of the thirteenth century].
>
> "*Rabbi Yitzchok of Acco was a student and colleague of the Ramban,*[2] *and one of the foremost Kabbalists of his time. He is quoted often in Rabbi Eliyahu de Vidas' great* mussar classic, Reishit Chochmah. *He was also contemporary to the publication of the* Zohar, *and is renowned as the individual who investigated (and verified) its authenticity.*
>
> "*A number of years ago, as part of a research project, I got my hands on a photocopy of one of Rabbi Yitzchak's important*

---

1. The most recent Kabbalistic works do not make reference to the idea. This is because two of the modern giants of Kabbalah, the AR"I HaKodesh and Rav Moshe Cordevero, believed that the cycles referred not to real worlds, but spiritual ones. Rav Kaplan argues that this should not rule out accepting the view that was quite common with earlier Kabbalistic thinkers.

2. According to Chida in his *Shem HaG'dolim*; he was certainly a member of the circle of Ramban's disciples.

works, Otzar HaChaim (*Lenin State Library, Moscow, Guenzberg Collection #775*). This is the only complete copy of the manuscript, which is itself several centuries old, in existence. I was almost overwhelmed when I discovered an entirely new interpretation of the concept of Sabbatical cycles in this manuscript.

"Rabbi Yitzchok writes that since these Sabbatical cycles existed before Adam, their chronology must be measured not by human years, but by Divine years. Since, according to many midrashic sources, a Divine day is a thousand earthly years, then a Divine year, consisting of 365 1/4 days, is equal to 365, 250 years. Therefore, when the Sefer HaT'munah states that the world is 42,000 years old, it is not speaking of human years, but of Divine years. This will have some startling consequences.

"Thus, according to Rabbi Yitzchok of Acco, the universe would be 42,000 x 365,250 years old. This is a highly significant figure. From all calculations based on the expanding universe and other cosmological observation, modern science has concluded that the big bang occurred approximately fifteen billion years ago. But here we see the same figure presented in a Torah source written over 700 years ago!

"I am sure that many will find this highly controversial. However, it is important to know that such a classical opinion exists. One of the most important Kabbalists of seven centuries ago calculated the age of the universe, and came to the same conclusion as modern science."

## III. Rav Avraham Yitzchok Hacohen Kook; Evolution and B'reishit, Chapter I

Rav Kook, the great Sage and Kabbalist, while not embracing evolution, stressed that acceptance of evolution was not necessarily incomparable with *B'reishit*. Where evolution to be established as scientific fact, the message of *B'reishit* would remain the same. This selection from *Igrot HaRayah* (number 91) demonstrates what he held about the "conflict" between science and Torah, and about the progress of science itself.

*"That there were many epochs before the counting of our present one* [that could account for our discovery of paleontological remains] *is commonplace to the earlier Kabbalists... We are not fully dependent on this argument, though, because even if it became apparent that life* [in our epoch] *came into being through the evolution of one species from another, there is no contradiction* [to the Torah]. *Our chronology follows the simple sense of the text, which has far greater value to us than knowledge of antiquity...The Torah's intent regarding the events of creation is certainly undisclosed, and it speaks in allusions and allegory.*

*"Surely all realize that* ma-asei b'reishit *are among the 'Secrets of the Torah.' If those matters were to be understood simply and plainly, what 'secrets' would there be? The* Midrash *already stated: To relate the true powers of creation to flesh and blood is impossible. Therefore, Scripture simply stated, 'in the beginning, God created...'*

*"Every idea has its own weight; there is a reason for the timing of its discovery...The ancient Jewish community had to contend with idolaters, to make known that the quality of Man's actions was not insignificant, even though individual man was dwarfed by the world around him. Imagine if people then had also known about the myriad worlds that modern science presents to us! Man would have thought of himself and his civilization as inconsequential,*[1] *and he never would have developed a sense of the greatness and splendor of his existence. It is only today, having long come to terms with the greatness that surrounds, that he is no longer frightened by the proportions of any other similar greatness..."*[2]

---

1. Rav Kook does not refer here, of course, to the *G'dolim* of the past, whose understanding of *emet* surpasses our imagination. He means the average man in the street, who was not always possessed of philosophical sophistication. Compare the argument of *Chovot HaL'vavot, Sha-ar HaBitachon, chapt.* 4, sect. six, that the Torah omits explicit mention of an afterlife because those who left Egypt and received the Torah initially lacked the sophistication to deal with such abstraction.

2. For the complete text in English of this letter, see, *Rav A.Y. Kook Selected Letters*, trans. and ed. by Tzvi Feldman ("Torah and Science Letter One" pp. 3-10), Ma-aleh Adumim, 1986.

*Professor Nathan Aviezer*

# The Revolution in Evolutionary Thinking: Role of Divine Providence

FOR THE RELIGIOUS JEW, IT IS AN ARTICLE OF FAITH THAT GOD intervenes in human affairs. On a larger scale, God's role is unquestioned in determining the fate of *Klal Yisrael*. In the present essay, this idea will be extended to the very existence of human beings.

It has often been stressed that Divine intervention in human affairs need not take the form of the miraculous. The occurrence of a series of extremely unlikely events that extricate one from an otherwise completely hopeless situation is to be regarded as a sign of *Hashgachah* (Divine Providence), even though the laws of nature have not been violated in bringing about the salvation. (Consider the story of Purim.) For the Torah Jew, such events are not perceived as mere "lucky accidents," but rather as the hallmark of the Almighty.

This understanding of *Hashgachah* leads us directly to the question that is central to our discussion: Did the human species result from straightforward, almost predictable evolutionary processes, without any sign of the "extremely unexpected?" We shall see that the answer of leading evolutionary biologists is a resounding "No!" Fundamental discoveries within the last two decades have led to a revolution in the thinking of most biologists. Indeed, it is now recognized that the events that led to the appearance of human beings on this planet were so utterly unexpected that the word "luck" (or its equivalent) appears repeatedly in scientific articles dealing with these events.

Until the 1970s, it was generally believed that biological evolution occurred through a slow and gradual process, whereby those creatures that are "less fit" are gradually replaced by other creatures that are "more fit" to survive the "struggle for existence." This is the principle of gradualism — the gradual change in species through the "survival of the fittest," which is, of course, the underlying premise of Darwin's Theory of Evolution, as well as its 20th-century version — neo-Darwinism.

Recently, there has been a significant change in thinking among evolutionary biologists as a result of the extensive fossil evidence that has ruled decisively against gradualism. It is instructive to quote the world's foremost paleontologists.

Professor Stephen J. Gould of Harvard University writes: "The history of most fossil species includes two features particularly inconsistent with gradualism."[1] Another recognized authority is Professor Steven Stanley of Johns Hopkins University, who has recently written a book to emphasize the vast difference between previously accepted ideas about the gradual evolution of species and the recent fossil evidence. Stanley makes this point repeatedly throughout his book: "Darwin and the many architects of modern neo-Darwinism would have been confounded by the fossil evidence . . . they would have been shocked . . .

"It was a gradualistic view of evolution that led Darwin and others on their fruitless search. . .believing only in slow persistent evolution.

"The [fossil] record has now answered. . .with solid evidence . . . confronting gradualism with an insolvable problem."[2]

An extremely important aspect of the evidence against gradualism relates to the extinction of species. Why do some species disappear while others survive?

The Darwinism answer is, of course, enshrined in the process known as the "survival of the fittest." Darwin himself emphasized throughout his famous book, *The Origin of Species,* that the mechanism he proposes is a slow and gradual one, writing: "Species and groups of species gradually disappear. . .the extinction of a whole group of species is generally a slower process."[3]

---

1. S.J. Gould, 1980. *The Panda's Thumb* (W.W. Norton, New York), p. 151.

2. S.M. Stanley, 1981, *The New Evolutionary Timetable* (Basic Books, New York), pp. 89, 90, 114.

3. C. Darwin. 1859, *The Origin of Species* (reprint edition: Mentor, New York), pp. 316, 317.

It is the above Darwinian view of the gradual extinction of species that has recently been so completely overturned. Evolutionary biologists now emphasize the repeated occurrence of worldwide "mass extinctions" in which the vast majority of all the world's species abruptly disappear. It has become recognized that such mass extinctions have occurred repeatedly in the past and have played a central role in determining the composition of the animal kingdom. These important events have been the subject of numerous recent scientific articles and books. For example, *Scientific American* has published two articles that are entitled, respectively: "The Mass Extinctions of the Late Mesozoic" (issue of January 1982), "Mass Extinctions in the Ocean" (issue of June 1984).

The January 1992 issue of the *New Scientist* contains an article on the largest mass extinction of all, entitled: "The Day the World Nearly Died." The entire November 1989 issue of *Philosophical Transactions of the Royal Society of London* was devoted to a series of articles on "Evolution and Mass Extinctions." And finally, Professor Kenneth J. Hsu chose the following title for his 1986 book of mass extinctions: *The Great Dying*.

In summary, the sudden catastrophic disappearance of most of the world's species has become an accepted fact to every professional biologist. Particularly relevant to our discussion of Divine Providence is the most famous of the mass extinctions, in which all of the world's dinosaurs suddenly disappeared. What caused this abrupt demise of all the dinosaurs, together with most other species?

After years of debate, the riddle was solved in 1980 when Nobel laureate Luis Alvarez and his son, Walter, showed that a giant meteor from outer space collided with the Earth to cause this worldwide catastrophe. This explanation for the mass extinctions — the impact of meteors or comets colliding with the Earth — is known as the "impact theory." The scientific evidence in support of the impact theory has accumulated rapidly. In 1987, Professor Luis Alvarez demonstrated that there are at least 15 independent pieces of scientific data that support the theory, and he concluded his article with the following definite statement: "I see no way to escape the conclusion that the [mass] extinction of the dinosaurs was triggered by the impact of a 10-kilometer-diameter [meteor]...This is the only existing theory that agrees with all the observations."[1]

---

1. L.W. Alvarez, July 1987, *Physics Today*, Vol. 40, pp. 30, 33.

A point of central importance in our discussion of the impact theory is that the collision between a meteor and the Earth was a matter of *sheer luck.* In particular, the destruction caused by the collision has *nothing* to do with the Darwinian principle of the "survival of the fittest." This has been repeatedly stressed by leading paleontologists. For example, Professor David M. Raup of the University of Chicago, past president of the American Paleontological Society, has taken precisely this point as his central theme in a famous article, appropriately entitled: "Extinctions: Bad Genes or Bad Luck?" In his article, Raup emphasizes again and again the role played by "luck" in such catastrophes, writing: "The extinction of a given species or higher group is more bad luck than bad genes."[1]

"Pure chance would favor some biologic groups over others — all in the absence of conventional Darwinian selection between species." Professor S.J. Gould of Harvard University has also noted the important rule played by "luck" in mass extinctions, writing: "If extinctions can demolish more than 90% of all species, then we must be losing groups forever by pure bad luck."[2] Professor G. U. Yule of the University of Oxford puts it in the following way: "The species exterminated were killed out not because of any inherent defects but simply because they had the ill-luck to stand in the way of the cataclysm."[3]

And finally, we quote Professor David Jablonski of the University of Chicago, a world authority on the subject of mass extinctions: "When a mass extinction strikes, it is not the most fit [species] that survive; often it is the most fortunate. Species that had been barely hanging on...inherit the earth."[4]

The point that these paleontologists are making is quite simple: If a giant meteor suddenly falls from the sky and wipes out some species, while permitting other species to survive and eventually flourish, then the former species were plagued with "bad luck," whereas the latter species were blessed with "good luck." In particular, the Darwinian concept of the "survival of the fittest" plays no role whatsoever during

---

1. D.M. Raup, 1981, *Acta Geologica Hispanica,* Vol. 16, pp. 26, 29.

2. S.J. Gould, 1985, *The Flamingo's Smile* (W. W. Norton, New York), p. 242.

3. G.U. Yule, 1981, *Philosophical Transactions of the Royal Society of London,* Vol. 213, p. 24.

4. D. Jablonski, June 1989, *National Geographic,* Vol. 175, p. 673.

mass extinctions. When they occur, survival is determined by "pure luck" or, as we Jews would say, by Divine Providence.

Returning to our central thesis, it has recently become widely recognized that the existence of the human species on the planet Earth would not have been possible without the occurrence of the extremely "lucky" impact of a meteor from outer space that killed off all the world's dinosaurs. Nobel laureate Luis Alvarez connects these two phenomena in the following way: "From our human point of view, that impact was arguably one of the most important single events in the history of our planet. Had it not taken place, the largest mammals alive today might still resemble the rat-like creatures that were scurrying around trying to avoid being devoured by the dinosaurs."[1]

Professor Gould has devoted an entire book to this theme, stating again and again how "lucky" it is that human beings exist at all. Emphasizing that the very existence of human beings as reasoning creatures is *extremely improbable* from the scientific point of view, Gould writes: "Consciousness would not have [appeared] on our planet if a cosmic catastrophe had not claimed the dinosaurs as victims. In an entirely literal sense, we owe our existence, as large and reasoning mammals, to our lucky stars.

"Wind back the 'tape of life' to the early days...and let it play again from an identical starting point, and the chance becomes vanishingly small that anything like human intelligence would grace the replay."[2]

As the above discussion makes clear, recent fossil data have led many leading biologists to conclude that the existence of reasoning creatures — human beings — was due to an extremely improbable event, which they attribute to unusual "good luck." Of course, the religious Jew perceives such "luck" as the unmistakable signature of Divine Providence. Thus current scientific findings have given new meaning to the Torah statement that Man is the handiwork of the Creator. "And God said, 'Let us make a man...' " (*Bereishit* 1:26).

I would like to conclude by stating my own viewpoint regarding biological evolution and Darwin's theory. When discussing Darwin's theory of evolution and neo-Darwinism, one must carefully distinguish between fact and *theory*. It is a fact that species have changed in the course of time. This fact, which is based on overwhelming fossil

---

1. L.W. Alvarez, July 1987, *Physics Today,* Vol. 40, p. 33.
2. S.J. Gould, 1989, *Wonderful Life* (W.W. Norton, New York), pp. 14, 318.

evidence, as well as on much additional evidence (such as the "molecular clock" for DNA), was known long before Darwin published his famous book in 1859. Moreover, as I have already discussed at length in a different context,[1] careful reading of the Biblical text shows that the first chapter of *Bereishit* is, in fact, consistent with the idea that present-day animals developed from earlier animals.

Darwin's book introduced the *theory* that species gradually evolved from one to another through such agencies as the survival of the fittest, the struggle for existence, natural selection and adaptation. It is this theory that is incompatible with the Torah outlook, for the following reason. If it were true that all species continually evolve gradually and inexorably from primitive forms into more complex forms, following a uniform, almost predictable, progression, then there would seem to be no place — and no need — for the Creator. In contrast to the theory of gradual evolution, the Torah describes the Animal Kingdom as the direct result of *Hashgachah*. The Torah thus implies that it should be impossible to predict new species on the basis of earlier species. In particular, the existence of human beings should appear as a completely unexpected and extremely improbable phenomenon.

As an observant Jew, I am inspired by the fact that it is the latter view — the Torah view — that has become widely accepted throughout the scientific community, whereas the former (gradualistic) view has been generally discarded as being incompatible with the sensitive fossil evidence. The current scientific position has been admirably summarized by Professor Gould as follows: "It fills us with a new kind of amazement (because of the improbability of the event) that human beings [exist] at all."[2]

I too am "filled with amazement" when contemplating the works of the Creator.

Indeed, it has become abundantly clear that the Torah Jew of the 20th century need not stand opposed to the mainstream of modern science.

Finally, it should be emphasized that the fossil evidence discussed in this essay is by no means the only illustration from modern science of how *Hashgachah* is directly responsible for the very existence of human beings. I have shown elsewhere[3] that it has become increasingly

---

1. N. Aviezer, 1990, *In the Beginning* (Ktav, Hoboken), Chap. 5, Part II.
2. S.J. Gould, 1989, *Wonderful Life* (W.W. Norton, New York), p. 289.
3. N. Aviezer, 1990, *In the Beginning* (Ktav, Hoboken).

obvious to scientists that there are a great many quite stringent requirements of nature that are necessary for the existence of Man — and somehow they all *just happen* to occur. This phenomenon has attracted considerable scientific interest and has been named the "Anthropic Principle." The numerous "accidents of nature" that just seemed to happen for our benefit are so remarkable that many scientists have commented on them. Particularly perceptive are the words of Professor Freeman J. Dyson, a world-famous physicist from the Institute for Advanced Study in Princeton, who writes: "As we look out into the universe and identify the many accidents of physics and astronomy that have worked together for our benefit, it almost seems as if the universe must in some sense have known that we were coming."[1]

The signs of Divine Providence have become evident throughout the physical universe. *Ma gadlu ma-asecha, Hashem, mi'od amuku machshevotecha (Psalms 92:6).*

---

1. F.J. Dyson, September 1971, *Scientific American,* Vol. 225, p.59.

Dr. Gerald L. Schroeder

# The Age of Our Universe:
## Six Days AND 15 Billion Years

*Harmony Between
Torah and Science*

ARMONY, RATHER THAN DISCORD, IS TO BE FOUND BEtween science and the teachings of the Torah provided one has an in-depth understanding of both science and the Torah. I have attempted to demonstrate this in GENESIS AND THE BIG BANG: *The Discovery of Harmony Between Modern Science and the Bible,* recently published by Bantam Books.

Of the many topics of possible conflict between theological and scientific opinion, the age of the universe seems to make front-page news almost daily. Scientists tell us that the universe appeared with a big bang some ten to twenty billion years ago. This age has been established using such unrelated phenomena as the rate of travel of distant stars and the frigid -270 degrees centigrade (approximately -450 degrees Fahrenheit) temperature of deep space. In contrast to this very great age, the opening chapter of the Torah tells us in no uncertain terms that the universe and all it contains was fashioned in the six days of *Genesis.*

To reach an accord between the two ages, we might say that *Genesis* days are really measured in billions of years per day. After all, *Psalms* 90:4 does say: "A thousand years in Your (God's) sight are as yesterday, as a watch that passes in the night." That might convince a "believer," but such arguments are likely to evoke a chortle by a skeptic as a weak attempt to find a similarity between science and theology. Remember what W.C. Fields said: "One night I spent a week in Philadelphia." That was strictly a subjective sensation and had no physical reality. True harmony must be based on stronger ground than these arguments provide.

First, let us establish that there is no one "correct" Earthly age for the matter of our universe. The big bang produced hydrogen and helium and very little of any other elements. That is because of a fortunate instability in deuterium, the isotope of hydrogen that falls between hydrogen and helium. Had such an instability not existed, the high pressures that existed just after the big bang would have fused all the hydrogen into heavy elements. Stars make their heat by fusing hydrogen into helium. Had deuterium been more stable than it is, there would be no hydrogen remaining from the big bang to make today's stars "burn." No stars would mean a very cold Earth and no chance of life.

"The Sun appeared on the fourth day. Rabbi Abahu said: From this we learn that during the first three days, the Holy One Blessed be His Name, used to make and destroy worlds [stars]" (*Genesis Rabba*). The elements that make up the proteins and fats and bones of our bodies, the air we breathe, were made from the original hydrogen and helium, but made long after the big bang. These elements were made in exploding stars (supernovae). The force of a star's explosion fuses helium nuclei, building them into heavier elements much as a child adds one Lego piece to another. The supernova spews these newly formed elements into space. Over eons of time, this stardust, drawn together by gravity, forms new stars which in turn fuse more hydrogen into helium for their heat and die in a supernova explosion. More stardust is formed. These supernovae were the sources of the elements in the solar system. We have no idea how many supernovae contributed their dust to the nebula that eventually condensed to form the solar system; however, the large amounts of heavy elements in the solar system mean that the Sun cannot be a first-generation star. This sounds very much like what Rabbi Abahu hinted at 1600 years ago.

Einstein's Law of General Relativity teaches us an extraordinary fact: the flow of time is not the same at all places. The rate that time passes depends upon the strength of the local gravitational field which in turn depends upon the amount of matter in the area. Each star that exploded and contributed its stardust to the nebula that was to become the solar system had its own particularly mass and so its own particular gravitational field. That means each of these by-gone stars had its own particular clock, its own particular rate at which time passed. Within our universe there are billions upon billions of stars and so there are billions upon billions of cosmic clocks. Each records time *exactly* correctly for its own particular gravity, but each clock ticks at a rate very different from the other clocks of the universe. Because the elements of the Earth and the solar system originated in an unknown multitude of supernovae, there is no one age that is the "true" age of the Earth. Physically, we are the residue, the dust, of many stars. Truly, the elements of our bodies, our planet and the entire universe are a mix of many different ages. The idea of a fifteen-billion-year age for our universe is a totally anthropocentric projection. It is the imposition of measurements made by clocks ticking and tocking at a rate fixed by the gravity and velocity of our planet, the Earth, onto objects and events existing at very different gravities and velocities.

In pursuing this line of reasoning, I have stumbled onto a fact that is almost unnerving. The fact flows from the Law of General Relativity. Changes in the flow of time caused by differences in forces of gravity can be calculated. These differences are known as time dilation. Unlike time dilation due to motion (based on Einstein's Law of Special Relativity), where one cannot tell who is really moving and who is standing still — Think of yourself at a stoplight. The car next to you slowly rolls forward, or is it your car rolling backward? Sometimes you cannot tell — with gravitational time dilation, we can always tell whose clock is faster and whose is slower because we can tell who has the higher gravitational field. Because of this absolute determination of a gravitational field, we can calculate the effect of the mass of the universe on the flow of time, and decide whose duration is longer, whose shorter.

The slowing down of a clock in a strong gravitational field relative to a clock at a place where there is little or no gravity is proportional to the square root of the gravitational force. This, in turn, is proportional to the mass of weight causing the gravity, divided by the radius of the sphere in which the mass is held. It may sound complicated, but it is simple mathematics.

The unnerving surprise comes when we put numbers into Einstein's equation for gravitational time dilation. The estimated mass of the universe is approximately $10^{55}$ grams. (That number is a one with fifty-five zeros after it and reads as ten billion billion billion billion billion billion grams.) This is unchanging. Both science and the Torah (see Nachmanides commentary on *Genesis* 1:1 and 1:26) tell us that there was only one creation of matter. All the mass and energy of the universe appeared at the instant of the creation (the big bang). Unlike the matter of the universe, the radius of the universe is not constant. The universe has been in a state of rapid expansion since its creation in a tiny speck of space (Nachmanides, *Genesis* 1:1) in the blast of the big bang.

Today the radius is approximately ten billion light years. At the time the Sun and Earth were forming, the start of the third day by the biblical calendar, the universe's radius was some two to three billion light years. (This is still huge beyond human imagination. A single light year, the distance that light travels in a year, is approximately six thousand billion miles long.) The powerful gravitational potential at the hypothetical edge of the universe, with its $10^{55}$ grams of weight contained in a sphere having a radius of two to three billion light years, would slow a clock by a ratio of approximately one thousand billion, relative to a clock operating at the gravitational potential produced by the Earth. In terms of days and years and millennia, this dilation reduces fifteen billion years to...six days!

It may just be that science and the Torah are *both* exactly correct. The fifteen-billion-year measurement of the age of the universe is made by clocks working in the Earth's current gravitational field. The six-day age of the universe, stated in *Genesis*, is for a system that encompassed all of the universe, such as would be the perspective for an infinite Creator. Note well that from the time that the *neshamah*, the soul of life (*Genesis* 2:7), is given to mankind and thereafter, the dates of events described in the Torah match dates derived from archaeological finds. It seems that from the start of humanity and thereafter, the calendar of mankind became that of the Creator's. "The truth has sprung from the Earth" (*Psalms* 85:12).

# ⋹ Sources of Faith

> *"Faith was lost,*
> *it was removed from their mouths"*
> *(Jeremiah 7:28).*
>
> *The prophet's plaint has been*
> *interpreted by Reb Mordechai Lechovitz*
> *as a question and answer:*
> *Why was faith lost?*
> *Because it was no longer discussed.*

☐ *Credo of Credence*
☐ *Reflections on Emunah*
☐ *The Source of Faith Is Faith Itself*

*Rabbi Aharon Feldman*

# Credo of Credence

ALTHOUGH I GREW UP IN A RELIGIOUS HOUSEHOLD AND WENT to a Jewish day school, America in the late forties and early fifties was no place for a nice Jewish boy to grow into Jewish manhood. The pressures against remaining a Torah-observant Jew were enormous. The public attitude, the implied message of teachers, media and books made Torah appear irrelevant.

Non-conformism had not yet become conformist. Academia looked with disdain upon any religion; psychiatry proclaimed it a neurosis. Wherever one went, there was hostility to keeping *mitzvot*. An act as innocent as going to the barbershop could end with the barber lecturing his captive audience on why Torah was no longer applicable in modern times.

There were few contemporary models with whom a young person could identify and who could give him the courage to battle the entire world. Most English-speaking rabbis were weak, uninspiring models with little Torah knowledge and little to offer in their sermons beyond bland comments on current events. They so abjectly prostrated themselves before the secular culture that it was sometimes difficult to figure what kept them religious.

Growing up in those years was an experience in loneliness. Nevertheless I am thankful for the times into which I was born. My life has been immeasurably enriched by the tortuous route I had to take. I had to know and to decide why I was going to remain a religious Jew.

The source of a Jew's *emunah* (faith in Judaism) is the belief that God revealed His Torah to the Jewish people. It is not difficult to arrive at this belief; on the contrary, trying to explain one's Jewishness while rejecting the truth of Torah is the problematic feat.

As the famous quotation by Emperor Franz Josef's court theologian has it, the existence of the Jewish people is the most powerful proof of the existence of God. It is also the greatest proof of the truth of Judaism's beliefs. If the stories in the Torah did not happen, what caused the entire Jewish people to believe that they did occur? What would anyone have gained by inventing them? Why would he have exposed himself to the predictions which the Torah makes about the future of the Jewish people: how could he have known that they would enter *Eretz Yisrael*, that they would be expelled and remain a nation forever? How could the stiff-necked Jewish people have allowed stories like the Exodus from Egypt and the forty-year sojourn in the desert to be foisted upon them if they did not occur?

I would often strengthen myself by rereading the parts of the Torah — in particular *Parashat Va-etchanan* — which deals with the giving of the Torah and its predictions about Jewish destiny. I could not escape the conclusion that they were not concoctions of a human mind.

Besides the testimony of the Torah, the greatest evidence that the events related in the Torah actually occurred is the manner in which they have entered the collective historical consciousness of the Jewish people. No one questions if George Washington, Shakespeare or Alexander the Great really existed because there is a national consciousness which agrees that they did. For the same reason, no one could question the Exodus or the Revelation of the Torah; they exist in the national Jewish consciousness to the same degree of reality.

Logical arguments are the beginnings of *emunah*, but they are not its full-fledged manifestation. The Sages refer to certain people as *"ketaney amana"* (small in faith);[1] they are not *apikorsim* (heretics) but merely "small in faith." *Emunah* is something which must grow; one must become "large in faith." This means reaching a point where one is so convinced of the truth of something that it appears absurd for it not to be true.

For example, how does a person know that his mother will not stab him during his sleep and steal his money? Not logic, but a combination of indicators from past behavior of the mother — how she nurtured him and concerned herself for a lifetime with his welfare — make the

---

1. *Sotah* 48b.

thought that she would murder him absurd. None of these indicators is foolproof; nevertheless, most sons sleep comfortably in their mothers' homes because of this belief. They have a "largeness of faith" in their mothers.

The same is true about Judaism. The arguments from Jewish history and from the contents of the Torah are powerful, but they are not enough. Ultimately, *emunah* must reach a point where one feels that any other explanation is absurd.

This sort of *emunah* slowly grows on an individual as a result of one's personal experience with Torah. The richness of the experience of a *Seder* night, of a Yom Kippur, of a Jewish marriage are so real, so obviously a contact with a higher level of experience, that they cannot be illusions.

More than anything else, the greatest catalyst for the development of *emunah* is the study of Torah. It is told that when someone came to the great Reb Chaim Brisker with problems in *emunah,* he would advise him to learn Torah with more intensity and that the problems would disappear. In our times, we have seen this advice borne out. In *yeshivot* for *baalei teshuvah* it is a fact that the intense study of *Gemara* and *Rishonim* is the most effective medium for inspiring young people to return to their heritage. My personal feeling is that the remarkable phenomenon has something supernatural about it, something related to the promise to Moshe Rabbeinu that the Jewish people "will believe in you forever."[1] But one need not subscribe to my feelings. There is a rational explanation as well.

To study Torah is to come into contact with the heartbeat of the Jewish nation. One perceives the uncompromising manner in which the Jewish tradition was transmitted; one appreciates the greatness of its Sages. One senses the Torah's depth, its consistency, its scope and its power; one hears its ring of truth.

For many people, *aggadata* (the non-halachic parts of Talmud) have an even more forceful effect. One sees the cosmic message of Torah for mankind; what existence is all about, why the Jewish people exists, what went wrong with mankind, and — most important — the principles by which one can set one's own life aright. The message which the Torah has for mankind and for each individual makes sense on every level of existence; as an individual, as a parent, as a son or daughter, as

---

1. *Sh'mot* 19:9.

a member of a community, as a Jew, as a human being. In addition, one sees how these ideas harmonize with all aspects of the Torah and concur with past and present Jewish history.

Like the illustration of the mother given above, Torah proves itself in too many situations to be anything but genuine.

I remember one passage of Torah in particular which I studied in those years which led me to conclude, "this so obviously could not have been contrived." At the beginning of his commentary to *Shir HaShirim* (*The Song of Songs*), the Vilna Gaon explains Verse 2, "He has kissed me with the kisses of His mouth," which the Sages say is a metaphor for the first two of the Ten Commandments.[1] In the course of his terse discussion, he demonstrates the following:

1. How these two commandments represent two aspects of the revelation of God's will, described as God's love.
2. How all of the Torah is nothing more than an elaboration of these two commandments; namely, that all positive commandments of the Torah are developments of the first of these commandments and all negative prohibitions, of the second.
3. How these two aspects of revelation are symbolized by the last two letters of God's four-lettered name, *vav* and *hei*. All positive commandments depend on the *vav* and all negative commandments on the *hei*.[2]
4. Since these two aspects of revelation (and the letters upon which they depend) reflect a masculine and a feminine relationship of God to His world, this is why the letter *vav* is the suffix used in Hebrew for the masculine and *hei* is used for the feminine (e.g., *oto* and *otah*).
5. That this has a bearing on the fact that women are exempted from certain positive commandments but not from any negative commandments.
6. That the two aspects of Torah, the Oral and the Written Torah, are expressions of these two aspects of revelation.

---

1. *Shir HaShirim Rabba* 1:4.
2. God's Name describes His revelation to mankind and the last two letters describe Him as the revealer of His will in the Torah. See A. Feldman, *The Juggler and The King* (Feldheim, 1990), 2.4, where the concept appears in a context unrelated to the present commentary.

7. That the numerical value of these two letters (six and five, respectfully) are the reason for the number of orders (six) in the Oral Torah (the *Mishnah*) and the number of books (five) in the Written Torah.

8. How this relates to the statement by the Sages which says that the eleven *mitzvot* in *Tehillim,* Chapter 6, summarize the entire Torah.[1] This psalm contains six positive commandments and five negative commandments. Again, six is the value of *vav* which symbolizes positive commandments and five, the value of *hei* which symbolizes negative commandments.

9. All of this is by way of explaining the above verse. The metaphor "kisses" is used because with a kiss one uses one's mouth to express one's love. Similarly, the first two commandments are expressions of God's love of His people which the Jews heard from the mouth of God Himself,[2] unlike the other commandments.

10. The word used for "his mouth" in this verse is *pihu* rather than the ordinarily used *piv* to hint at the fact that these kisses were an expression of both the *vav* and the *hei* of God's name.

The sheer abundance and scope of ideas in a commentary to a single verse is dizzying. With one sweep, it shows the unity and interrelationships of the Hagiagrapha, the Written Torah, the *Midrash,* the Oral Law, the Names of God (a topic of *Kabbalah*), and the usage and numerical value of Hebrew letters. As I subsequently discovered, such unity and scope in the wisdom of the Torah is quite usual. The Torah itself is the greatest evidence of its authenticity.

I know a famous Israeli whose "conversion" to *teshuvah* was — and still is, many years later — a *cause celebre* for the Israeli media. He still exercises a powerful influence on public opinion and on the *baal teshuvah* movement. His background and mine could not have been more different. He was an Israeli — who grew up on an anti-religious *kibbutz* — whose name became a household word in the entertainment

---

1. *Makkot* 24a.
2. *Shir HaShirim Rabba* I. Only the first two commandments were spoken by God in the first person; i.e., the Jews heard them, as it were, from God's mouth Himself. The other commandments were spoken by Moshe who referred to God in the third person.

world. I was, again, a nice Jewish boy who had grown up in a religious atmosphere and had gone to *yeshivot*.

Once, in the course of a conversation, he revealed to me what was the final stroke in his acceptance of Torah. "It was the Vilna Gaon's commentary to the beginning of *Shir HaShirim*. It was simultaneously so beautifully consistent with so many varied ideas, I decided then and there, 'It so obviously could not have been contrived.' "

*Dr. Judith Grunfeld*

# Reflections on Emunah

How can I write about *emunah*? I do not feel competent to deal with so great and deep a subject. I only know that our people have been rooted in *emunah* like a sturdy, weatherbeaten tree that is firmly rooted in solid ground, constantly shooting out plants alive with growth.

But I have been asked to draw upon "any personal events which challenged... faith or played a crucial part in solidifying it." This touches a cord. Where have I experienced *emunah?*

My mind travels back many years. Pictures of long ago stir and come to life. I am a 16 year-old girl. Life is peaceful and unharassed in those days at the beginning of the century. I love sunshine, beauty of summergreen and the reflection of idealistic romance. And then something happens. My brother, age 18, has caught the flu which is sweeping Germany. My parents, by his bedside, storm the heavens with their prayers and supplications. To no avail. He is laid to rest on *Erev Shabbos*, a beloved son, a pure soul, a part of the strong fabric of our solid family unit and my first encounter with death. The world had suddenly become dark for me as never before and my mother's tears burnt wounds into my hitherto idealistic, cloudless existence. And then — but a few hours later, we all come to the Shabbos table. The silver was shining, the *challos* were presiding, *zemiros* were sung, light filled the room, the golden soup was shared — the Shabbos Queen had shed her radiance unaltered. We filed into togetherness and the pain, which should have reached its peak, was prevented from rising to the top. Shabbos had triumphed, had smoothed us into harmony and had dipped our hearts into the radiance that flooded the room. This happened over 70 years ago and while I write this down, having since gone through a number of tribulations, including the terror of the world's worst human catastrophic time — I feel the tears still rising . . . in reverence of this long past experience that my parents in their *emunah* had given me. Something of this experience has never left me, it forged my inner triumphant strength that stood by me all along through many a difficult period in life.

So how is *emunah* defined? Is it in the quiver of the heart when grappling with the infinite or is it in the glitter of the tears that well up when we humbly accept our unfathomable destiny?

In our mundane, everyday life, we sometimes encounter moments of elation and mental inspiration. We then reach beyond the banality of our routine and feel confronted with a super individual vision far beyond our temporal experience. I remember such moments (which appear as ordinary happenings when I try to recall or retell them) and their impact was so strong that something of it accompanied me through life.

Why should I now, after the passage of 60 years, so vividly and clearly remember sitting on the green grass of the Carpathian mountains next to a woman twice my age, whom I have only just met after coming from Frankfurt to Poland? While listening to her plans for women's education, I feel overcome and lifted up to a height of vision — a vision which has not lost its magic momentum even today, so many decades later.

This woman was the then unknown Sarah Schenierer, and while she spoke to me, initiating me into her plans, the radiance of her presence was strongly communicating itself to me. I became a part of the magic web that embraced her and wider spheres beyond her. From that moment onwards, I handed myself over to the task of weaving the net of education spread out before me, and I have seen it spread out into a world-embracing and widely acknowledged blessed movement. The sensation of this experience, so sudden, so far reaching and so sincerely presented has never left me. I have lived and relived this encounter countless times, and every time it touches me anew in its incredible power of sincerity. The basis of it all — *emunah*, strong, unshakable and solid.

It seems that the seedlings of *emunah* are not just private sensations, not just personal gifts. They are slumbering in us and may remain unrecognized and unknown until they are touched by the kiss of an event or an encounter with fate. Words from a pure source may serve as a magic key to unlock those sensations. Inbuilt genetic disposition may also contribute, as a gift of grace. We may not be the beginners of *emunah* in our hearts — it may have been passed on to us from beyond time and some may be more richly endowed with it than others.

Can we define *emunah*? Can we define a colour? We can only point at it and say "this rose is red." This is something that is positive to the eye, it is refreshing, it is attractive, it is loud — but it will never be possible to define any colour. To a blind man there is no way of presenting it — there is no bridge of understanding to one bereft of sight.

What is *emunah*? *Emunah* is when you are told to jump into the roaring sea, and that "it will be safe." When all hesitated, Nachshon Ben Aminadav did the jump. He went down in history with this fearless jump where reason based on experience had abdicated. It was a jump of *emunah* — reality was overrun.

With *emunah* we become sure that the unbelievable will happen and has happened in the past.

One feels divine guidance, the hand behind the mechanics of life. *Emunah* will sprout in elite moments, may they be moments of joy or of helpless devastation. It has its bright chances when marriage under the sky is seen as enchanted immortalization of life itself. When two people are blended into a unit under the canopy, then continuation is handed over to the yet unborn. In the seven marriage blessings we have the visionary ecstasy of joining *Gan Eden* through the new couple, directly with the days of *Mashiach*. Thus *emunah* makes life transparent. *Emunah* is potentially an extension of the mundane life. Mundane life contains treasures of holiness which come out at sparking times and develop into a tapestry which, when woven tightly enough, gives us purpose of life, strength without strain, harmony beyond our planning and elevation without conscious effort.

When a mother gives birth, she is not just a woman giving birth to a child, she is a descendant sliding gradually into ancestry. She is leading into further flowering which in turn will bring the song and music of life, pointing far beyond the temporal moment. Deep down, the essence of it all is *emunah*. *Emunah* lifts us up, makes us ignore the stumbling block in our way, the thorns that rend our garments and our skin. It directs our glance towards a height we shall never really reach. It hurts and soothes at the same time. It must have been in Gittel (and in so many like her), the staunch Beth Jacob girl in the Cracow Ghetto, when she gathered her children around her, took them by the hand and said to them: "Do not be afraid, my *kinderlach,* we go now together to Hashem." And with confident step, her children by her side, she walked directly towards the commanding SS officer of the extermination squad. They were in the next group felled to the ground and no one ever saw the wings of *bitachon* on which Gittel had floated.

I have been told this account by a surviving eyewitness: how Gittel and her children walked towards their end. Gittel had been my student 60 years ago in Sarah Schenierer's first Beth Jacob Seminary in Cracow. What is it that grips me now, some 50 years later, when I recount it, that I feel so totally humble, hinged to a sublime existence?

☙ ☙ ☙

There is not much time for the ordinary person for holiness. We have to deal with so many mundane things, routine takes most of the time. But suddenly we feel there are moments that give their sparks and when I come face to face with those sparks, my feelings are all aglow. I am ready for the encounter and while I am aware of this readiness, all bent to hold on to it . . . it escapes me and I am a creature earthbound, fumbling for the security of earth. "My beloved eludes me" *(Shir HaShirim 5:6).* Is there a trace of *emunah* anywhere to be found? Maybe our sparks of *emunah* experience are linked to each other, one here, one there, one of the *Ne'ilah* hour, one of an encounter with hope, with disaster, and together they all form a mighty power, breaking in full force of ecstasy like lava breaks out of a mountain and floods all around. . .How dare I analyze *emunah,* I can barely tentatively touch the surface, perhaps not even this.

*Yaacov Avinu* saw a ladder standing on earth, its top reaching to heaven. Our Jewish home is founded on *emunah* and it is the place on which the world hinges. The distance from the profane to the sacred is so small. It is incalculable. Our house was shaken to the ground, but it has proved its strength. The hinges never broke. It needed the raging hurricane to make us aware of its indestructibility and with it the indestructibility of our people. Perhaps *emunah* are the rungs that lead from the earth to heaven.

*Rabbi Aharon Lichtenstein*

# The Source of Faith Is Faith Itself

"WHO PROP, THOU ASK'ST, IN THESE BAD DAYS, MY mind?" Thus opened Matthew Arnold an early sonnet, *To A Friend*. I believe that, unlike the Rambam, I do not generally experience the days as bad; and I am quite certain that if I did, Arnold's choices — Homer, Epictetus and Sophocles — would not provide the requisite solace. But as to the formulation of the question: In my case, at least, the critical factor is indeed "who" rather than "what."

Without question, during my formative years and, to a lesser extent, beyond, the source and bulwark of my commitment was not so much a cluster of abstract factors or arguments as key persons. This may make my response less valuable for readers who have no access to my sources of strength and inspiration. Moreover, such a response raises obvious questions about determinism and inequity which, in a different context, would need to be addressed philosophically. But any other would be not only partial but false.

I refer, of course. to those who, in the words of the *Mishnah*, put me on the path to temporal and eternal life: my parents, *zecher tzaddikim l'verachah*, who were also my primary (in several senses of the term) teachers; and my *rebbeim*, of whom three — Rav Hutner *zecher tzaddik l'verachah*, the Rav *zecher tzaddik l'verachah*, and *yibadel l'chaim aruchim*, Rav Aaron Soleveichik, *shlita* — stand out far above the rest. At home, I received trust and strength, imbibed (although did not always implement in youth) a work ethic, and initially breathed an atmosphere within which a balance between criticism and rootedness was consistently maintained. Both my parents, each in his own way, habitually raised serious questions about the religious world or about various textual or philosophic aspects of Torah — but always radiated a sense of profoundly engaged commitment.

The impact of my *rebbeim* was obviously varied. That of the first two is presumably self-evident. They — the Rav, as *rabbi muvhak*, in particular — both limned the contours of my religious and intellectual universe and filled it with content. In addition, they communicated a powerful sense of relation to the past, immediate and distant, of *k'illu kiblah mehar Sinai,* of being and becoming a link in the unbroken chain of the *mesorah.* Perhaps more needs to be said, however, about my relation to Reb Aaron. From him too, I learned much, but above all, he served as a role model. The *Rosh Yeshiva* (as his *talmidim* invariably called Rav Hutner), *gavra d'mistafina minei* par excellence, simply overwhelmed. The Rav overawed. I could entertain no rational illusions about attaining their status or stature. But Reb Aaron, while an inspiring vision, yet somehow seemed within reach, and truly presented a model. It wasn't so much what he said or did. I was simply enthralled by what he was — a remarkable fusion of mastery and simplicity, of vigor and humility and, above all, a pillar of radical integrity. To an extent probably far beyond what he knew or could even have imagined, he was to me, for many years, a polestar. Upon attaining fuller maturity, I came to realize that the notion that I could attain his level was pretentiously vainglorious. But his hold upon me, and the ambition and commitment it generated, have not waned to this day.

What I received from all my mentors, at home or in *yeshivot,* was the key to confronting life, particularly modern life, in all its complexity: the recognition that it was not so necessary to have all the answers as to learn to live with the questions. Regardless of what issues — moral, theological, textual or historical — vexed me, I was confident that they had been raised by masters far sharper and wiser than myself; and if they had remained impregnably steadfast in their commitment, so should and could I. I intuited that, his categorical formulations and imperial certitude notwithstanding, Rav Hutner had surely confronted whatever questions occurred to me. Later, I felt virtually certain the Rav had, so that the depth and intensity of their *avodat Hashem* was doubly reassuring.

Newman has emphasized the difference between difficulty and doubt, noting that of all his beliefs, the existence of God was the most fraught with philosophical questions, and yet none was borne in upon his mind and heart with greater certitude. This is the crucial distinction between judging faith and its tents as an outsider or probing its contents while firmly ensconced within. The bulwark of my mentors' support assured that my own situation would be the latter; and the motto I inscribed in my college notebook was David's plea: *Tuv taam vadaat lamdeni key b'mitzvotecha he'emanti.* Answers, I of course continued — and continue — to seek, and have found many. But commitment has not been conditioned upon them. I have never been attracted to fideism and I regard Tartullian's *credo quia absurdum est* as alien to the spirit of Judaism. Clearly, however, faith cannot be contingent upon having all the answers. Its essence is implied in Rav Yohanan's rejoinder to a student who had initially ridiculed a palpably implausible statement but who then recanted upon finding empirical support for it: "Ne'er do well, had you not seen, you would not have believed. You ridicule the words of the wise" (*Baba Batra,* 75a).

The source of my support was not confined to my immediate *rebbeim.* At one point, during my late teens, I was troubled by certain ethical questions concerning Amalek, *ir hanidachat,* etc. I then recalled having recently read that Rav Chaim Brisker would awaken nightly to see if someone hadn't place a foundling at his doorstep. I knew that I slept quite soundly, and I concluded that if such a paragon of *chesed* coped with these *halachot,* evidently the source of my anxiety did not lie in my greater sensitivity but in my weaker faith. And I set myself to enhancing it.

That faith has been persistently reinforced by Jewish history. And this, in two respects. First, I have envisioned Providence as revealed and refracted through its uniqueness, in the spirit of the response *Chazal* ascribe to *Anshei Knesset Hagedolah*: "These are His awesome effects, for were it not for awe of God, how could one nation survive among the nations?" (*Yoma,* 69b). Of course, I realized that, from a purely logical standpoint, one could rejoin with an analogue to Newman's statement that he saw design in nature because he believed in God, not vice versa. But given the substratum of faith, our singular history has provided much reinforcement. Secondly, it has served as a corpus with which — to some extent, even through which — to identify, and on whose behalf to continue. That sense has received added impetus through the

Holocaust. Some may regard this as paradoxical; but it is thoroughly genuine — and from my perspective, not paradoxical at all. The theological philosophic difficulties posed by this frightful *hester panim* are self-evident. They are, however, so insoluble and intractable that a person of faith is led to look beyond their sheer magnitude to evoke and formulate a practical response. For me, that has meant a redoubled commitment — a sense of mission to take the flickering torch from my predecessors and move with it toward our common goals.

The greatest source of faith, however, has been the *Ribbono Shel Olam* Himself.

At the level of rational demonstration, this is, of course, patently circular. I hold no brief for Anselm's ontological proof and I recognized the theoretical possibility of self-delusion long before I had ever heard of Feuerbach. Existentially, however, nothing has been more authentic than the encounter with *Avinu Malkeinu,* the source and ground of all being. Nothing more sustaining, nothing more strengthening, nothing more vivifying.

Encounter, of course, has been varied. In part, it has been channeled — primarily through *talmud Torah* (this is no doubt an aspect of *maor shebah,* "the light within it," of which *Chazal* spoke) but also through *tefillah* and the performance of *mitzvot*; or, if you will, by the halachic regimen in its totality. In part, it has been random — moments of illumination while getting on a crowded bus or watching children play in a park at twilight. Obviously, it has also been greatly varied in intensity. In its totality, however, whatever the form and content, it has been the ultimate basis of spiritual life.

This will obviously provide little guidance for those to whom attaining encounter is precisely the problem. To those "struggling to develop faith" one can, however, proffer first the reassuring assertion of the religious significance of the quest *per se,* as in the footsteps of *Avraham Avinu,* they have already become *mevakshei Hashem;* second, the prospective hope of successful resolution, as "The Lord is good unto them that yearn for Him, to the soul that seeketh Him" (*Eichah* 3:25); and third, the counsel to focus persistently, in terms of Coleridge's familiar distinction, upon faith rather than belief, upon experiential trust, dependence and submission more than upon catechetical dogmatics. Intellectual assent is normative and essential; but, at the personal level, it is generally not the key. In the final analysis, the primary human source of faith is faith itself.